MznLnx

Missing Links Exam Preps

Exam Prep for

Marketing 10e: Marketing in the 21st Century

Evans & Berman, 10th Edition

The MznLnx Exam Prep is your link from the texbook and lecture to your exams.
The MznLnx Exam Preps are unauthorized and comprehensive reviews of your textbooks.

All material provided by MznLnx and Rico Publications (c) 2010
Textbook publishers and textbook authors do not particpate in or contribute to these reviews.

MznLnx

Rico
Publications

Exam Prep for Marketing 10e: Marketing in the 21st Century
10th Edition
Evans & Berman

Publisher: Raymond Houge
Assistant Editor: Michael Rouger
Text and Cover Designer: Lisa Buckner
Marketing Manager: Sara Swagger
Project Manager, Editorial Production: Jerry Emerson
Art Director: Vernon Lowerui

Product Manager: Dave Mason
Editorial Assitant: Rachel Guzmanji
Pedagogy: Debra Long
Cover Image: Jim Reed/Getty Images
Text and Cover Printer: City Printing, Inc.
Compositor: Media Mix, Inc.

(c) 2010 Rico Publications
ALL RIGHTS RESERVED. No part of this work covered by the copyright may be reproduced or used in any form or by an means--graphic, electronic, or mechanical, including photocopying, recording, taping, Web distribution, information storage, and retrieval systems, or in any other manner--without the written permission of the publisher.

Printed in the United States
ISBN:

For more information about our products, contact us at:
Dave.Mason@RicoPublications.com

For permission to use material from this text or product, submit a request online to:
Dave.Mason@RicoPublications.com

Contents

CHAPTER 1
Marketing Today — 1

CHAPTER 2
The Environment in Which Marketing Operates — 8

CHAPTER 3
Developing and Enacting Strategic Marketing Plans — 21

CHAPTER 4
Information for Marketing Decisions — 29

CHAPTER 5
Societal, Ethical, and Consumer Issues — 38

CHAPTER 6
Global Aspects of Marketing — 48

CHAPTER 7
Marketing and the Internet — 57

CHAPTER 8
Final Consumers — 66

CHAPTER 9
Organizational Consumers — 77

CHAPTER 10
Developing a Target Market Strategy — 85

CHAPTER 11
Basic Concepts in Product Planning — 94

CHAPTER 12
Goods Versus Services Planning — 106

CHAPTER 13
Conceiving, Developing, and Managing Products — 113

CHAPTER 14
Value Chain Management and Logistics — 124

CHAPTER 15
Wholesaling — 136

CHAPTER 16
Retailing — 141

CHAPTER 17
Integrated Marketing Communications — 150

CHAPTER 18
Advertising and Public Relations — 159

CHAPTER 19
Personal Selling and Sales Promotion — 167

CHAPTER 20
Considerations in Price Planning — 176

Contents (Cont.)

CHAPTER 21
Developing and Applying a Pricing Strategy — 185
CHAPTER 22
Pulling It All Together: Integrating and Analyzing the Marketing Plan — 193
ANSWER KEY — 203

TO THE STUDENT

COMPREHENSIVE

The *MznLnx* Exam Prep series is designed to help you pass your exams. Editors at MznLnx review your textbooks and then prepare these practice exams to help you master the textbook material. Unlike study guides, workbooks, and practice tests provided by the texbook publisher and textbook authors, *MznLnx* gives you **all** of the material in each chapter in exam form, not just samples, so you can be sure to nail your exam.

MECHANICAL

The MznLnx Exam Prep series creates exams that will help you learn the subject matter as well as test you on your understanding. Each question is designed to help you master the concept. Just working through the exams, you gain an understanding of the subject--its a simple mechanical process that produces success.

INTEGRATED STUDY GUIDE AND REVIEW

MznLnx is not just a set of exams designed to test you, its also a comprehensive review of the subject content. Each exam question is also a review of the concept, making sure that you will get the answer correct without having to go to other sources of material. You learn as you go! Its the easiest way to pass an exam.

HUMOR

Studying can be tedious and dry. MznLnx's instructional design includes moderate humor within the exam questions on occassion, to break the tedium and revitalize the brain

Chapter 1. Marketing Today

1. _____ is a broad label that refers to any individuals or households that use goods and services generated within the economy. The concept of a _____ is used in different contexts, so that the usage and significance of the term may vary.

A _____ is a person who uses any product or service.

   a. 6-3-5 Brainwriting
   b. Power III
   c. 180SearchAssistant
   d. Consumer

2. _____, a business term, is a measure of how products and services supplied by a company meet or surpass customer expectation. It is seen as a key performance indicator within business and is part of the four perspectives of a Balanced Scorecard.

In a competitive marketplace where businesses compete for customers, _____ is seen as a key differentiator and increasingly has become a key element of business strategy.

   a. Customer satisfaction
   b. Psychological pricing
   c. Customer base
   d. Supplier diversity

3. _____ is defined by the American _____ Association as the activity, set of institutions, and processes for creating, communicating, delivering, and exchanging offerings that have value for customers, clients, partners, and society at large. The term developed from the original meaning which referred literally to going to market, as in shopping, or going to a market to sell goods or services.

_____ practice tends to be seen as a creative industry, which includes advertising, distribution and selling.

   a. Marketing myopia
   b. Customer acquisition management
   c. Product naming
   d. Marketing

4. A _____ is a list of the general tasks and responsibilities of a position. Typically, it also includes to whom the position reports, specifications such as the qualifications needed by the person in the job, salary range for the position, etc. A _____ is usually developed by conducting a job analysis, which includes examining the tasks and sequences of tasks necessary to perform the job.

   a. Job description
   b. Power III
   c. 180SearchAssistant
   d. 6-3-5 Brainwriting

5. _____ is one of the four elements of marketing mix. An organization or set of organizations (go-betweens) involved in the process of making a product or service available for use or consumption by a consumer or business user.

The other three parts of the marketing mix are product, pricing, and promotion.

   a. Better Living Through Chemistry
   b. Japan Advertising Photographers' Association
   c. Distribution
   d. Comparison-Shopping agent

6. _____ is a business discipline which is focused on the practical application of marketing techniques and the management of a firm's marketing resources and activities. Marketing managers are often responsible for influencing the level, timing, and composition of customer demand accepted definition of the term. In part, this is because the role of a marketing manager can vary significantly based on a business' size, corporate culture, and industry context.
   a. Door-to-door
   b. Performance-based advertising
   c. Business structure
   d. Marketing management

7. _____ is one of the four Ps of the marketing mix. The other three aspects are product, promotion, and place. It is also a key variable in microeconomic price allocation theory.
   a. Relationship based pricing
   b. Price
   c. Competitor indexing
   d. Pricing

8. _____ is the ongoing process of identifying and articulating market requirements that define a product's feature set.
   a. Targeted advertising
   b. Product planning
   c. Market intelligence
   d. Brand parity

9. _____ in organizations and public policy is both the organizational process of creating and maintaining a plan; and the psychological process of thinking about the activities required to create a desired goal on some scale. As such, it is a fundamental property of intelligent behavior. This thought process is essential to the creation and refinement of a plan, or integration of it with other plans, that is, it combines forecasting of developments with the preparation of scenarios of how to react to them.
   a. Power III
   b. 180SearchAssistant
   c. 6-3-5 Brainwriting
   d. Planning

10. A _____ is a plan of action designed to achieve a particular goal.

   _____ is different from tactics. In military terms, tactics is concerned with the conduct of an engagement while _____ is concerned with how different engagements are linked.

   a. Power III
   b. Strategy
   c. 6-3-5 Brainwriting
   d. 180SearchAssistant

11. _____ or consumer demand or consumption is also known as personal consumption expenditure. It is the largest part of aggregate demand or effective demand at the macroeconomic level. There are two variants of consumption in the aggregate demand model, including induced consumption and autonomous consumption.
   a. Consumer spending
   b. Power III
   c. Deregulation
   d. Value added

12. In economics, _____ is the desire to own something and the ability to pay for it. The term _____ signifies the ability or the willingness to buy a particular commodity at a given point of time.

   a. Discretionary spending
   b. Market system
   c. Demand
   d. Market dominance

13. _____ is the deliberate attempt to manage the public's perception of a subject. The subjects of _____ include people (for example, politicians and performing artists), goods and services, organizations of all kinds, and works of art or entertainment.

From a marketing perspective, _____ is one component of promotion.

- a. Pearson's chi-square
- b. Publicity
- c. Little value placed on potential benefits
- d. Brando

14. _____ refers to 'controlling human or societal behaviour by rules or restrictions.' _____ can take many forms: legal restrictions promulgated by a government authority, self-_____, social _____, co-_____ and market _____. One can consider _____ as actions of conduct imposing sanctions (such as a fine.) This action of administrative law, or implementing regulatory law, may be contrasted with statutory or case law.
- a. Regulation
- b. CAN-SPAM
- c. Non-conventional trademark
- d. Rule of four

15. _____ is the provision of service to customers before, during and after a purchase.

According to Turban et al., '_____ is a series of activities designed to enhance the level of customer satisfaction - that is, the feeling that a product or service has met the customer expectation.'

Its importance varies by product, industry and customer.

- a. Facing
- b. Customer service
- c. COPC Inc.
- d. Customer experience

16. _____ is an advertisement in which a particular product specifically mentions a competitor by name for the express purpose of showing why the competitor is inferior to the product naming it.

This should not be confused with parody advertisements, where a fictional product is being advertised for the purpose of poking fun at the particular advertisement, nor should it be confused with the use of a coined brand name for the purpose of comparing the product without actually naming an actual competitor. ('Wikipedia tastes better and is less filling than the Encyclopedia Galactica.')

In the 1980s, during what has been referred to as the cola wars, soft-drink manufacturer Pepsi ran a series of advertisements where people, caught on hidden camera, in a blind taste test, chose Pepsi over rival Coca-Cola.

- a. Heavy-up
- b. GL-70
- c. Cost per conversion
- d. Comparative advertising

17. _____ is a type of trade in which goods or services are directly exchanged for other goods and/or services, without the use of money. It can be bilateral or multilateral, and usually exists parallel to monetary systems in most developed countries, though to a very limited extent. _____ usually replaces money as the method of exchange in times of monetary crisis, when the currency is unstable and devalued by hyperinflation.

a. Black market
c. Mixed economy
b. Barter
d. Market economy

18. A _____ is a written document that details the necessary actions to achieve one or more marketing objectives. It can be for a product or service, a brand, or a product line. _____s cover between one and five years.
   a. Prosumer
   b. Disruptive technology
   c. Marketing strategy
   d. Marketing plan

19. In economics, business, retail, and accounting, a _____ is the value of money that has been used up to produce something, and hence is not available for use anymore. In economics, a _____ is an alternative that is given up as a result of a decision. In business, the _____ may be one of acquisition, in which case the amount of money expended to acquire it is counted as _____.
   a. Transaction cost
   b. Fixed costs
   c. Variable cost
   d. Cost

20. _____ is a form of marketing developed from direct response marketing campaigns conducted in the 1970's and 1980's which emphasizes customer retention and satisfaction, rather than a dominant focus on 'point of sale' transactions.

_____ differs from other forms of marketing in that it recognizes the long term value to the firm of keeping customers, as opposed to direct or 'Intrusion' marketing, which focuses upon acquisition of new clients by targeting majority demographics based upon prospective client lists.

_____ refers to long-term and mutually beneficial arrangement wherein both buyer and seller focus on value enhancement through the certain of more satisfying exchange.This approach attempts to transcend the simple purchase exchange process with customer to make more meaningful and richer contact by providing a more holistic, personalized purchase, and use orn consumption experience to create stronger ties.

   a. Guerrilla Marketing
   b. Global marketing
   c. Diversity marketing
   d. Relationship marketing

21. The general definition of an _____ is an evaluation of a person, organization, system, process, project or product. _____s are performed to ascertain the validity and reliability of information; also to provide an assessment of a system's internal control. The goal of an _____ is to express an opinion on the person/organization/system (etc) in question, under evaluation based on work done on a test basis.
   a. Audit
   b. ADTECH
   c. ACNielsen
   d. AMAX

22. _____ , according to The American Marketing Association, is 'a planning process designed to assure that all brand contacts received by a customer or prospect for a product, service, or organization are relevant to that person and consistent over time.' (Marketing Power Dictionary)

_____ is a term used to describe a holistic approach to marketing. It aims to ensure consistency of message and the complementary use of media. The concept includes online and offline marketing channels.

a. AMAX
b. ACNielsen
c. Integrated marketing communications
d. ADTECH

23. _____ involves disseminating information about a product, product line, brand, or company. It is one of the four key aspects of the marketing mix. (The other three elements are product marketing, pricing, and distribution). P>_____ is generally sub-divided into two parts:

- Above the line _____: Promotion in the media (e.g. TV, radio, newspapers, Internet and Mobile Phones) in which the advertiser pays an advertising agency to place the ad
- Below the line _____: All other _____. Much of this is intended to be subtle enough for the consumer to be unaware that _____ is taking place. E.g. sponsorship, product placement, endorsements, sales _____, merchandising, direct mail, personal selling, public relations, trade shows

a. Promotion
b. Bottling lines
c. Cashmere Agency
d. Davie Brown Index

24. _____, or Value optimized pricing is a business strategy. It sets selling prices on the perceived value to the customer, rather than on the actual cost of the product, the market price, competitors prices, or the historical price.

The goal of _____ is to align price with value delivered.

a. Service-profit chain
b. Jobbing house
c. Money back guarantee
d. Value-based pricing

25. _____ is a measure of the strength of a brand, product, service relative to competitive offerings. There is often a geographic element to the competitive landscape. In defining _____, you must see to what extent a product, brand, or firm controls a product category in a given geographic area.

a. Market dominance
b. Productivity
c. Discretionary spending
d. Market system

26. _____ refers to messages and related media used to communicate with a market. Those who practice advertising, branding, direct marketing, graphic design, marketing, packaging, promotion, publicity, sponsorship, public relations, sales, sales promotion and online marketing are termed marketing communicators, _____ managers, or more briefly as marcom managers.

a. Merchandising
b. Marketing communication
c. Sales promotion
d. Merchandise

27. _____ is a form of communication that typically attempts to persuade potential customers to purchase or to consume more of a particular brand of product or service. 'While now central to the contemporary global economy and the reproduction of global production networks, it is only quite recently that _____ has been more than a marginal influence on patterns of sales and production. The formation of modern _____ was intimately bound up with the emergence of new forms of monopoly capitalism around the end of the 19th and beginning of the 20th century as one element in corporate strategies to create, organize and where possible control markets, especially for mass produced consumer goods.

a. ACNielsen
b. ADTECH
c. AMAX
d. Advertising

28. _____ is a contract between two parties, one being the employer and the other being the employee. An employee may be defined as: 'A person in the service of another under any contract of hire, express or implied, oral or written, where the employer has the power or right to control and direct the employee in the material details of how the work is to be performed.' Black's Law Dictionary page 471 (5th ed. 1979.)

   a. ADTECH
   b. AMAX
   c. ACNielsen
   d. Employment

29. _____ is the equation of personal happiness with consumption and the purchase of material possessions.

The term is often associated with criticisms of consumption starting with Thorstein Veblen.

Veblen's subject of examination, the newly emergent middle class arising at the turn of the twentieth century, comes to full fruition by the end of the twentieth century through the process of globalization.

In economics, _____ refers to economic policies placing emphasis on consumption.

   a. Power III
   b. 6-3-5 Brainwriting
   c. 180SearchAssistant
   d. Consumerism

30. The verb _____ or grant _____ means to give permission. The noun _____ refers to that permission as well as to the document memorializing that permission. _____ may be granted by a party to another party as an element of an agreement between those parties.

   a. 6-3-5 Brainwriting
   b. 180SearchAssistant
   c. Power III
   d. License

31. The _____ is an economic and political union of 27 member states, located primarily in Europe. It was established by the Treaty of Maastricht on 1 November 1993 upon the foundations of the pre-existing European Economic Community. With almost 500 million citizens, the _____ combined generates an estimated 30% share (US$16.8 trillion in 2007) of the nominal gross world product.

   a. ADTECH
   b. Eurozone
   c. ACNielsen
   d. European Union

32. Consumer market research is a form of applied sociology that concentrates on understanding the behaviours, whims and preferences, of consumers in a market-based economy, and aims to understand the effects and comparative success of marketing campaigns. The field of consumer _____ as a statistical science was pioneered by Arthur Nielsen with the founding of the ACNielsen Company in 1923.

Thus _____ is the systematic and objective identification, collection, analysis, and dissemination of information for the purpose of assisting management in decision making related to the identification and solution of problems and opportunities in marketing.

   a. Focus group
   b. Marketing research process
   c. Marketing research
   d. Logit analysis

33. _____ is a set of six steps which defines the tasks to be accomplished in conducting a marketing research study. These include problem definition, developing an approach to problem, research design formulation, field work, data preparation and analysis, and report generation and presentation.
   a. Simple random sampling   b. Preference-rank translation
   c. Market analysis   d. Marketing research process

34. A _____ is an entity that provides services to other entities. Usually this refers to a business that provides subscription or web service to other businesses or individuals. Examples of these services include Internet access, Mobile phone operator, and web application hosting.
   a. Cross-selling   b. Yield management
   c. Service provider   d. Freebie marketing

Chapter 2. The Environment in Which Marketing Operates

1. _____ is defined by the American _____ Association as the activity, set of institutions, and processes for creating, communicating, delivering, and exchanging offerings that have value for customers, clients, partners, and society at large. The term developed from the original meaning which referred literally to going to market, as in shopping, or going to a market to sell goods or services.

   _____ practice tends to be seen as a creative industry, which includes advertising, distribution and selling.

   a. Marketing
   b. Customer acquisition management
   c. Marketing myopia
   d. Product naming

2. The _____ is a marketing term and refers to all of the forces outside of marketing that affect marketing management's ability to build and maintain successful relationships with target customers. The _____ consists of both the macroenvironment and the microenvironment.

   The microenvironment refers to the forces that are close to the company and affect its ability to serve its customers.

   a. Psychographic
   b. Customer franchise
   c. Market environment
   d. Business-to-consumer

3. A supply chain is the system of organizations, people, technology, activities, information and resources involved in moving a product or service from _____ to customer. Supply chain activities transform natural resources, raw materials and components into a finished product that is delivered to the end customer. In sophisticated supply chain systems, used products may re-enter the supply chain at any point where residual value is recyclable.
   a. Rebate
   b. Supplier
   c. Bringin' Home the Oil
   d. Product line extension

4. _____ is one of the four elements of marketing mix. An organization or set of organizations (go-betweens) involved in the process of making a product or service available for use or consumption by a consumer or business user.

   The other three parts of the marketing mix are product, pricing, and promotion.

   a. Japan Advertising Photographers' Association
   b. Distribution
   c. Better Living Through Chemistry
   d. Comparison-Shopping agent

5. _____ describes the situation when output from (or information about the result of) an event or phenomenon in the past will influence the same event/phenomenon in the present or future. When an event is part of a chain of cause-and-effect that forms a circuit or loop, then the event is said to 'feed back' into itself.

   _____ is also a synonym for:

   - _____ Signal; the information about the initial event that is the basis for subsequent modification of the event.
   - _____ Loop; the causal path that leads from the initial generation of the _____ signal to the subsequent modification of the event.

Chapter 2. The Environment in Which Marketing Operates

_____ is a mechanism, process or signal that is looped back to control a system within itself. Such a loop is called a _____ loop.

- a. Power III
- b. Feedback
- c. 180SearchAssistant
- d. 6-3-5 Brainwriting

6. Organizational culture is not the same as _____. It is wider and deeper concepts, something that an organization 'is' rather than what it 'has' (according to Buchanan and Huczynski.)

_____ is the total sum of the values, customs, traditions and meanings that make a company unique.

- a. Cross-functional team
- b. Power III
- c. 180SearchAssistant
- d. Corporate culture

7. _____ is difficult to define. For example, in 1952, Alfred Kroeber and Clyde Kluckhohn compiled a list of 164 definitions of '_____' in _____: A Critical Review of Concepts and Definitions. However, the word '_____' is most commonly used in three basic senses:

- excellence of taste in the fine arts and humanities
- an integrated pattern of human knowledge, belief, and behavior that depends upon the capacity for symbolic thought and social learning
- the set of shared attitudes, values, goals, and practices that characterizes an institution, organization or group.

When the concept first emerged in eighteenth- and nineteenth-century Europe, it connoted a process of cultivation or improvement, as in agriculture or horticulture. In the nineteenth century, it came to refer first to the betterment or refinement of the individual, especially through education, and then to the fulfillment of national aspirations or ideals.

- a. African Americans
- b. Culture
- c. AStore
- d. Albert Einstein

8. _____ is the state or fact of exclusive rights and control over property, which may be an object, land/real estate, or some other kind of property (like government-granted monopolies collectively referred to as intellectual property.) It is embodied in an _____ right also referred to as title.

_____ is the key building block in the development of the capitalist socio-economic system.

- a. AMAX
- b. ADTECH
- c. ACNielsen
- d. Ownership

Chapter 2. The Environment in Which Marketing Operates

9. _____ is when a large distribution channel member (usually a retailer), buys from a manufacturer in bulk and puts its own name on the product. This strategy is only practical when the retailer does very high levels of volume. The advantages to the retailer are:

- more freedom and flexibility in pricing
- more control over product attributes and quality
- higher margins (or lower selling price)
- eliminates much of the manufacturer's promotional costs

The advantages to the manufacturer are:

- reduced promotional costs
- stability of sales volume (at least while the contract is operative)

- Kumar, Nirmalya; Steenkamp, Jan-Benedict E.M., Private Label Strategy - How to Meet the Store Brand Challenge. Harvard Business Press 2007

- private label
- brand management
- brand
- product management
- marketing

a. Promotion
c. Customization
b. Rural market
d. Private branding

10. _____ is a form of communication that typically attempts to persuade potential customers to purchase or to consume more of a particular brand of product or service. 'While now central to the contemporary global economy and the reproduction of global production networks, it is only quite recently that _____ has been more than a marginal influence on patterns of sales and production. The formation of modern _____ was intimately bound up with the emergence of new forms of monopoly capitalism around the end of the 19th and beginning of the 20th century as one element in corporate strategies to create, organize and where possible control markets, especially for mass produced consumer goods.

a. AMAX
c. ACNielsen
b. ADTECH
d. Advertising

11. A _____ is a collection of symbols, experiences and associations connected with a product, a service, a person or any other artifact or entity.

_____s have become increasingly important components of culture and the economy, now being described as 'cultural accessories and personal philosophies'.

Some people distinguish the psychological aspect of a _____ from the experiential aspect.

Chapter 2. The Environment in Which Marketing Operates

a. Brand
b. Brand equity
c. Store brand
d. Brandable software

12. The term _____ is used to describe countries that have a high level of development according to some criteria. Which criteria, and which countries are classified as being developed, is a contentious issue and there is fierce debate about this. Economic criteria have tended to dominate discussions.

a. Completely randomized designs
b. Brando
c. Bringin' Home the Oil
d. Developed country

13. _____, also referred to as i-marketing, web marketing, online marketing is the marketing of products or services over the Internet.

The Internet has brought many unique benefits to marketing, one of which being lower costs for the distribution of information and media to a global audience. The interactive nature of _____, both in terms of providing instant response and eliciting responses, is a unique quality of the medium.

a. ACNielsen
b. ADTECH
c. Internet marketing
d. AMAX

14. A _____ is a process that can allow an organization to concentrate its limited resources on the greatest opportunities to increase sales and achieve a sustainable competitive advantage. A _____ should be centered around the key concept that customer satisfaction is the main goal.

A _____ is most effective when it is an integral component of corporate strategy, defining how the organization will successfully engage customers, prospects, and competitors in the market arena.

a. Cyberdoc
b. Marketing strategy
c. Psychographic
d. Societal marketing

15. A _____ is a plan of action designed to achieve a particular goal.

_____ is different from tactics. In military terms, tactics is concerned with the conduct of an engagement while _____ is concerned with how different engagements are linked.

a. 6-3-5 Brainwriting
b. Strategy
c. Power III
d. 180SearchAssistant

Chapter 2. The Environment in Which Marketing Operates

16. _____ involves disseminating information about a product, product line, brand, or company. It is one of the four key aspects of the marketing mix. (The other three elements are product marketing, pricing, and distribution). P>_____ is generally sub-divided into two parts:

- Above the line _____: Promotion in the media (e.g. TV, radio, newspapers, Internet and Mobile Phones) in which the advertiser pays an advertising agency to place the ad
- Below the line _____: All other _____. Much of this is intended to be subtle enough for the consumer to be unaware that _____ is taking place. E.g. sponsorship, product placement, endorsements, sales _____, merchandising, direct mail, personal selling, public relations, trade shows

   a. Davie Brown Index   b. Cashmere Agency
   c. Promotion   d. Bottling lines

17. _____ is a rivalry between individuals, groups, nations for territory, a niche, or allocation of resources. It arises whenever two or more parties strive for a goal which cannot be shared. _____ occurs naturally between living organisms which co-exist in the same environment.

   a. Non-price competition   b. Competition
   c. Price competition   d. Price fixing

18. _____ in organizations and public policy is both the organizational process of creating and maintaining a plan; and the psychological process of thinking about the activities required to create a desired goal on some scale. As such, it is a fundamental property of intelligent behavior. This thought process is essential to the creation and refinement of a plan, or integration of it with other plans, that is, it combines forecasting of developments with the preparation of scenarios of how to react to them.

   a. Power III   b. 6-3-5 Brainwriting
   c. 180SearchAssistant   d. Planning

19. _____ is the equation of personal happiness with consumption and the purchase of material possessions.

The term is often associated with criticisms of consumption starting with Thorstein Veblen.

Veblen's subject of examination, the newly emergent middle class arising at the turn of the twentieth century, comes to full fruition by the end of the twentieth century through the process of globalization.

In economics, _____ refers to economic policies placing emphasis on consumption.

   a. Power III   b. Consumerism
   c. 6-3-5 Brainwriting   d. 180SearchAssistant

20. _____ consists of the sale of goods or merchandise from a fixed location, such as a department store or kiosk in small or individual lots for direct consumption by the purchaser. _____ may include subordinated services, such as delivery. Purchasers may be individuals or businesses.

   a. Retailing   b. Thrifting
   c. Charity shop   d. Warehouse store

Chapter 2. The Environment in Which Marketing Operates 13

21. _____ is a broad label that refers to any individuals or households that use goods and services generated within the economy. The concept of a _____ is used in different contexts, so that the usage and significance of the term may vary.

A _____ is a person who uses any product or service.

a. Power III
b. 6-3-5 Brainwriting
c. Consumer
d. 180SearchAssistant

22. _____ is an American magazine published monthly by Consumers Union. It publishes reviews and comparisons of consumer products and services based on reporting and results from its in-house testing laboratory. It also publishes cleaning and general buying guides.

a. Power III
b. Magalog
c. Crossing the Chasm
d. Consumer Reports

23. _____ is a branch of philosophy which seeks to address questions about morality, such as how a moral outcome can be achieved in a specific situation (applied _____), how moral values should be determined (normative _____), what moral values people actually abide by (descriptive _____), what the fundamental semantic, ontological, and epistemic nature of _____ or morality is (meta-_____), and how moral capacity or moral agency develops and what its nature is (moral psychology.)

Socrates was one of the first Greek philosophers to encourage both scholars and the common citizen to turn their attention from the outside world to the condition of man. In this view, Knowledge having a bearing on human life was placed highest, all other knowledge being secondary.

a. AMAX
b. Ethics
c. ACNielsen
d. ADTECH

24. In economics, a _____ exists when a specific individual or enterprise has sufficient control over a particular product or service to determine significantly the terms on which other individuals shall have access to it. Monopolies are thus characterized by a lack of economic competition for the good or service that they provide and a lack of viable substitute goods. The verb 'monopolize' refers to the process by which a firm gains persistently greater market share than what is expected under perfect competition.

a. 6-3-5 Brainwriting
b. 180SearchAssistant
c. Monopoly
d. Power III

25. A _____ is a written document that details the necessary actions to achieve one or more marketing objectives. It can be for a product or service, a brand, or a product line. _____s cover between one and five years.

a. Prosumer
b. Marketing strategy
c. Disruptive technology
d. Marketing plan

26. The phrase _____ refers to the aspect of corporate strategy, corporate finance and management dealing with the buying, selling and combining of different companies that can aid, finance, or help a growing company in a given industry grow rapidly without having to create another business entity.

Chapter 2. The Environment in Which Marketing Operates

An acquisition, also known as a takeover or a buyout, is the buying of one company (the 'target') by another. An acquisition may be friendly or hostile.

a. 6-3-5 Brainwriting
b. 180SearchAssistant
c. Power III
d. Mergers and acquisitions

27. _____ is a common market form. Many markets can be considered monopolistically competitive, often including the markets for restaurants, cereal, clothing, shoes and service industries in large cities. Short-run equilibrium of the firm under _____

Monopolistically competitive markets have the following characteristics:

- There are many producers and many consumers in a given market, and no business has total control over the market price.
- Consumers perceive that there are non-price differences among the competitors' products.
- There are few barriers to entry and exit.
- Producers have a degree of control over price.

Long-run equilibrium of the firm under _____

The characteristics of a monopolistically competitive market are almost the same as in perfect competition, with the exception of heterogeneous products, and that _____ involves a great deal of non-price competition (based on subtle product differentiation.) A firm making profits in the short run will break even in the long run because demand will decrease and average total cost will increase.

a. Macroeconomics
b. Recession
c. Gross domestic product
d. Monopolistic competition

28. An _____ is a market form in which a market or industry is dominated by a small number of sellers (oligopolists.) Because there are few participants in this type of market, each oligopolist is aware of the actions of the others. The decisions of one firm influence, and are influenced by, the decisions of other firms.

a. ACNielsen
b. ADTECH
c. AMAX
d. Oligopoly

29. Competitiveness is a comparative concept of the ability and performance of a firm, sub-sector or country to sell and supply goods and/or services in a given market. Although widely used in economics and business management, the usefulness of the concept, particularly in the context of national competitiveness, is vigorously disputed by economists, such as Paul Krugman .

The term may also be applied to markets, where it is used to refer to the extent to which the market structure may be regarded as perfectly _____.

Chapter 2. The Environment in Which Marketing Operates

a. Free trade zone
c. Customs union
b. Geographical pricing
d. Competitive

30. _____ is a process by which government's control over businesses and individuals is reduced or eliminated. It is the removal of some governmental controls over a market. _____ does not mean elimination of laws against fraud, but eliminating or reducing government control of how business is done, thereby moving toward a more free market.
a. Power III
c. Value added
b. Deregulation
d. Consumer spending

31. _____ is an organization's process of defining its strategy and making decisions on allocating its resources to pursue this strategy, including its capital and people. Various business analysis techniques can be used in _____, including SWOT analysis (Strengths, Weaknesses, Opportunities, and Threats) and PEST analysis (Political, Economic, Social, and Technological analysis) or STEER analysis involving Socio-cultural, Technological, Economic, Ecological, and Regulatory factors and EPISTEL (Environment, Political, Informatic, Social, Technological, Economic and Legal)

_____ is the formal consideration of an organization's future course. All _____ deals with at least one of three key questions:

1. 'What do we do?'
2. 'For whom do we do it?'
3. 'How do we excel?'

In business _____, the third question is better phrased 'How can we beat or avoid competition?'. (Bradford and Duncan, page 1.)

a. 180SearchAssistant
c. 6-3-5 Brainwriting
b. Power III
d. Strategic planning

32. The _____ is an economic and political union of 27 member states, located primarily in Europe. It was established by the Treaty of Maastricht on 1 November 1993 upon the foundations of the pre-existing European Economic Community. With almost 500 million citizens, the _____ combined generates an estimated 30% share (US$16.8 trillion in 2007) of the nominal gross world product.
a. Eurozone
c. European Union
b. ADTECH
d. ACNielsen

33. The _____ is an independent agency of the United States government, established in 1914 by the _____ Act. Its principal mission is the promotion of 'consumer protection' and the elimination and prevention of what regulators perceive to be harmfully 'anti-competitive' business practices, such as coercive monopoly.

The _____ Act was one of President Wilson's major acts against trusts.

a. 6-3-5 Brainwriting
c. Power III
b. Federal Trade Commission
d. 180SearchAssistant

34. _____ is one of the four Ps of the marketing mix. The other three aspects are product, promotion, and place. It is also a key variable in microeconomic price allocation theory.

Chapter 2. The Environment in Which Marketing Operates

a. Price
b. Relationship based pricing
c. Pricing
d. Competitor indexing

35. _____ is the act of marketing or advertising products or services to young people. In 2000, children under 13 years old impacted the spending of over $600 billion in the United States alone. This has created a large incentive to advertise to children which has led to the development to a multimillion dollar industry.
   a. Advertising to children
   b. Advertising research
   c. In-game advertising
   d. Industrial musical

36. A _____ or chief executive is typically the highest-ranking corporate officer (executive) or administrator in charge of total management of a corporation, company, organization reporting to the board of directors. In internal communication and press releases, many companies capitalize the term and those of other high positions, even when they are not proper nouns.

In some European Union countries, there are two separate boards, one executive board for the day-to-day business and one supervisory board for control purposes (elected by the shareholders.)

   a. Power III
   b. Decision Analyst
   c. Financial analyst
   d. Chief executive officer

37. The United States federal wage garnishment law, widely known as the _____ guards employees from discharge by their employers because their wages have been garnished in any one week. It was approved by the government in 1968. The Wage and Hour Division of the United States Department of Labor includes the Employment Standards Administration, who administers the act.
   a. 6-3-5 Brainwriting
   b. Consumer Credit Protection Act
   c. 180SearchAssistant
   d. Power III

38. The _____ is an American federal law (codified at 15 U.S.C. § 1681 et seq.) that regulates the collection, dissemination, and use of consumer credit information.
   a. Power III
   b. 6-3-5 Brainwriting
   c. Fair Credit Reporting Act
   d. 180SearchAssistant

39. The _____ is a US law that applies to labels on many consumer products. It requires the label to state:

- The identity of the product;
- The name and place of business of the manufacturer, packer, or distributor; and
- The net quantity of contents.

The contents statement must include both metric and U.S. customary units.

Passed under Lyndon B. Johnson in 1966, the law first took effect on July 1, 1967. The metric labeling requirement was added in 1992 and took effect on February 14, 1994.

   a. Fair Packaging and Labeling Act
   b. 180SearchAssistant
   c. 6-3-5 Brainwriting
   d. Power III

Chapter 2. The Environment in Which Marketing Operates

40. The _____ of 1914 (15 U.S.C §§ 41-58, as amended) established the Federal Trade Commission (FTC), a bipartisan body of five members appointed by the President of the United States for seven year terms. This Commission was authorized to issue Cease and Desist orders to large corporations to curb unfair trade practices. This Act also gave more flexibility to the US congress for judicial matters.
   a. Comparative negligence
   b. Gripe site
   c. Product liability
   d. Federal Trade Commission Act

41. _____ of consumer products (often supermarket goods) are distinguished by the absence of a brand name. They are identifed more by product characterstics.

    They may be manufactured by less [prominent companies], or manufactured on the same production line as a 'named' brand. _____ are usually priced below those products sold by supermarkets under their own brand (frequently referred to as 'store brands' or 'own brands'.)
   a. Generic brands
   b. Micro ads
   c. M80
   d. Gross Margin Return on Inventory Investment

42. _____ in economics and business is the result of an exchange and from that trade we assign a numerical monetary value to a good, service or asset. If I trade 4 apples for an orange, the _____ of an orange is 4 - apples. Inversely, the _____ of an apple is 1/4 oranges.
   a. Contribution margin-based pricing
   b. Pricing
   c. Discounts and allowances
   d. Price

43. _____ exists when sales of identical goods or services are transacted at different prices from the same provider. In a theoretical market with perfect information, no transaction costs or prohibition on secondary exchange (or re-selling) to prevent arbitrage, _____ can only be a feature of monopoly and oligopoly markets, where market power can be exercised. Otherwise, the moment the seller tries to sell the same good at different prices, the buyer at the lower price can arbitrage by selling to the consumer buying at the higher price but with a tiny discount.
   a. Penetration pricing
   b. Price
   c. Resale price maintenance
   d. Price discrimination

44. The _____ of 1936 (or Anti-Price Discrimination Act, 15 U.S.C. § 13) is a United States federal law that prohibits what were considered, at the time of passage, to be anticompetitive practices by producers, specifically price discrimination. It grew out of practices in which chain stores were allowed to purchase goods at lower prices than other retailers.
   a. Fair Debt Collection Practices Act
   b. Robinson-Patman Act
   c. Trademark infringement
   d. Registered trademark symbol

45. A _____ or trade mark, identified by the symbols ™ (not yet registered) and ® (registered) business organization or other legal entity to identify that the products and/or services to consumers with which the _____ appears originate from a unique source of origin, and to distinguish its products or services from those of other entities. A _____ is a type of intellectual property, and typically a name, word, phrase, logo, symbol, design, image, or a combination of these elements. There is also a range of non-conventional _____s comprising marks which do not fall into these standard categories.
   a. Risk management
   b. Power III
   c. 180SearchAssistant
   d. Trademark

Chapter 2. The Environment in Which Marketing Operates

46. _____ was originally coined by Austrian psychologist Alfred Adler in 1929. The current broader sense of the word dates from 1961.

In sociology, a _____ is the way a person lives.

   a. 6-3-5 Brainwriting
   b. 180SearchAssistant
   c. Lifestyle
   d. Power III

47. _____ are final goods specifically intended for the mass market. For instance, _____ do not include investment assets, like precious antiques, even though these antiques are final goods.

Manufactured goods are goods that have been processed by way of machinery.

   a. Free good
   b. Power III
   c. Durable good
   d. Consumer Goods

48. The _____ was enacted in 1972 by the United States Congress. It established the United States Consumer Product Safety Commission as an independent agency of the United States federal government and defined its basic authority. The act gives CPSC the power to develop safety standards and pursue recalls for products that present unreasonable or substantial risks of injury or death to consumers.

   a. 180SearchAssistant
   b. 6-3-5 Brainwriting
   c. Power III
   d. Consumer Product Safety Act

49. _____ is a form of government regulation which protects the interests of consumers. For example, a government may require businesses to disclose detailed information about products--particularly in areas where safety or public health is an issue, such as food. _____ is linked to the idea of consumer rights (that consumers have various rights as consumers), and to the formation of consumer organizations which help consumers make better choices in the marketplace.

   a. Sound trademark
   b. Federal Bureau of Investigation
   c. Trademark dilution
   d. Consumer Protection

50. The _____, 15 U.S.C. § 1692 et seq., is a United States statute added in 1978 as Title VIII of the Consumer Credit Protection Act. Its purposes are to eliminate abusive practices in the collection of consumer debts, to promote fair debt collection and to provide consumers with an avenue for disputing and obtaining validation of debt information in order to ensure the information's accuracy.

   a. Fair Debt Collection Practices Act
   b. Mediation
   c. Fair trade law
   d. Service mark

51. _____ is the realization of an application idea, model, design, specification, standard, algorithm an _____ is a realization of a technical specification or algorithm as a program, software component, or other computer system. Many _____s may exist for a given specification or standard.

   a. AMAX
   b. ADTECH
   c. ACNielsen
   d. Implementation

52. _____ is the practice of individuals including commercial businesses, governments and institutions, facilitating the sale of their products or services to other companies or organizations that in turn resell them, use them as components in products or services they offer _____ is also called business-to-_____ for short. (Note that while marketing to government entities shares some of the same dynamics of organizational marketing, B2G Marketing is meaningfully different.)

a. Law of disruption
b. Business marketing
c. Disruptive technology
d. Mass marketing

53. _____ is a method of direct marketing in which a salesperson solicits to prospective customers to buy products or services, either over the phone or through a subsequent face to face or Web conferencing appointment scheduled during the call.

_____ can also include recorded sales pitches programmed to be played over the phone via automatic dialing. _____ has come under fire in recent years, being viewed as an annoyance by many.

a. Phishing
b. Directory Harvest Attack
c. Telemarketing
d. Joe job

54. _____ is a measure of the strength of a brand, product, service relative to competitive offerings. There is often a geographic element to the competitive landscape. In defining _____, you must see to what extent a product, brand, or firm controls a product category in a given geographic area.

a. Discretionary spending
b. Productivity
c. Market system
d. Market dominance

55. _____ is an advertisement in which a particular product specifically mentions a competitor by name for the express purpose of showing why the competitor is inferior to the product naming it.

This should not be confused with parody advertisements, where a fictional product is being advertised for the purpose of poking fun at the particular advertisement, nor should it be confused with the use of a coined brand name for the purpose of comparing the product without actually naming an actual competitor. ('Wikipedia tastes better and is less filling than the Encyclopedia Galactica.')

In the 1980s, during what has been referred to as the cola wars, soft-drink manufacturer Pepsi ran a series of advertisements where people, caught on hidden camera, in a blind taste test, chose Pepsi over rival Coca-Cola.

a. GL-70
b. Cost per conversion
c. Heavy-up
d. Comparative advertising

56. The _____ or gross domestic income (GDI) is one of the measures of national income and output for a given country's economy. It is the total value of all final goods and services produced in a particular economy; the dollar value of all goods and services produced within a country's borders in a given year. _____ can be defined in three ways, all of which are conceptually identical.

a. Macroeconomics
b. Leading indicator
c. Microeconomics
d. Gross Domestic Product

Chapter 2. The Environment in Which Marketing Operates

57. _____ is a term used in marketing as well as the title of an important marketing paper written by Theodore Levitt. This paper was first published in 1960 in the Harvard Business Review; a journal of which he was an editor.

Some commentators have suggested that its publication marked the beginning of the modern marketing movement.

- a. Business marketing
- b. Marketing performance measurement and management
- c. Corporate image
- d. Marketing myopia

58. _____ is the ongoing process of identifying and articulating market requirements that define a product's feature set.
- a. Targeted advertising
- b. Brand parity
- c. Market intelligence
- d. Product planning

59. _____s function as professionals who deal with trade, dealing in commodities that they do not produce themselves, in order to produce profit.

_____s can be of two types:

1. A wholesale _____ operates in the chain between producer and retail _____. Some wholesale _____s only organize the movement of goods rather than move the goods themselves.
2. A retail _____ or retailer, sells commodities to consumers (including businesses.) A shop owner is a retail _____.

A _____ class characterizes many pre-modern societies. Its status can range from high (even achieving titles like that of _____ prince or nabob) to low, such as in Chinese culture, due to the soiling capabilities of profiting from 'mere' trade, rather than from the labor of others reflected in agricultural produce, craftsmanship, and tribute.

In the United States, '_____' is defined (under the Uniform Commercial Code) as any person while engaged in a business or profession or a seller who deals regularly in the type of goods sold.

- a. RFM
- b. Retail loss prevention
- c. Trade credit
- d. Merchant

Chapter 3. Developing and Enacting Strategic Marketing Plans

1. _____ is a form of communication that typically attempts to persuade potential customers to purchase or to consume more of a particular brand of product or service. 'While now central to the contemporary global economy and the reproduction of global production networks, it is only quite recently that _____ has been more than a marginal influence on patterns of sales and production. The formation of modern _____ was intimately bound up with the emergence of new forms of monopoly capitalism around the end of the 19th and beginning of the 20th century as one element in corporate strategies to create, organize and where possible control markets, especially for mass produced consumer goods.
   a. ADTECH
   b. Advertising
   c. AMAX
   d. ACNielsen

2. _____ is defined by the American _____ Association as the activity, set of institutions, and processes for creating, communicating, delivering, and exchanging offerings that have value for customers, clients, partners, and society at large. The term developed from the original meaning which referred literally to going to market, as in shopping, or going to a market to sell goods or services.

   _____ practice tends to be seen as a creative industry, which includes advertising, distribution and selling.

   a. Customer acquisition management
   b. Marketing myopia
   c. Product naming
   d. Marketing

3. The _____ is generally accepted as the use and specification of the four p's describing the strategic position of a product in the marketplace. One version of the origins of the _____ starts in 1948 when James Culliton said that a marketing decision should be a result of something similar to a recipe. This version continued in 1953 when Neil Borden, in his American Marketing Association presidential address, took the recipe idea one step further and coined the term 'Marketing-Mix'.
   a. 180SearchAssistant
   b. Marketing mix
   c. 6-3-5 Brainwriting
   d. Power III

4. _____ in organizations and public policy is both the organizational process of creating and maintaining a plan; and the psychological process of thinking about the activities required to create a desired goal on some scale. As such, it is a fundamental property of intelligent behavior. This thought process is essential to the creation and refinement of a plan, or integration of it with other plans, that is, it combines forecasting of developments with the preparation of scenarios of how to react to them.
   a. Power III
   b. Planning
   c. 6-3-5 Brainwriting
   d. 180SearchAssistant

5. _____ is an organization's process of defining its strategy and making decisions on allocating its resources to pursue this strategy, including its capital and people. Various business analysis techniques can be used in _____, including SWOT analysis (Strengths, Weaknesses, Opportunities, and Threats) and PEST analysis (Political, Economic, Social, and Technological analysis) or STEER analysis involving Socio-cultural, Technological, Economic, Ecological, and Regulatory factors and EPISTEL (Environment, Political, Informatic, Social, Technological, Economic and Legal)

Chapter 3. Developing and Enacting Strategic Marketing Plans

_____ is the formal consideration of an organization's future course. All _____ deals with at least one of three key questions:

1. 'What do we do?'
2. 'For whom do we do it?'
3. 'How do we excel?'

In business _____, the third question is better phrased 'How can we beat or avoid competition?'. (Bradford and Duncan, page 1.)

a. 180SearchAssistant
b. 6-3-5 Brainwriting
c. Strategic planning
d. Power III

6. _____ is the management of the flow of goods, information and other resources, including energy and people, between the point of origin and the point of consumption in order to meet the requirements of consumers (frequently, and originally, military organizations.) _____ involves the integration of information, transportation, inventory, warehousing, material-handling, and packaging. _____ is a channel of the supply chain which adds the value of time and place utility.
   a. Logistics
   b. 6-3-5 Brainwriting
   c. 180SearchAssistant
   d. Power III

7. In economic models, the _____ time frame assumes no fixed factors of production. Firms can enter or leave the marketplace, and the cost (and availability) of land, labor, raw materials, and capital goods can be assumed to vary. In contrast, in the short-run time frame, certain factors are assumed to be fixed, because there is not sufficient time for them to change.
   a. Power III
   b. 180SearchAssistant
   c. 6-3-5 Brainwriting
   d. Long-run

8. A _____ is a written document that details the necessary actions to achieve one or more marketing objectives. It can be for a product or service, a brand, or a product line. _____s cover between one and five years.
   a. Marketing strategy
   b. Disruptive technology
   c. Prosumer
   d. Marketing plan

9. _____ consists of the sale of goods or merchandise from a fixed location, such as a department store or kiosk in small or individual lots for direct consumption by the purchaser. _____ may include subordinated services, such as delivery. Purchasers may be individuals or businesses.
   a. Charity shop
   b. Warehouse store
   c. Thrifting
   d. Retailing

10. A _____ is a formal statement of a set of business goals, the reasons why they are believed attainable, and the plan for reaching those goals. It may also contain background information about the organization or team attempting to reach those goals.

The business goals may be defined for for-profit or for non-profit organizations.

Chapter 3. Developing and Enacting Strategic Marketing Plans

a. Product marketing
b. Digital strategy
c. Logistics management
d. Business plan

11. _____ is one of the four elements of marketing mix. An organization or set of organizations (go-betweens) involved in the process of making a product or service available for use or consumption by a consumer or business user.

The other three parts of the marketing mix are product, pricing, and promotion.

a. Japan Advertising Photographers' Association
b. Better Living Through Chemistry
c. Comparison-Shopping agent
d. Distribution

12. _____ is understood as a business unit within the overall corporate identity which is distinguishable from other business because it serves a defined external market where management can conduct strategic planning in relation to products and markets. When companies become really large, they are best thought of as being composed of a number of businesses (or _____s.)

In the broader domain of strategic management, the phrase '_____' came into use in the 1960s, largely as a result of General Electric's many units.

a. Business strategy
b. Corporate strategy
c. Cost leadership
d. Strategic business unit

13. _____ is a marketing term, and involves evaluating the situation and trends in a particular company's market. _____ is often called the 'three c's', which refers to the three major elements that must be studied:

- Customers
- Costs
- Competition

The number of 'c's' is sometimes extended to four, five, or even six, with 'Collaboration', 'Company', and 'Competitive advantage'.

- Marketing mix
- SWOT analysis

a. Power III
b. 180SearchAssistant
c. 6-3-5 Brainwriting
d. Situation analysis

14. A supply chain is the system of organizations, people, technology, activities, information and resources involved in moving a product or service from _____ to customer. Supply chain activities transform natural resources, raw materials and components into a finished product that is delivered to the end customer. In sophisticated supply chain systems, used products may re-enter the supply chain at any point where residual value is recyclable.

a. Bringin' Home the Oil
b. Rebate
c. Product line extension
d. Supplier

15. _____ is a broad label that refers to any individuals or households that use goods and services generated within the economy. The concept of a _____ is used in different contexts, so that the usage and significance of the term may vary.

A _____ is a person who uses any product or service.

   a. 180SearchAssistant   b. Consumer
   c. Power III   d. 6-3-5 Brainwriting

16. _____ is the study of when, why, how, where and what people do or do not buy products. It blends elements from psychology, sociology,social psychology, anthropology and economics. It attempts to understand the buyer decision making process, both individually and in groups. It studies characteristics of individual consumers such as demographics and behavioural variables in an attempt to understand people's wants. It also tries to assess influences on the consumer from groups such as family, friends, reference groups, and society in general.

   a. Consumer behavior   b. Communal marketing
   c. Consumer confidence   d. Multidimensional scaling

17. _____ or _____ data refers to selected population characteristics as used in government, marketing or opinion research, or the _____ profiles used in such research. Note the distinction from the term 'demography' Commonly-used _____ include race, age, income, disabilities, mobility (in terms of travel time to work or number of vehicles available), educational attainment, home ownership, employment status, and even location.

   a. Albert Einstein   b. African Americans
   c. AStore   d. Demographic

18. _____ is a contract between two parties, one being the employer and the other being the employee. An employee may be defined as: 'A person in the service of another under any contract of hire, express or implied, oral or written, where the employer has the power or right to control and direct the employee in the material details of how the work is to be performed.' Black's Law Dictionary page 471 (5th ed. 1979.)

   a. ACNielsen   b. ADTECH
   c. AMAX   d. Employment

19. _____ is a list for goods and materials held available in stock by a business. It is also used for a list of the contents of a household and for a list for testamentary purposes of the possessions of someone who has died. In accounting _____ is considered an asset.

   a. ADTECH   b. ACNielsen
   c. Ending Inventory   d. Inventory

20. In economics, _____ is the desire to own something and the ability to pay for it. The term _____ signifies the ability or the willingness to buy a particular commodity at a given point of time .

   a. Demand   b. Market dominance
   c. Market system   d. Discretionary spending

21. _____ is an advertisement in which a particular product specifically mentions a competitor by name for the express purpose of showing why the competitor is inferior to the product naming it.

Chapter 3. Developing and Enacting Strategic Marketing Plans 25

This should not be confused with parody advertisements, where a fictional product is being advertised for the purpose of poking fun at the particular advertisement, nor should it be confused with the use of a coined brand name for the purpose of comparing the product without actually naming an actual competitor. ('Wikipedia tastes better and is less filling than the Encyclopedia Galactica.')

In the 1980s, during what has been referred to as the cola wars, soft-drink manufacturer Pepsi ran a series of advertisements where people, caught on hidden camera, in a blind taste test, chose Pepsi over rival Coca-Cola.

a. Cost per conversion
b. Comparative advertising
c. Heavy-up
d. GL-70

22. In grammar, the _____ is the form of an adjective or adverb which denotes the degree or grade by which a person, thing and is used in this context with a subordinating conjunction, such as than, as...as, etc.

The structure of a _____ in English consists normally of the positive form of the adjective or adverb, plus the suffix -er e.g. 'he is taller than his father is', or 'the village is less picturesque than the town nearby'.

a. 6-3-5 Brainwriting
b. Comparative
c. Power III
d. 180SearchAssistant

23. Organizational culture is not the same as _____. It is wider and deeper concepts, something that an organization 'is' rather than what it 'has' (according to Buchanan and Huczynski.)

_____ is the total sum of the values, customs, traditions and meanings that make a company unique.

a. Power III
b. 180SearchAssistant
c. Corporate culture
d. Cross-functional team

24. _____ is difficult to define. For example, in 1952, Alfred Kroeber and Clyde Kluckhohn compiled a list of 164 definitions of '_____' in _____: A Critical Review of Concepts and Definitions. However, the word '_____' is most commonly used in three basic senses:

- excellence of taste in the fine arts and humanities
- an integrated pattern of human knowledge, belief, and behavior that depends upon the capacity for symbolic thought and social learning
- the set of shared attitudes, values, goals, and practices that characterizes an institution, organization or group.

When the concept first emerged in eighteenth- and nineteenth-century Europe, it connoted a process of cultivation or improvement, as in agriculture or horticulture. In the nineteenth century, it came to refer first to the betterment or refinement of the individual, especially through education, and then to the fulfillment of national aspirations or ideals.

Chapter 3. Developing and Enacting Strategic Marketing Plans

    a. African Americans   b. Albert Einstein
    c. AStore   d. Culture

25. _____ is the equation of personal happiness with consumption and the purchase of material possessions.

The term is often associated with criticisms of consumption starting with Thorstein Veblen.

Veblen's subject of examination, the newly emergent middle class arising at the turn of the twentieth century, comes to full fruition by the end of the twentieth century through the process of globalization.

In economics, _____ refers to economic policies placing emphasis on consumption.

    a. 180SearchAssistant   b. 6-3-5 Brainwriting
    c. Consumerism   d. Power III

26. _____ is a branch of philosophy which seeks to address questions about morality, such as how a moral outcome can be achieved in a specific situation (applied _____), how moral values should be determined (normative _____), what moral values people actually abide by (descriptive _____), what the fundamental semantic, ontological, and epistemic nature of _____ or morality is (meta-_____), and how moral capacity or moral agency develops and what its nature is (moral psychology.)

Socrates was one of the first Greek philosophers to encourage both scholars and the common citizen to turn their attention from the outside world to the condition of man. In this view, Knowledge having a bearing on human life was placed highest, all other knowledge being secondary.

    a. ADTECH   b. AMAX
    c. Ethics   d. ACNielsen

27. The phrase _____, according to the Organization for Economic Co-operation and Development, refers to 'creative work undertaken on a systematic basis in order to increase the stock of knowledge, including knowledge of man, culture and society, and the use of this stock of knowledge to devise new applications [sic]' Though it is questionable that an organization is needed for this definition, as it is quite obvious that _____ refers to the _____ of something.

New product design and development is more often than not a crucial factor in the survival of a company. In an industry that is fast changing, firms must continually revise their design and range of products.

    a. 6-3-5 Brainwriting   b. 180SearchAssistant
    c. Research and development   d. Power III

28. In business, a _____ is a product or a business unit that generates unusually high profit margins: so high that it is responsible for a large amount of a company's operating profit. This profit far exceeds the amount necessary to maintain the _____ business, and the excess is used by the business for other purposes.

Chapter 3. Developing and Enacting Strategic Marketing Plans   27

A firm is said to be acting as a _____ when its earnings per share (EPS) is equal to its dividends per share (DPS), or in other words, when a firm pays out 100% of its free cash flow (FCF) to its shareholders as dividends at the end of each accounting term.

- a. Goal setting
- b. Crisis management
- c. Corporate transparency
- d. Cash cow

29. A _____ strategy targets non-buying customers in currently targeted segments. It also targets new customers in new segments. (Winer)

A marketing manager has to think about the following questions before implementing a _____ strategy: Is it profitable? Will it require the introduction of new or modified products? Is the customer and channel well enough researched and understood?

The marketing manager uses these four groups to give more focus to the market segment decision: existing customers, competitor customers, non-buying in current segments, new segments.

- a. Perceptual mapping
- b. Kano model
- c. Commercial planning
- d. Market development

30. _____ is one of the four growth strategies of the Product-Market Growth Matrix defined by Ansoff. _____ occurs when a company enters/penetrates a market with current products. The best way to achieve this is by gaining competitors' customers (part of their market share.)
- a. Pasar pagi
- b. Horizontal market
- c. Marketization
- d. Market penetration

31. A _____ is a process that can allow an organization to concentrate its limited resources on the greatest opportunities to increase sales and achieve a sustainable competitive advantage. A _____ should be centered around the key concept that customer satisfaction is the main goal.

A _____ is most effective when it is an integral component of corporate strategy, defining how the organization will successfully engage customers, prospects, and competitors in the market arena.

- a. Psychographic
- b. Cyberdoc
- c. Marketing strategy
- d. Societal marketing

32. A _____ is a plan of action designed to achieve a particular goal.

_____ is different from tactics. In military terms, tactics is concerned with the conduct of an engagement while _____ is concerned with how different engagements are linked.

- a. Power III
- b. 180SearchAssistant
- c. Strategy
- d. 6-3-5 Brainwriting

Chapter 3. Developing and Enacting Strategic Marketing Plans

33. In business and engineering, new _____ is the term used to describe the complete process of bringing a new product or service to market. There are two parallel paths involved in the Nproduct development process: one involves the idea generation, product design, and detail engineering; the other involves market research and marketing analysis. Companies typically see new _____ as the first stage in generating and commercializing new products within the overall strategic process of product life cycle management used to maintain or grow their market share.
    a. New product screening
    b. Specification tree
    c. New product development
    d. Product development

34. The U.S. _____ is an independent agency of the United States government which holds primary responsibility for enforcing the federal securities laws and regulating the securities industry, the nation's stock and options exchanges, and other electronic securities markets. The SEC was created by section 4 of the Securities Exchange Act of 1934 (now codified as 15 U.S.C. Â§ 78d and commonly referred to as the 1934 Act.)
    a. 6-3-5 Brainwriting
    b. Securities and Exchange Commission
    c. Power III
    d. 180SearchAssistant

35. _____ refer to a collection of facts usually collected as the result of experience, observation or experiment or a set of premises. This may consist of numbers, words particularly as measurements or observations of a set of variables. _____ are often viewed as a lowest level of abstraction from which information and knowledge are derived.
    a. Mean
    b. Pearson product-moment correlation coefficient
    c. Sample size
    d. Data

Chapter 4. Information for Marketing Decisions

1. _____ is understood as a business unit within the overall corporate identity which is distinguishable from other business because it serves a defined external market where management can conduct strategic planning in relation to products and markets. When companies become really large, they are best thought of as being composed of a number of businesses (or _____s.)

In the broader domain of strategic management, the phrase '_____' came into use in the 1960s, largely as a result of General Electric's many units.

   a. Business strategy
   b. Cost leadership
   c. Corporate strategy
   d. Strategic business unit

2. _____ is defined by the American _____ Association as the activity, set of institutions, and processes for creating, communicating, delivering, and exchanging offerings that have value for customers, clients, partners, and society at large. The term developed from the original meaning which referred literally to going to market, as in shopping, or going to a market to sell goods or services.

_____ practice tends to be seen as a creative industry, which includes advertising, distribution and selling.

   a. Customer acquisition management
   b. Marketing
   c. Product naming
   d. Marketing myopia

3. Consumer market research is a form of applied sociology that concentrates on understanding the behaviours, whims and preferences, of consumers in a market-based economy, and aims to understand the effects and comparative success of marketing campaigns. The field of consumer _____ as a statistical science was pioneered by Arthur Nielsen with the founding of the ACNielsen Company in 1923.

Thus _____ is the systematic and objective identification, collection, analysis, and dissemination of information for the purpose of assisting management in decision making related to the identification and solution of problems and opportunities in marketing.

   a. Focus group
   b. Marketing research process
   c. Logit analysis
   d. Marketing research

4. In economics, _____ is the desire to own something and the ability to pay for it. The term _____ signifies the ability or the willingness to buy a particular commodity at a given point of time.

   a. Demand
   b. Market dominance
   c. Market system
   d. Discretionary spending

5. _____ is an advertisement in which a particular product specifically mentions a competitor by name for the express purpose of showing why the competitor is inferior to the product naming it.

This should not be confused with parody advertisements, where a fictional product is being advertised for the purpose of poking fun at the particular advertisement, nor should it be confused with the use of a coined brand name for the purpose of comparing the product without actually naming an actual competitor. ('Wikipedia tastes better and is less filling than the Encyclopedia Galactica.')

In the 1980s, during what has been referred to as the cola wars, soft-drink manufacturer Pepsi ran a series of advertisements where people, caught on hidden camera, in a blind taste test, chose Pepsi over rival Coca-Cola.

a. Heavy-up
b. GL-70
c. Cost per conversion
d. Comparative advertising

6. _____ refer to a collection of facts usually collected as the result of experience, observation or experiment or a set of premises. This may consist of numbers, words particularly as measurements or observations of a set of variables. _____ are often viewed as a lowest level of abstraction from which information and knowledge are derived.

a. Pearson product-moment correlation coefficient
b. Data
c. Sample size
d. Mean

7. _____ , according to Cornish, 'the process of acquiring and analyzing information in order to understand the market (both existing and potential customers); to determine the current and future needs and preferences, attitudes and behavior of the market; and to assess changes in the business environment that may affect the size and nature of the market in the future.' ('Product', 1997, p147.)

This figure shows how the interaction between variables from producers, communication channels, and consumers vary the effectiveness of _____ which affects the performance of the sales of a new product. The product is central in a circle because it helps to direct what information is gathered and how.

a. Line extension
b. Co-branding
c. Brand parity
d. Market intelligence

8. _____ is a broad label that refers to any individuals or households that use goods and services generated within the economy. The concept of a _____ is used in different contexts, so that the usage and significance of the term may vary.

A _____ is a person who uses any product or service.

a. Power III
b. 6-3-5 Brainwriting
c. 180SearchAssistant
d. Consumer

9. _____ is a form of government regulation which protects the interests of consumers. For example, a government may require businesses to disclose detailed information about products--particularly in areas where safety or public health is an issue, such as food. _____ is linked to the idea of consumer rights (that consumers have various rights as consumers), and to the formation of consumer organizations which help consumers make better choices in the marketplace.

a. Federal Bureau of Investigation
b. Consumer Protection
c. Trademark dilution
d. Sound trademark

10. _____ is the process of extracting hidden patterns from data. As more data is gathered, with the amount of data doubling every three years, _____ is becoming an increasingly important tool to transform this data into information. It is commonly used in a wide range of profiling practices, such as marketing, surveillance, fraud detection and scientific discovery.

Chapter 4. Information for Marketing Decisions

a. 180SearchAssistant
b. Power III
c. Structure mining
d. Data mining

11. _____ is a form of marketing developed from direct response marketing campaigns conducted in the 1970's and 1980's which emphasizes customer retention and satisfaction, rather than a dominant focus on 'point of sale' transactions.

_____ differs from other forms of marketing in that it recognizes the long term value to the firm of keeping customers, as opposed to direct or 'Intrusion' marketing, which focuses upon acquisition of new clients by targeting majority demographics based upon prospective client lists.

_____ refers to long-term and mutually beneficial arrangement wherein both buyer and seller focus on value enhancement through the certain of more satisfying exchange. This approach attempts to transcend the simple purchase exchange process with customer to make more meaningful and richer contact by providing a more holistic, personalized purchase, and use orn consumption experience to create stronger ties.

a. Guerrilla Marketing
b. Global marketing
c. Diversity marketing
d. Relationship marketing

12. _____ is the ability of an individual or group to seclude themselves or information about themselves and thereby reveal themselves selectively. The boundaries and content of what is considered private differ among cultures and individuals, but share basic common themes. _____ is sometimes related to anonymity, the wish to remain unnoticed or unidentified in the public realm.

a. 180SearchAssistant
b. 6-3-5 Brainwriting
c. Power III
d. Privacy

13. Combining Existing _____ Sources with New Primary Data Sources

Imagine that we could get hold of a good collection of surveys taken in earlier years, such as detailed studies about changes going on in this phase and hopefully additional studies in the years to come. Analyzing this data base over time could give us a good picture of what changes actually have taken place in the orientation of the population and of the extent to which new technical concepts did have an impact on subgroups of the population. Furthermore, data archives can help to prepare studies on change over time by monitoring what questions have been asked in earlier years and alerting principal investigators to important questions which should be repeated in planned research projects.

a. Secondary data
b. 6-3-5 Brainwriting
c. Power III
d. 180SearchAssistant

14. A _____ is a written document that details the necessary actions to achieve one or more marketing objectives. It can be for a product or service, a brand, or a product line. _____s cover between one and five years.

a. Prosumer
b. Disruptive technology
c. Marketing strategy
d. Marketing plan

15. _____ is an organization's process of defining its strategy and making decisions on allocating its resources to pursue this strategy, including its capital and people. Various business analysis techniques can be used in _____, including SWOT analysis (Strengths, Weaknesses, Opportunities, and Threats) and PEST analysis (Political, Economic, Social, and Technological analysis) or STEER analysis involving Socio-cultural, Technological, Economic, Ecological, and Regulatory factors and EPISTEL (Environment, Political, Informatic, Social, Technological, Economic and Legal)

_____ is the formal consideration of an organization's future course. All _____ deals with at least one of three key questions:

1. 'What do we do?'
2. 'For whom do we do it?'
3. 'How do we excel?'

In business _____, the third question is better phrased 'How can we beat or avoid competition?'. (Bradford and Duncan, page 1.)

a. 180SearchAssistant
b. Power III
c. 6-3-5 Brainwriting
d. Strategic planning

16. _____ is the process of comparing the cost, cycle time, productivity, or quality of a specific process or method to another that is widely considered to be an industry standard or best practice. The result is often a business case for making changes in order to make improvements. The term _____ was first used by cobblers to measure ones feet for shoes.

a. Benchmarking
b. Switching cost
c. Business strategy
d. Strategic group

17. _____ in organizations and public policy is both the organizational process of creating and maintaining a plan; and the psychological process of thinking about the activities required to create a desired goal on some scale. As such, it is a fundamental property of intelligent behavior. This thought process is essential to the creation and refinement of a plan, or integration of it with other plans, that is, it combines forecasting of developments with the preparation of scenarios of how to react to them.

a. Power III
b. Planning
c. 6-3-5 Brainwriting
d. 180SearchAssistant

18. _____ is a term for unprocessed data, it is also known as primary data. It is a relative term _____ can be input to a computer program or used in manual analysis procedures such as gathering statistics from a survey.

a. Shoppers Food ' Pharmacy
b. Raw data
c. Product manager
d. Chief marketing officer

19. _____ is a form of communication that typically attempts to persuade potential customers to purchase or to consume more of a particular brand of product or service. 'While now central to the contemporary global economy and the reproduction of global production networks, it is only quite recently that _____ has been more than a marginal influence on patterns of sales and production. The formation of modern _____ was intimately bound up with the emergence of new forms of monopoly capitalism around the end of the 19th and beginning of the 20th century as one element in corporate strategies to create, organize and where possible control markets, especially for mass produced consumer goods.

Chapter 4. Information for Marketing Decisions

a. ACNielsen
b. ADTECH
c. AMAX
d. Advertising

20. _____ is a rivalry between individuals, groups, nations for territory, a niche, or allocation of resources. It arises whenever two or more parties strive for a goal which cannot be shared. _____ occurs naturally between living organisms which co-exist in the same environment.
   a. Non-price competition
   b. Price fixing
   c. Price competition
   d. Competition

21. _____ is a measure of the strength of a brand, product, service relative to competitive offerings. There is often a geographic element to the competitive landscape. In defining _____, you must see to what extent a product, brand, or firm controls a product category in a given geographic area.
   a. Discretionary spending
   b. Productivity
   c. Market system
   d. Market dominance

22. _____ is a term used to describe a process of preparing and collecting data - for example as part of a process improvement or similar project.

_____ usually takes place early on in an improvement project, and is often formalised through a _____ Plan which often contains the following activity.

1. Pre collection activity - Agree goals, target data, definitions, methods
2. Collection - _____
3. Present Findings - usually involves some form of sorting analysis and/or presentation.

A formal _____ process is necessary as it ensures that data gathered is both defined and accurate and that subsequent decisions based on arguments embodied in the findings are valid . The process provides both a baseline from which to measure from and in certain cases a target on what to improve. Types of _____ 1-By mail questionnaires 2-By personal interview

- Six sigma
- Sampling (statistics)

   a. Data collection
   b. 6-3-5 Brainwriting
   c. Power III
   d. 180SearchAssistant

23. _____ is a type of research conducted because a problem has not been clearly defined. _____ helps determine the best research design, data collection method and selection of subjects. Given its fundamental nature, _____ often concludes that a perceived problem does not actually exist.
   a. Intent scale translation
   b. ACNielsen
   c. IDDEA
   d. Exploratory research

24. _____ is a set of six steps which defines the tasks to be accomplished in conducting a marketing research study. These include problem definition, developing an approach to problem, research design formulation, field work, data preparation and analysis, and report generation and presentation.

a. Preference-rank translation
c. Market analysis
b. Marketing research process
d. Simple random sampling

25. In economics, an externality or spillover of an economic transaction is an impact on a party that is not directly involved in the transaction. In such a case, prices do not reflect the full costs or benefits in production or consumption of a product or service. A positive impact is called an _____ benefit, while a negative impact is called an _____ cost.
   a. AMAX
   c. ACNielsen
   b. ADTECH
   d. External

26. _____ is a specialized form of marketing research conducted to improve the efficiency of advertising. According to MarketConscious.com, 'It may focus on a specific ad or campaign, or may be directed at a more general understanding of how advertising works or how consumers use the information in advertising. It can entail a variety of research approaches, including psychological, sociological, economic, and other perspectives.'

1879 - N.W. Ayer conducts custom research in an attempt to win the advertising business of Nichols-Shepard Co., a manufacturer of agricultural machinery.

   a. INVISTA
   c. Advertising Research
   b. Electrolux
   d. American Medical Association

27. _____ is a way of expressing knowledge or belief that an event will occur or has occurred. In mathematics the concept has been given an exact meaning in _____ theory, that is used extensively in such areas of study as mathematics, statistics, finance, gambling, science, and philosophy to draw conclusions about the likelihood of potential events and the underlying mechanics of complex systems.
   a. Data
   c. Probability
   b. Linear regression
   d. Heteroskedastic

28. A sample is a subject chosen from a population for investigation. A _____ is one chosen by a method involving an unpredictable component. Random sampling can also refer to taking a number of independent observations from the same probability distribution, without involving any real population.
   a. 180SearchAssistant
   c. Selection bias
   b. Random sample
   d. Power III

Chapter 4. Information for Marketing Decisions 35

29. A number of different _____s are indicated below.

- Randomized controlled trial
    - Double-blind randomized trial
    - Single-blind randomized trial
    - Non-blind trial
- Nonrandomized trial (quasi-experiment)
    - Interrupted time series design (measures on a sample or a series of samples from the same population are obtained several times before and after a manipulated event or a naturally occurring event) - considered a type of quasi-experiment

- Cohort study
    - Prospective cohort
    - Retrospective cohort
    - Time series study
- Case-control study
    - Nested case-control study
- Cross-sectional study
    - Community survey (a type of cross-sectional study)

When choosing a _____, many factors must be taken into account. Different types of studies are subject to different types of bias. For example, recall bias is likely to occur in cross-sectional or case-control studies where subjects are asked to recall exposure to risk factors.

a. Power III
c. Longitudinal studies
b. 180SearchAssistant
d. Study design

30. _____ is that part of statistical practice concerned with the selection of individual observations intended to yield some knowledge about a population of concern, especially for the purposes of statistical inference. Each observation measures one or more properties (weight, location, etc.) of an observable entity enumerated to distinguish objects or individuals.
a. Sampling
c. AStore
b. Richard Buckminster 'Bucky' Fuller
d. Sports Marketing Group

31. _____ is either an activity of a living being (such as a human), consisting of receiving knowledge of the outside world through the senses, or the recording of data using scientific instruments. The term may also refer to any datum collected during this activity.

The scientific method requires _____s of nature to formulate and test hypotheses.

a. AMAX
c. ADTECH
b. ACNielsen
d. Observation

32. _____ in economics and business is the result of an exchange and from that trade we assign a numerical monetary value to a good, service or asset. If I trade 4 apples for an orange, the _____ of an orange is 4 - apples. Inversely, the _____ of an apple is 1/4 oranges.

a. Discounts and allowances
b. Contribution margin-based pricing
c. Price
d. Pricing

33. _____ exists when sales of identical goods or services are transacted at different prices from the same provider. In a theoretical market with perfect information, no transaction costs or prohibition on secondary exchange (or re-selling) to prevent arbitrage, _____ can only be a feature of monopoly and oligopoly markets, where market power can be exercised. Otherwise, the moment the seller tries to sell the same good at different prices, the buyer at the lower price can arbitrage by selling to the consumer buying at the higher price but with a tiny discount.
   a. Resale price maintenance
   b. Price discrimination
   c. Price
   d. Penetration pricing

34. _____ is the imitation of some real thing, state of affairs, or process. The act of simulating something generally entails representing certain key characteristics or behaviors of a selected physical or abstract system.

   _____ is used in many contexts, including the modeling of natural systems or human systems in order to gain insight into their functioning.

   a. Simulation
   b. 180SearchAssistant
   c. Power III
   d. 6-3-5 Brainwriting

35. _____ is one of the four Ps of the marketing mix. The other three aspects are product, promotion, and place. It is also a key variable in microeconomic price allocation theory.
   a. Price
   b. Pricing
   c. Competitor indexing
   d. Relationship based pricing

36. _____ is a type of a rating scale designed to measure the connotative meaning of objects, events, and concepts. The connotations are used to derive the attitude towards the given object, event or concept.

   Osgood's _____ was designed to measure the connotative meaning of concepts.

   a. Semantic differential
   b. Likert scale
   c. Power III
   d. Factor analysis

37. In economics, business, retail, and accounting, a _____ is the value of money that has been used up to produce something, and hence is not available for use anymore. In economics, a _____ is an alternative that is given up as a result of a decision. In business, the _____ may be one of acquisition, in which case the amount of money expended to acquire it is counted as _____.
   a. Transaction cost
   b. Variable cost
   c. Fixed costs
   d. Cost

38. _____ is a process of gathering, modeling, and transforming data with the goal of highlighting useful information, suggesting conclusions, and supporting decision making. _____ has multiple facets and approaches, encompassing diverse techniques under a variety of names, in different business, science, and social science domains.

   Data mining is a particular _____ technique that focuses on modeling and knowledge discovery for predictive rather than purely descriptive purposes.

a. Power III
c. 6-3-5 Brainwriting
b. Data analysis
d. 180SearchAssistant

Chapter 5. Societal, Ethical, and Consumer Issues

1. _____ is a broad label that refers to any individuals or households that use goods and services generated within the economy. The concept of a _____ is used in different contexts, so that the usage and significance of the term may vary.

A _____ is a person who uses any product or service.

- a. Power III
- b. 180SearchAssistant
- c. 6-3-5 Brainwriting
- d. Consumer

2. _____ is the equation of personal happiness with consumption and the purchase of material possessions.

The term is often associated with criticisms of consumption starting with Thorstein Veblen.

Veblen's subject of examination, the newly emergent middle class arising at the turn of the twentieth century, comes to full fruition by the end of the twentieth century through the process of globalization.

In economics, _____ refers to economic policies placing emphasis on consumption.

- a. 180SearchAssistant
- b. Consumerism
- c. Power III
- d. 6-3-5 Brainwriting

3. _____, a business term, is a measure of how products and services supplied by a company meet or surpass customer expectation. It is seen as a key performance indicator within business and is part of the four perspectives of a Balanced Scorecard.

In a competitive marketplace where businesses compete for customers, _____ is seen as a key differentiator and increasingly has become a key element of business strategy.

- a. Supplier diversity
- b. Customer base
- c. Psychological pricing
- d. Customer satisfaction

4. _____ is a branch of philosophy which seeks to address questions about morality, such as how a moral outcome can be achieved in a specific situation (applied _____), how moral values should be determined (normative _____), what moral values people actually abide by (descriptive _____), what the fundamental semantic, ontological, and epistemic nature of _____ or morality is (meta-_____), and how moral capacity or moral agency develops and what its nature is (moral psychology.)

Socrates was one of the first Greek philosophers to encourage both scholars and the common citizen to turn their attention from the outside world to the condition of man. In this view, Knowledge having a bearing on human life was placed highest, all other knowledge being secondary.

- a. ACNielsen
- b. ADTECH
- c. AMAX
- d. Ethics

Chapter 5. Societal, Ethical, and Consumer Issues 39

5. _____ is a form of communication that typically attempts to persuade potential customers to purchase or to consume more of a particular brand of product or service. 'While now central to the contemporary global economy and the reproduction of global production networks, it is only quite recently that _____ has been more than a marginal influence on patterns of sales and production. The formation of modern _____ was intimately bound up with the emergence of new forms of monopoly capitalism around the end of the 19th and beginning of the 20th century as one element in corporate strategies to create, organize and where possible control markets, especially for mass produced consumer goods.
   a. ACNielsen
   b. ADTECH
   c. AMAX
   d. Advertising

6. In economics, _____ is the desire to own something and the ability to pay for it. The term _____ signifies the ability or the willingness to buy a particular commodity at a given point of time.

   a. Market dominance
   b. Discretionary spending
   c. Market system
   d. Demand

7. _____ is the examining of goods or services from retailers with the intent to purchase at that time. _____ is an activity of selection and/or purchase. In some contexts it is considered a leisure activity as well as an economic one.
   a. Discount store
   b. Hawkers
   c. Khodebshchik
   d. Shopping

8. _____ is a rivalry between individuals, groups, nations for territory, a niche, or allocation of resources. It arises whenever two or more parties strive for a goal which cannot be shared. _____ occurs naturally between living organisms which co-exist in the same environment.
   a. Non-price competition
   b. Price fixing
   c. Price competition
   d. Competition

9. _____ is one of the four elements of marketing mix. An organization or set of organizations (go-betweens) involved in the process of making a product or service available for use or consumption by a consumer or business user.

   The other three parts of the marketing mix are product, pricing, and promotion.

   a. Japan Advertising Photographers' Association
   b. Better Living Through Chemistry
   c. Comparison-Shopping agent
   d. Distribution

10. _____ is a contract between two parties, one being the employer and the other being the employee. An employee may be defined as: 'A person in the service of another under any contract of hire, express or implied, oral or written, where the employer has the power or right to control and direct the employee in the material details of how the work is to be performed.' Black's Law Dictionary page 471 (5th ed. 1979.)
    a. AMAX
    b. ACNielsen
    c. Employment
    d. ADTECH

11. _____ was originally coined by Austrian psychologist Alfred Adler in 1929. The current broader sense of the word dates from 1961.

In sociology, a _____ is the way a person lives.

a. Lifestyle
b. Power III
c. 180SearchAssistant
d. 6-3-5 Brainwriting

12. _____ is defined by the American _____ Association as the activity, set of institutions, and processes for creating, communicating, delivering, and exchanging offerings that have value for customers, clients, partners, and society at large. The term developed from the original meaning which referred literally to going to market, as in shopping, or going to a market to sell goods or services.

_____ practice tends to be seen as a creative industry, which includes advertising, distribution and selling.

a. Marketing myopia
b. Product naming
c. Customer acquisition management
d. Marketing

13. _____ in organizations and public policy is both the organizational process of creating and maintaining a plan; and the psychological process of thinking about the activities required to create a desired goal on some scale. As such, it is a fundamental property of intelligent behavior. This thought process is essential to the creation and refinement of a plan, or integration of it with other plans, that is, it combines forecasting of developments with the preparation of scenarios of how to react to them.

a. Power III
b. 6-3-5 Brainwriting
c. Planning
d. 180SearchAssistant

14. _____ is an advertisement in which a particular product specifically mentions a competitor by name for the express purpose of showing why the competitor is inferior to the product naming it.

This should not be confused with parody advertisements, where a fictional product is being advertised for the purpose of poking fun at the particular advertisement, nor should it be confused with the use of a coined brand name for the purpose of comparing the product without actually naming an actual competitor. ('Wikipedia tastes better and is less filling than the Encyclopedia Galactica.')

In the 1980s, during what has been referred to as the cola wars, soft-drink manufacturer Pepsi ran a series of advertisements where people, caught on hidden camera, in a blind taste test, chose Pepsi over rival Coca-Cola.

a. GL-70
b. Heavy-up
c. Cost per conversion
d. Comparative advertising

15. The U.S. _____ is an independent agency of the United States government which holds primary responsibility for enforcing the federal securities laws and regulating the securities industry, the nation's stock and options exchanges, and other electronic securities markets. The SEC was created by section 4 of the Securities Exchange Act of 1934 (now codified as 15 U.S.C. § 78d and commonly referred to as the 1934 Act.)

a. Securities and Exchange Commission
b. 6-3-5 Brainwriting
c. Power III
d. 180SearchAssistant

Chapter 5. Societal, Ethical, and Consumer Issues

16. According to the American Marketing Association, _____ is the marketing of products that are presumed to be environmentally safe. Thus _____ incorporates a broad range of activities, including product modification, changes to the production process, packaging changes, as well as modifying advertising. Yet defining _____ is not a simple task where several meanings intersect and contradict each other; an example of this will be the existence of varying social, environmental and retail definitions attached to this term.

   a. Value proposition
   b. Customer Interaction Tracker
   c. Commercialization
   d. Green marketing

17. A _____ is a relatively new executive level position at a corporation, company, organization typically reporting directly to the CEO or board of directors. The _____ is responsible for a brand's image, experience, and promise, and propagating it throughout all aspects of the company. The brand officer oversees marketing, advertising, design, public relations and customer service departments.

   a. Power III
   b. Financial analyst
   c. Chief executive officer
   d. Chief brand officer

18. The _____ is a marketing term and refers to all of the forces outside of marketing that affect marketing management's ability to build and maintain successful relationships with target customers. The _____ consists of both the macroenvironment and the microenvironment.

The microenvironment refers to the forces that are close to the company and affect its ability to serve its customers.

   a. Business-to-consumer
   b. Market environment
   c. Psychographic
   d. Customer franchise

19. The _____ is an international financial institution that provides financial and technical assistance to developing countries for development programs (e.g. bridges, roads, schools, etc.) with the stated goal of reducing poverty.

The _____ differs from the _____ Group, in that the _____ comprises only two institutions:

- International Bank for Reconstruction and Development (IBRD)
- International Development Association (IDA)

Whereas the latter incorporates these two in addition to three more:

- International Finance Corporation (IFC)
- Multilateral Investment Guarantee Agency (MIGA)
- International Centre for Settlement of Investment Disputes (ICSID)

John Maynard Keynes (right) represented the UK at the conference, and Harry Dexter White represented the US.

The _____ was created following the ratification of the United Nations Monetary and Financial Conference of the Bretton Woods agreement. The concept was originally conceived in July 1944 at the United Nations Monetary and Financial Conference.

Chapter 5. Societal, Ethical, and Consumer Issues

a. 180SearchAssistant
b. 6-3-5 Brainwriting
c. Power III
d. World Bank

20. Human beings are also considered to be _____ because they have the ability to change raw materials into valuable _____. The term Human _____ can also be defined as the skills, energies, talents, abilities and knowledge that are used for the production of goods or the rendering of services. While taking into account human beings as _____, the following things have to be kept in mind:

- The size of the population
- The capabilities of the individuals in that population

Many _____ cannot be consumed in their original form. They have to be processed in order to change them into more usable commodities.

a. 180SearchAssistant
b. Power III
c. 6-3-5 Brainwriting
d. Resources

21. _____ is the process of a product becoming obsolete and/or non-functional after a certain period or amount of use in a way that is planned or designed by the manufacturer. _____ has potential benefits for a producer because the product fails and the consumer is under pressure to purchase again, whether from the same manufacturer (a replacement part or a newer model), or from a competitor which might also rely on _____. The purpose of _____ is to hide the real cost per use from the consumer, and charge a higher price than they would otherwise be willing to pay (or would be unwilling to spend all at once.)

a. Power III
b. 180SearchAssistant
c. 6-3-5 Brainwriting
d. Planned obsolescence

22. In economics, business, retail, and accounting, a _____ is the value of money that has been used up to produce something, and hence is not available for use anymore. In economics, a _____ is an alternative that is given up as a result of a decision. In business, the _____ may be one of acquisition, in which case the amount of money expended to acquire it is counted as _____.

a. Variable cost
b. Fixed costs
c. Transaction cost
d. Cost

23. _____ is one of the four aspects of promotional mix. (The other three parts of the promotional mix are advertising, personal selling, and publicity/public relations.) Media and non-media marketing communication are employed for a pre-determined, limited time to increase consumer demand, stimulate market demand or improve product availability.

a. New Media Strategies
b. Marketing communication
c. Merchandise
d. Sales promotion

24. _____ is the idea that the moral worth of an action is determined solely by its contribution to overall utility: that is, its contribution to happiness or pleasure as summed among all persons. It is thus a form of consequentialism, meaning that the moral worth of an action is determined by its outcome: put simply, the ends justify the means. Utility, the good to be maximized, has been defined by various thinkers as happiness or pleasure (versus suffering or pain), although preference utilitarians like Peter Singer define it as the satisfaction of preferences.

a. Albert Einstein
b. AStore
c. Utilitarianism
d. African Americans

25. _____ involves disseminating information about a product, product line, brand, or company. It is one of the four key aspects of the marketing mix. (The other three elements are product marketing, pricing, and distribution). P>_____ is generally sub-divided into two parts:

- Above the line _____: Promotion in the media (e.g. TV, radio, newspapers, Internet and Mobile Phones) in which the advertiser pays an advertising agency to place the ad
- Below the line _____: All other _____. Much of this is intended to be subtle enough for the consumer to be unaware that _____ is taking place. E.g. sponsorship, product placement, endorsements, sales _____, merchandising, direct mail, personal selling, public relations, trade shows

a. Davie Brown Index
b. Cashmere Agency
c. Bottling lines
d. Promotion

26. _____ refers to a type of marketing involving the cooperative efforts of a 'for profit' business and a non-profit organization for mutual benefit. The term is sometimes used more broadly and generally to refer to any type of marketing effort for social and other charitable causes, including in-house marketing efforts by non-profit organizations. Cause marketing differs from corporate giving (philanthropy) as the latter generally involves a specific donation that is tax deductible, while cause marketing is a marketing relationship generally not based on a donation.

a. Global marketing
b. Diversity marketing
c. Digital marketing
d. Cause-related marketing

27. _____ is subcontracting a process, such as product design or manufacturing, to a third-party company. The decision to outsource is often made in the interest of lowering cost or making better use of time and energy costs, redirecting or conserving energy directed at the competencies of a particular business, or to make more efficient use of land, labor, capital, (information) technology and resources. _____ became part of the business lexicon during the 1980s.

a. Intangible assets
b. ACNielsen
c. Outsourcing
d. In-house

28. _____ is the tendency to believe that one's own race or ethnic group is the most important and that some or all aspects of its culture are superior to those of other groups. Since within this ideology, individuals will judge other groups in relation to their own particular ethnic group or culture, especially with concern to language, behavior, customs, and religion. These ethnic distinctions and sub-divisions serve to define each ethnicity's unique cultural identity.

a. African Americans
b. AStore
c. Albert Einstein
d. Ethnocentrism

29. _____ is a measure of the strength of a brand, product, service relative to competitive offerings. There is often a geographic element to the competitive landscape. In defining _____, you must see to what extent a product, brand, or firm controls a product category in a given geographic area.

a. Productivity
b. Market dominance
c. Market system
d. Discretionary spending

Chapter 5. Societal, Ethical, and Consumer Issues

30. A personal and cultural _____ is a relative ethic _____, an assumption upon which implementation can be extrapolated. A _____ system is a set of consistent _____s and measures that is soo not true. A principle _____ is a foundation upon which other _____s and measures of integrity are based.
    a. Supreme Court of the United States
    b. Value
    c. Perceptual maps
    d. Package-on-Package

31. In 1962, President John F. Kennedy presented a speech to the United States Congress in which he extolled four basic consumer rights, later called The _____.

    While later expanded, the original six basic beliefs of consumer protection are the most widely recognized.

    In 1985, the concept of consumer rights was endorsed by the United Nations and expanded to included eight basic rights.

    a. Consumer bill of rights
    b. 180SearchAssistant
    c. Power III
    d. 6-3-5 Brainwriting

32. _____ is an independent, nonprofit testing and information organization serving consumers in the United States. Its mission is to test products, inform the public, and protect consumers. Its income is derived from the sale of its magazine Consumer Reports and other services, and from noncommercial contributions, grants, and fees.
    a. Consumers Union
    b. Goodyear Tire ' Rubber Company
    c. JPMorgan Chase ' Co.
    d. Checkoff

33. False advertising or _____ is the use of false or misleading statements in advertising. As advertising has the potential to persuade people into commercial transactions that they might otherwise avoid, many governments around the world use regulations to control false, deceptive or misleading advertising. Truth in labeling refers to essentially the same concept, that customers have the right to know what they are buying, and that all necessary information should be on the label.
    a. Misleading advertising
    b. Fine print
    c. Power III
    d. Deceptive advertising

34. Competitiveness is a comparative concept of the ability and performance of a firm, sub-sector or country to sell and supply goods and/or services in a given market. Although widely used in economics and business management, the usefulness of the concept, particularly in the context of national competitiveness, is vigorously disputed by economists, such as Paul Krugman .

    The term may also be applied to markets, where it is used to refer to the extent to which the market structure may be regarded as perfectly _____.

    a. Free trade zone
    b. Customs union
    c. Geographical pricing
    d. Competitive

35. _____ is a form of government regulation which protects the interests of consumers. For example, a government may require businesses to disclose detailed information about products--particularly in areas where safety or public health is an issue, such as food. _____ is linked to the idea of consumer rights (that consumers have various rights as consumers), and to the formation of consumer organizations which help consumers make better choices in the marketplace.

Chapter 5. Societal, Ethical, and Consumer Issues

a. Sound trademark
b. Consumer Protection
c. Federal Bureau of Investigation
d. Trademark dilution

36. An _____ is quite usually a standard guarantee from the seller of a product that specifies the extent to which the quality or performance of the product is assured and states the conditions under which the product can be returned, replaced, or repaired. It is often given in the form of a specific, written 'Warranty' document. However, a warranty may also arise by operation of law based upon the seller's description of the goods, and perhaps their source and quality, and any material deviation from that specification would violate the guarantee.
   a. Imperial Group v. Philip Morris
   b. Energy Star
   c. Office for Harmonization in the Internal Market
   d. Express warranty

37. _____ is one of the four Ps of the marketing mix. The other three aspects are product, promotion, and place. It is also a key variable in microeconomic price allocation theory.
   a. Relationship based pricing
   b. Price
   c. Competitor indexing
   d. Pricing

38. _____s function as professionals who deal with trade, dealing in commodities that they do not produce themselves, in order to produce profit.

_____s can be of two types:

1. A wholesale _____ operates in the chain between producer and retail _____. Some wholesale _____s only organize the movement of goods rather than move the goods themselves.
2. A retail _____ or retailer, sells commodities to consumers (including businesses.) A shop owner is a retail _____.

A _____ class characterizes many pre-modern societies. Its status can range from high (even achieving titles like that of _____ prince or nabob) to low, such as in Chinese culture, due to the soiling capabilities of profiting from 'mere' trade, rather than from the labor of others reflected in agricultural produce, craftsmanship, and tribute.

In the United States, '_____' is defined (under the Uniform Commercial Code) as any person while engaged in a business or profession or a seller who deals regularly in the type of goods sold.

   a. Trade credit
   b. Retail loss prevention
   c. RFM
   d. Merchant

39. The United States _____ is an independent agency of the United States government created in 1972 through the Consumer Product Safety Act to protect 'against unreasonable risks of injuries associated with consumer products.' As of 2006 its acting chairman is Nancy Nord, a Republican. The other commissioner is Thomas Hill Moore, a Democrat. Normally the board has three commissioners.
   a. 180SearchAssistant
   b. Consumer Product Safety Commission
   c. 6-3-5 Brainwriting
   d. Power III

Chapter 5. Societal, Ethical, and Consumer Issues

40. The U.S. _____ is an agency of the United States Department of Health and Human Services and is responsible for regulating and supervising the safety of foods, dietary supplements, drugs, vaccines, biological medical products, blood products, medical devices, radiation-emitting devices, veterinary products, and cosmetics. The FDA also enforces section 361 of the Public Health Service Act and the associated regulations, including sanitation requirements on interstate travel as well as specific rules for control of disease on products ranging from pet turtles to semen donations for assisted reproductive medicine techniques.

The FDA is an agency within the United States Department of Health and Human Services responsible for protecting and promoting the nation's public health.

- a. 180SearchAssistant
- b. Power III
- c. 6-3-5 Brainwriting
- d. Food and Drug Administration

41. In marketing, _____ has come to mean the process by which marketers try to create an image or identity in the minds of their target market for its product, brand, or organization. It is the 'relative competitive comparison' their product occupies in a given market as perceived by the target market.

Re-_____ involves changing the identity of a product, relative to the identity of competing products, in the collective minds of the target market.

- a. GE matrix
- b. Containerization
- c. Moratorium
- d. Positioning

42. A _____ is a type of wholesale merchant business that buys goods and bulk products from importers, other wholesalers and then sells to retailers. _____s can deal in any commodity destined for the retail market. Typical categories are food, lumber, hardware, fuel, and textiles.

- a. Refusal to deal
- b. Chief privacy officer
- c. Tacit collusion
- d. Jobbing house

43. _____ in economics and business is the result of an exchange and from that trade we assign a numerical monetary value to a good, service or asset. If I trade 4 apples for an orange, the _____ of an orange is 4 - apples. Inversely, the _____ of an apple is 1/4 oranges.

- a. Contribution margin-based pricing
- b. Pricing
- c. Discounts and allowances
- d. Price

44. The _____ is an independent agency of the United States government, established in 1914 by the _____ Act. Its principal mission is the promotion of 'consumer protection' and the elimination and prevention of what regulators perceive to be harmfully 'anti-competitive' business practices, such as coercive monopoly.

The _____ Act was one of President Wilson's major acts against trusts.

- a. Power III
- b. 6-3-5 Brainwriting
- c. 180SearchAssistant
- d. Federal Trade Commission

45. A _____ is the price one pays as remuneration for services, especially the honorarium paid to a doctor, lawyer, consultant, or other member of a learned profession. _____s usually allow for overhead, wages, costs, and markup.

Traditionally, professionals in Great Britain received a _____ in contradistinction to a payment, salary, or wage, and would often use guineas rather than pounds as units of account.

a. Transfer pricing
c. Price war

b. Price shading
d. Fee

Chapter 6. Global Aspects of Marketing

1. _____ is difficult to define. For example, in 1952, Alfred Kroeber and Clyde Kluckhohn compiled a list of 164 definitions of '_____' in _____: A Critical Review of Concepts and Definitions. However, the word '_____' is most commonly used in three basic senses:

- excellence of taste in the fine arts and humanities
- an integrated pattern of human knowledge, belief, and behavior that depends upon the capacity for symbolic thought and social learning
- the set of shared attitudes, values, goals, and practices that characterizes an institution, organization or group.

When the concept first emerged in eighteenth- and nineteenth-century Europe, it connoted a process of cultivation or improvement, as in agriculture or horticulture. In the nineteenth century, it came to refer first to the betterment or refinement of the individual, especially through education, and then to the fulfillment of national aspirations or ideals.

   a. African Americans   b. Albert Einstein
   c. AStore   d. Culture

2. _____ is exchange of capital, goods, and services across international borders or territories. In most countries, it represents a significant share of gross domestic product (GDP.) While _____ has been present throughout much of history , its economic, social, and political importance has been on the rise in recent centuries.
   a. ACNielsen   b. ADTECH
   c. Incoterms   d. International trade

3. The Oxford University Press defines _____ as 'marketing on a worldwide scale reconciling or taking commercial advantage of global operational differences, similarities and opportunities in order to meet global objectives.' Oxford University Press' Glossary of Marketing Terms.

Here are three reasons for the shift from domestic to _____ as given by the authors of the textbook, _____ Management--3rd Edition by Masaaki Kotabe and Kristiaan Helsen, 2004.

One of the product categories in which global competition has been easy to track is in U.S. automotive sales.

   a. Diversity marketing   b. Digital marketing
   c. Guerrilla Marketing   d. Global marketing

4. _____ Management is the succession of strategies used by management as a product goes through its _____. The conditions in which a product is sold changes over time and must be managed as it moves through its succession of stages.

The _____ goes through many phases, involves many professional disciplines, and requires many skills, tools and processes.

   a. Supplier diversity   b. Customer satisfaction
   c. Chain stores   d. Product life cycle

Chapter 6. Global Aspects of Marketing

5. _____ is a form of communication that typically attempts to persuade potential customers to purchase or to consume more of a particular brand of product or service. 'While now central to the contemporary global economy and the reproduction of global production networks, it is only quite recently that _____ has been more than a marginal influence on patterns of sales and production. The formation of modern _____ was intimately bound up with the emergence of new forms of monopoly capitalism around the end of the 19th and beginning of the 20th century as one element in corporate strategies to create, organize and where possible control markets, especially for mass produced consumer goods.
   a. ACNielsen
   b. AMAX
   c. Advertising
   d. ADTECH

6. In economics, _____ is the desire to own something and the ability to pay for it. The term _____ signifies the ability or the willingness to buy a particular commodity at a given point of time .

   a. Discretionary spending
   b. Demand
   c. Market dominance
   d. Market system

7. _____ is a measure of the strength of a brand, product, service relative to competitive offerings. There is often a geographic element to the competitive landscape. In defining _____, you must see to what extent a product, brand, or firm controls a product category in a given geographic area.
   a. Productivity
   b. Discretionary spending
   c. Market system
   d. Market dominance

8. _____ is defined by the American _____ Association as the activity, set of institutions, and processes for creating, communicating, delivering, and exchanging offerings that have value for customers, clients, partners, and society at large. The term developed from the original meaning which referred literally to going to market, as in shopping, or going to a market to sell goods or services.

   _____ practice tends to be seen as a creative industry, which includes advertising, distribution and selling.

   a. Product naming
   b. Customer acquisition management
   c. Marketing myopia
   d. Marketing

9. In grammar, the _____ is the form of an adjective or adverb which denotes the degree or grade by which a person, thing and is used in this context with a subordinating conjunction, such as than, as...as, etc.

   The structure of a _____ in English consists normally of the positive form of the adjective or adverb, plus the suffix -er e.g. 'he is taller than his father is', or 'the village is less picturesque than the town nearby'.

   a. Power III
   b. Comparative
   c. 6-3-5 Brainwriting
   d. 180SearchAssistant

10. _____ is a broad label that refers to any individuals or households that use goods and services generated within the economy. The concept of a _____ is used in different contexts, so that the usage and significance of the term may vary.

    A _____ is a person who uses any product or service.

Chapter 6. Global Aspects of Marketing

a. Power III
b. 6-3-5 Brainwriting
c. 180SearchAssistant
d. Consumer

11. _____ or _____ data refers to selected population characteristics as used in government, marketing or opinion research, or the _____ profiles used in such research. Note the distinction from the term 'demography' Commonly-used _____ include race, age, income, disabilities, mobility (in terms of travel time to work or number of vehicles available), educational attainment, home ownership, employment status, and even location.

a. Demographic
b. AStore
c. Albert Einstein
d. African Americans

12. The _____ is a model used to represent the process of explaining the transformation of countries from high birth rates and high death rates to low birth rates and low death rates as part of the economic development of a country from a pre-industrial to an industrialized economy. It is based on an interpretation begun in 1929 by the American demographer Warren Thompson of prior observed changes, or transitions, in birth and death rates in industrialized societies over the past two hundred years.

Most developed countries are beyond stage three of the model; the majority of developing countries are in stage 2 or stage 3.

a. Power III
b. 6-3-5 Brainwriting
c. 180SearchAssistant
d. Demographic transition model

13. _____s is the social science that studies the production, distribution, and consumption of goods and services. The term _____s comes from the Ancient Greek oá¼°κονομῐα from oá¼¶κος (oikos, 'house') + vÏŒμος (nomos, 'custom' or 'law'), hence 'rules of the house(hold)'. Current _____ models developed out of the broader field of political economy in the late 19th century, owing to a desire to use an empirical approach more akin to the physical sciences.

a. Industrial organization
b. ACNielsen
c. ADTECH
d. Economic

14. _____ is an advertisement in which a particular product specifically mentions a competitor by name for the express purpose of showing why the competitor is inferior to the product naming it.

This should not be confused with parody advertisements, where a fictional product is being advertised for the purpose of poking fun at the particular advertisement, nor should it be confused with the use of a coined brand name for the purpose of comparing the product without actually naming an actual competitor. ('Wikipedia tastes better and is less filling than the Encyclopedia Galactica.')

In the 1980s, during what has been referred to as the cola wars, soft-drink manufacturer Pepsi ran a series of advertisements where people, caught on hidden camera, in a blind taste test, chose Pepsi over rival Coca-Cola.

a. Heavy-up
b. GL-70
c. Cost per conversion
d. Comparative advertising

Chapter 6. Global Aspects of Marketing

15. The _____ or gross domestic income (GDI) is one of the measures of national income and output for a given country's economy. It is the total value of all final goods and services produced in a particular economy; the dollar value of all goods and services produced within a country's borders in a given year. _____ can be defined in three ways, all of which are conceptually identical.

   a. Leading indicator
   b. Macroeconomics
   c. Gross Domestic Product
   d. Microeconomics

16. _____ is a rivalry between individuals, groups, nations for territory, a niche, or allocation of resources. It arises whenever two or more parties strive for a goal which cannot be shared. _____ occurs naturally between living organisms which co-exist in the same environment.

   a. Price fixing
   b. Non-price competition
   c. Competition
   d. Price competition

17. In economics and sociology, an _____ is any factor (financial or non-financial) that enables or motivates a particular course of action, or counts as a reason for preferring one choice to the alternatives. It is an expectation that encourages people to behave in a certain way. Since human beings are purposeful creatures, the study of _____ structures is central to the study of all economic activity (both in terms of individual decision-making and in terms of co-operation and competition within a larger institutional structure.)

   a. ADTECH
   b. AMAX
   c. ACNielsen
   d. Incentive

18. Competitiveness is a comparative concept of the ability and performance of a firm, sub-sector or country to sell and supply goods and/or services in a given market. Although widely used in economics and business management, the usefulness of the concept, particularly in the context of national competitiveness, is vigorously disputed by economists, such as Paul Krugman .

The term may also be applied to markets, where it is used to refer to the extent to which the market structure may be regarded as perfectly _____.

   a. Customs union
   b. Geographical pricing
   c. Free trade zone
   d. Competitive

19. The _____ is an international organization whose stated aims are to facilitate cooperation in international law, international security, economic development, social progress, human rights and achieving world peace. The _____ was founded in 1945 after World War II to replace the League of Nations, to stop wars between countries and to provide a platform for dialogue.

There are currently 192 member states, including nearly every recognized independent state in the world.

   a. ACNielsen
   b. ADTECH
   c. AMAX
   d. United Nations

20. The _____ is an international organization designed to supervise and liberalize international trade. The _____ came into being on 1 January 1995, and is the successor to the General Agreement on Tariffs and Trade (GATT), which was created in 1947, and continued to operate for almost five decades as a de facto international organization.

Chapter 6. Global Aspects of Marketing

The _____ deals with the rules of trade between nations at a near-global level; it is responsible for negotiating and implementing new trade agreements, and is in charge of policing member countries' adherence to all the _____ agreements, signed by the majority of the world's trading nations and ratified in their parliaments.

a. Merchandise Mart
c. Population Reference Bureau
b. World Trade Organization
d. BSI Group

21. However, there can be problems even with just using numerical averages to compare material standards of living, as opposed to, for instance, a Pareto index (a measure of the breadth of income or wealth distribution.) Standards of living are perhaps inherently subjective. As an example, countries with a very small, very rich upper class and a very large, very poor lower class may have a high mean level of income, even though the majority of people have a low '_____'.

a. Power III
c. 180SearchAssistant
b. 6-3-5 Brainwriting
d. Standard of living

22. The _____ is an international financial institution that provides financial and technical assistance to developing countries for development programs (e.g. bridges, roads, schools, etc.) with the stated goal of reducing poverty.

The _____ differs from the _____ Group, in that the _____ comprises only two institutions:

- International Bank for Reconstruction and Development (IBRD)
- International Development Association (IDA)

Whereas the latter incorporates these two in addition to three more:

- International Finance Corporation (IFC)
- Multilateral Investment Guarantee Agency (MIGA)
- International Centre for Settlement of Investment Disputes (ICSID)

John Maynard Keynes (right) represented the UK at the conference, and Harry Dexter White represented the US.

The _____ was created following the ratification of the United Nations Monetary and Financial Conference of the Bretton Woods agreement. The concept was originally conceived in July 1944 at the United Nations Monetary and Financial Conference.

a. 180SearchAssistant
c. Power III
b. 6-3-5 Brainwriting
d. World Bank

23. Organizational culture is not the same as _____. It is wider and deeper concepts, something that an organization 'is' rather than what it 'has' (according to Buchanan and Huczynski.)

_____ is the total sum of the values, customs, traditions and meanings that make a company unique.

Chapter 6. Global Aspects of Marketing

a. Cross-functional team
b. Power III
c. Corporate culture
d. 180SearchAssistant

24. _____ is a search engine marketing product where the search engine company charges fees related to inclusion of websites in their search index. _____ products are provided by most search engine companies, the most notable exception being Google.
   a. Paid inclusion
   b. Microsoft adCenter
   c. Hit inflation attack
   d. VoloMedia

25. _____ is the change in population over time, and can be quantified as the change in the number of individuals in a population using 'per unit time' for measurement. The term _____ can technically refer to any species, but almost always refers to humans, and it is often used informally for the more specific demographic term _____ rate , and is often used to refer specifically to the growth of the population of the world.

Simple models of _____ include the Malthusian Growth Model and the logistic model.

   a. 180SearchAssistant
   b. Population growth
   c. Power III
   d. 6-3-5 Brainwriting

26. The _____ is an economic and political union of 27 member states, located primarily in Europe. It was established by the Treaty of Maastricht on 1 November 1993 upon the foundations of the pre-existing European Economic Community. With almost 500 million citizens, the _____ combined generates an estimated 30% share (US$16.8 trillion in 2007) of the nominal gross world product.
   a. ADTECH
   b. Eurozone
   c. ACNielsen
   d. European Union

27. The _____ was the outcome of the failure of negotiating governments to create the International Trade Organization (ITO.) GATT was formed in 1947 and lasted until 1994, when it was replaced by the World Trade Organization. The Bretton Woods Conference had introduced the idea for an organization to regulate trade as part of a larger plan for economic recovery after World War II.
   a. General Agreement on Trade in Services
   b. Power III
   c. Trade pact
   d. General Agreement on Tariffs and Trade

28. A _____ is a tax imposed on goods when they are moved across a political boundary. They are usually associated with protectionism, the economic policy of restraining trade between nations. For political reasons, _____s are usually imposed on imported goods, although they may also be imposed on exported goods.
   a. Fiscal policy
   b. Tariff
   c. Power III
   d. Monetary policy

29. A _____ is a customs union with common policies on product regulation, and freedom of movement of the factors of production (capital and labour) and of enterprise. The goal is that the movement of capital, labour, goods, and services between the members is as easy as within them. This is the fourth stage of economic integration.
   a. Common Market
   b. Customs union
   c. Competitive
   d. Monetary union

Chapter 6. Global Aspects of Marketing

30. A _____ is an entity formed between two or more parties to undertake economic activity together. The parties agree to create a new entity by both contributing equity, and they then share in the revenues, expenses, and control of the enterprise. The venture can be for one specific project only, or a continuing business relationship such as the Fuji Xerox _____.

   a. Consumer protection
   b. Joint venture
   c. Trademark attorney
   d. Gripe site

31. _____s function as professionals who deal with trade, dealing in commodities that they do not produce themselves, in order to produce profit.

   _____s can be of two types:

   1. A wholesale _____ operates in the chain between producer and retail _____. Some wholesale _____s only organize the movement of goods rather than move the goods themselves.
   2. A retail _____ or retailer, sells commodities to consumers (including businesses.) A shop owner is a retail _____.

   A _____ class characterizes many pre-modern societies. Its status can range from high (even achieving titles like that of _____ prince or nabob) to low, such as in Chinese culture, due to the soiling capabilities of profiting from 'mere' trade, rather than from the labor of others reflected in agricultural produce, craftsmanship, and tribute.

   In the United States, '_____' is defined (under the Uniform Commercial Code) as any person while engaged in a business or profession or a seller who deals regularly in the type of goods sold.

   a. Retail loss prevention
   b. RFM
   c. Trade credit
   d. Merchant

32. _____ involves disseminating information about a product, product line, brand, or company. It is one of the four key aspects of the marketing mix. (The other three elements are product marketing, pricing, and distribution). P>_____ is generally sub-divided into two parts:

   - Above the line _____: Promotion in the media (e.g. TV, radio, newspapers, Internet and Mobile Phones) in which the advertiser pays an advertising agency to place the ad
   - Below the line _____: All other _____. Much of this is intended to be subtle enough for the consumer to be unaware that _____ is taking place. E.g. sponsorship, product placement, endorsements, sales _____, merchandising, direct mail, personal selling, public relations, trade shows

   a. Davie Brown Index
   b. Cashmere Agency
   c. Bottling lines
   d. Promotion

33. _____ is the state or fact of exclusive rights and control over property, which may be an object, land/real estate, or some other kind of property (like government-granted monopolies collectively referred to as intellectual property.) It is embodied in an _____ right also referred to as title.

   _____ is the key building block in the development of the capitalist socio-economic system.

a. ADTECH b. ACNielsen
c. AMAX d. Ownership

34. A _____ is a plan of action designed to achieve a particular goal.

_____ is different from tactics. In military terms, tactics is concerned with the conduct of an engagement while _____ is concerned with how different engagements are linked.

a. Strategy b. 180SearchAssistant
c. Power III d. 6-3-5 Brainwriting

35. _____ is one of the four elements of marketing mix. An organization or set of organizations (go-betweens) involved in the process of making a product or service available for use or consumption by a consumer or business user.

The other three parts of the marketing mix are product, pricing, and promotion.

a. Distribution b. Better Living Through Chemistry
c. Japan Advertising Photographers' Association d. Comparison-Shopping agent

36. _____ of consumer products (often supermarket goods) are distinguished by the absence of a brand name. They are identifed more by product characterstics.

They may be manufactured by less [prominent companies], or manufactured on the same production line as a 'named' brand. _____ are usually priced below those products sold by supermarkets under their own brand (frequently referred to as 'store brands' or 'own brands'.)

a. M80 b. Generic brands
c. Gross Margin Return on Inventory Investment d. Micro ads

37. A _____ or trade mark, identified by the symbols â„¢ (not yet registered) and Â® (registered) business organization or other legal entity to identify that the products and/or services to consumers with which the _____ appears originate from a unique source of origin, and to distinguish its products or services from those of other entities. A _____ is a type of intellectual property, and typically a name, word, phrase, logo, symbol, design, image, or a combination of these elements. There is also a range of non-conventional _____ s comprising marks which do not fall into these standard categories.

a. Power III b. Risk management
c. 180SearchAssistant d. Trademark

38. A _____ is a collection of symbols, experiences and associations connected with a product, a service, a person or any other artifact or entity.

_____ s have become increasingly important components of culture and the economy, now being described as 'cultural accessories and personal philosophies'.

Some people distinguish the psychological aspect of a _____ from the experiential aspect.

a. Store brand
b. Brandable software
c. Brand equity
d. Brand

39. A _____ is a written document that details the necessary actions to achieve one or more marketing objectives. It can be for a product or service, a brand, or a product line. _____s cover between one and five years.
   a. Marketing strategy
   b. Disruptive technology
   c. Prosumer
   d. Marketing plan

40. _____ is a branch of philosophy which seeks to address questions about morality, such as how a moral outcome can be achieved in a specific situation (applied _____), how moral values should be determined (normative _____), what moral values people actually abide by (descriptive _____), what the fundamental semantic, ontological, and epistemic nature of _____ or morality is (meta-_____), and how moral capacity or moral agency develops and what its nature is (moral psychology.)

Socrates was one of the first Greek philosophers to encourage both scholars and the common citizen to turn their attention from the outside world to the condition of man. In this view, Knowledge having a bearing on human life was placed highest, all other knowledge being secondary.

   a. ADTECH
   b. AMAX
   c. ACNielsen
   d. Ethics

41. _____ in organizations and public policy is both the organizational process of creating and maintaining a plan; and the psychological process of thinking about the activities required to create a desired goal on some scale. As such, it is a fundamental property of intelligent behavior. This thought process is essential to the creation and refinement of a plan, or integration of it with other plans, that is, it combines forecasting of developments with the preparation of scenarios of how to react to them.
   a. 6-3-5 Brainwriting
   b. 180SearchAssistant
   c. Power III
   d. Planning

42. _____ is the ongoing process of identifying and articulating market requirements that define a product's feature set.
   a. Market intelligence
   b. Brand parity
   c. Targeted advertising
   d. Product planning

43. In economics, '_____' can refer to any kind of predatory pricing. However, the word is now generally used only in the context of international trade law, where _____ is defined as the act of a manufacturer in one country exporting a product to another country at a price which is either below the price it charges in its home market or is below its costs of production. The term has a negative connotation, but advocates of free markets see '_____' as beneficial for consumers and believe that protectionism to prevent it would have net negative consequences.
   a. Hawkers
   b. Dumping
   c. Gold Key Matching Service
   d. Sample sales

Chapter 7. Marketing and the Internet

1. In economics, _____ is the desire to own something and the ability to pay for it. The term _____ signifies the ability or the willingness to buy a particular commodity at a given point of time.

   a. Market system
   b. Market dominance
   c. Discretionary spending
   d. Demand

2. _____ is a measure of the strength of a brand, product, service relative to competitive offerings. There is often a geographic element to the competitive landscape. In defining _____, you must see to what extent a product, brand, or firm controls a product category in a given geographic area.

   a. Discretionary spending
   b. Productivity
   c. Market system
   d. Market dominance

3. Electronic commerce, commonly known as _____ or eCommerce, consists of the buying and selling of products or services over electronic systems such as the Internet and other computer networks. The amount of trade conducted electronically has grown extraordinarily with wide-spread Internet usage. A wide variety of commerce is conducted in this way, spurring and drawing on innovations in electronic funds transfer, supply chain management, Internet marketing, online transaction processing, electronic data interchange (EDI), inventory management systems, and automated data collection systems.

   a. ACNielsen
   b. AMAX
   c. E-commerce
   d. ADTECH

4. The _____ is a very large set of interlinked hypertext documents accessed via the Internet. With a Web browser, one can view Web pages that may contain text, images, videos, and other multimedia and navigate between them using hyperlinks. Using concepts from earlier hypertext systems, the _____ was begun in 1992 by the English physicist Sir Tim Berners-Lee, now the Director of the _____ Consortium, and Robert Cailliau, a Belgian computer scientist, while both were working at CERN in Geneva, Switzerland.

   a. 180SearchAssistant
   b. 6-3-5 Brainwriting
   c. Power III
   d. World Wide Web

5. _____ is defined by the American _____ Association as the activity, set of institutions, and processes for creating, communicating, delivering, and exchanging offerings that have value for customers, clients, partners, and society at large. The term developed from the original meaning which referred literally to going to market, as in shopping, or going to a market to sell goods or services.

   _____ practice tends to be seen as a creative industry, which includes advertising, distribution and selling.

   a. Marketing
   b. Customer acquisition management
   c. Marketing myopia
   d. Product naming

6. _____ is an advertisement in which a particular product specifically mentions a competitor by name for the express purpose of showing why the competitor is inferior to the product naming it.

This should not be confused with parody advertisements, where a fictional product is being advertised for the purpose of poking fun at the particular advertisement, nor should it be confused with the use of a coined brand name for the purpose of comparing the product without actually naming an actual competitor. ('Wikipedia tastes better and is less filling than the Encyclopedia Galactica.')

In the 1980s, during what has been referred to as the cola wars, soft-drink manufacturer Pepsi ran a series of advertisements where people, caught on hidden camera, in a blind taste test, chose Pepsi over rival Coca-Cola.

a. Cost per conversion
b. Comparative advertising
c. Heavy-up
d. GL-70

7. _____ is a form of communication that typically attempts to persuade potential customers to purchase or to consume more of a particular brand of product or service. 'While now central to the contemporary global economy and the reproduction of global production networks, it is only quite recently that _____ has been more than a marginal influence on patterns of sales and production. The formation of modern _____ was intimately bound up with the emergence of new forms of monopoly capitalism around the end of the 19th and beginning of the 20th century as one element in corporate strategies to create, organize and where possible control markets, especially for mass produced consumer goods.

a. ADTECH
b. AMAX
c. ACNielsen
d. Advertising

8. In economics, business, retail, and accounting, a _____ is the value of money that has been used up to produce something, and hence is not available for use anymore. In economics, a _____ is an alternative that is given up as a result of a decision. In business, the _____ may be one of acquisition, in which case the amount of money expended to acquire it is counted as _____.

a. Variable cost
b. Fixed costs
c. Cost
d. Transaction cost

9. _____ is one of the four Ps of the marketing mix. The other three aspects are product, promotion, and place. It is also a key variable in microeconomic price allocation theory.

a. Price
b. Competitor indexing
c. Relationship based pricing
d. Pricing

10. A _____ is a plan of action designed to achieve a particular goal.

_____ is different from tactics. In military terms, tactics is concerned with the conduct of an engagement while _____ is concerned with how different engagements are linked.

a. 180SearchAssistant
b. Power III
c. 6-3-5 Brainwriting
d. Strategy

11. _____ is subcontracting a process, such as product design or manufacturing, to a third-party company. The decision to outsource is often made in the interest of lowering cost or making better use of time and energy costs, redirecting or conserving energy directed at the competencies of a particular business, or to make more efficient use of land, labor, capital, (information) technology and resources. _____ became part of the business lexicon during the 1980s.

a. In-house
b. Intangible assets
c. ACNielsen
d. Outsourcing

12. _____ is the provision of service to customers before, during and after a purchase.

According to Turban et al., '_____ is a series of activities designed to enhance the level of customer satisfaction - that is, the feeling that a product or service has met the customer expectation.'

Its importance varies by product, industry and customer.

a. Customer experience
c. Facing

b. COPC Inc.
d. Customer service

13. Consumer market research is a form of applied sociology that concentrates on understanding the behaviours, whims and preferences, of consumers in a market-based economy, and aims to understand the effects and comparative success of marketing campaigns. The field of consumer _____ as a statistical science was pioneered by Arthur Nielsen with the founding of the ACNielsen Company in 1923 .

Thus _____ is the systematic and objective identification, collection, analysis, and dissemination of information for the purpose of assisting management in decision making related to the identification and solution of problems and opportunities in marketing.

a. Focus group
c. Marketing Research

b. Marketing research process
d. Logit analysis

14. _____ is a market coverage strategy in which a firm decides to ignore market segment differences and go after the whole market with one offer.it is type of marketing (or attempting to sell through persuasion) of a product to a wide audience. The idea is to broadcast a message that will reach the largest number of people possible. Traditionally _____ has focused on radio, television and newspapers as the medium used to reach this broad audience.

a. Cyberdoc
c. Business-to-consumer

b. Marketspace
d. Mass marketing

15. _____, in marketing, manufacturing, and management, is the use of flexible computer-aided manufacturing systems to produce custom output. Those systems combine the low unit costs of mass production processes with the flexibility of individual customization.

'_____' is the new frontier in business competition for both manufacturing and service industries.

a. Flanking marketing warfare strategies
c. Power III

b. Vertical integration
d. Mass customization

16. On an intranet or B2E Enterprise Web portals, personalization is often based on user attributes such as department, functional area, or role. The term _____ in this context refers to the ability of users to modify the page layout or specify what content should be displayed.

Chapter 7. Marketing and the Internet

There are two categories of personalizations:

1. Rule-based
2. Content-based

Web personalization models include rules-based filtering, based on 'if this, then that' rules processing, and collaborative filtering, which serves relevant material to customers by combining their own personal preferences with the preferences of like-minded others. Collaborative filtering works well for books, music, video, etc.

a. Customization
b. Self branding
c. Cashmere Agency
d. Movin'

17. _____ is a list for goods and materials held available in stock by a business. It is also used for a list of the contents of a household and for a list for testamentary purposes of the possessions of someone who has died. In accounting _____ is considered an asset.

a. ADTECH
b. Inventory
c. Ending Inventory
d. ACNielsen

18. _____ refers to a business or organization attempting to acquire goods or services to accomplish the goals of the enterprise. Though there are several organizations that attempt to set standards in the _____ process, processes can vary greatly between organizations. Typically the word '_____' is not used interchangeably with the word 'procurement', since procurement typically includes Expediting, Supplier Quality, and Traffic and Logistics (T'L) in addition to _____.

a. Drop shipping
b. Purchasing
c. Supply network
d. Supply chain

19. _____, also referred to as i-marketing, web marketing, online marketing is the marketing of products or services over the Internet.

The Internet has brought many unique benefits to marketing, one of which being lower costs for the distribution of information and media to a global audience. The interactive nature of _____, both in terms of providing instant response and eliciting responses, is a unique quality of the medium.

a. AMAX
b. ADTECH
c. Internet marketing
d. ACNielsen

20. _____ is marketing using many different marketing channels to reach a customer. In this sense, a channel might be a retail store, a web site, a mail order catalogue, or direct personal communications by letter, email or text message. The objective of the company doing the marketing is to make it easy for a consumer to buy from them in whatever way is most appropriate.

a. Blitz QFD
b. Macromarketing
c. Buy one, get one free
d. Multichannel marketing

21. _____ is one of the four elements of marketing mix. An organization or set of organizations (go-betweens) involved in the process of making a product or service available for use or consumption by a consumer or business user.

Chapter 7. Marketing and the Internet

The other three parts of the marketing mix are product, pricing, and promotion.

a. Better Living Through Chemistry
b. Comparison-Shopping agent
c. Japan Advertising Photographers' Association
d. Distribution

22. In the Mediterranean Basin and the Near East, a _____ is a small, separated garden pavilion open on some or all sides. _____s were common in Persia, India, Pakistan, and in the Ottoman Empire from the 13th century onward. Today, there are many _____s in and around the Topkapı Palace in Istanbul, and they are still a relatively common sight in Greece.

a. Kiosk
b. 180SearchAssistant
c. Power III
d. 6-3-5 Brainwriting

23. A _____ is a process that can allow an organization to concentrate its limited resources on the greatest opportunities to increase sales and achieve a sustainable competitive advantage. A _____ should be centered around the key concept that customer satisfaction is the main goal.

A _____ is most effective when it is an integral component of corporate strategy, defining how the organization will successfully engage customers, prospects, and competitors in the market arena.

a. Societal marketing
b. Psychographic
c. Cyberdoc
d. Marketing strategy

24. _____ involves disseminating information about a product, product line, brand, or company. It is one of the four key aspects of the marketing mix. (The other three elements are product marketing, pricing, and distribution). P>_____ is generally sub-divided into two parts:

- Above the line _____: Promotion in the media (e.g. TV, radio, newspapers, Internet and Mobile Phones) in which the advertiser pays an advertising agency to place the ad
- Below the line _____: All other _____. Much of this is intended to be subtle enough for the consumer to be unaware that _____ is taking place. E.g. sponsorship, product placement, endorsements, sales _____, merchandising, direct mail, personal selling, public relations, trade shows

a. Bottling lines
b. Cashmere Agency
c. Davie Brown Index
d. Promotion

25. _____ is one of the four aspects of promotional mix. (The other three parts of the promotional mix are advertising, personal selling, and publicity/public relations.) Media and non-media marketing communication are employed for a pre-determined, limited time to increase consumer demand, stimulate market demand or improve product availability.

a. Sales promotion
b. New Media Strategies
c. Marketing communication
d. Merchandise

26. _____ is the realization of an application idea, model, design, specification, standard, algorithm an _____ is a realization of a technical specification or algorithm as a program, software component, or other computer system. Many _____s may exist for a given specification or standard.

a. ACNielsen
b. AMAX
c. ADTECH
d. Implementation

27. _____ refers to the structured transmission of data between organizations by electronic means. It is used to transfer electronic documents from one computer system to another (ie from one trading partner to another trading partner. It is more than mere E-mail; for instance, organizations might replace bills of lading and even checks with appropriate _____ messages.
   a. ACNielsen
   b. AMAX
   c. Electronic data interchange
   d. ADTECH

28. _____ describes the situation when output from (or information about the result of) an event or phenomenon in the past will influence the same event/phenomenon in the present or future. When an event is part of a chain of cause-and-effect that forms a circuit or loop, then the event is said to 'feed back' into itself.

_____ is also a synonym for:

- _____ Signal; the information about the initial event that is the basis for subsequent modification of the event.
- _____ Loop; the causal path that leads from the initial generation of the _____ signal to the subsequent modification of the event.

_____ is a mechanism, process or signal that is looped back to control a system within itself. Such a loop is called a _____ loop.

   a. Feedback
   b. 6-3-5 Brainwriting
   c. Power III
   d. 180SearchAssistant

29. _____ is the examining of goods or services from retailers with the intent to purchase at that time. _____ is an activity of selection and/or purchase. In some contexts it is considered a leisure activity as well as an economic one.
   a. Hawkers
   b. Shopping
   c. Khodebshchik
   d. Discount store

30. _____ refer to a collection of facts usually collected as the result of experience, observation or experiment or a set of premises. This may consist of numbers, words particularly as measurements or observations of a set of variables. _____ are often viewed as a lowest level of abstraction from which information and knowledge are derived.
   a. Sample size
   b. Pearson product-moment correlation coefficient
   c. Mean
   d. Data

31. _____ is a broad label that refers to any individuals or households that use goods and services generated within the economy. The concept of a _____ is used in different contexts, so that the usage and significance of the term may vary.

A _____ is a person who uses any product or service.

a. Power III
b. 180SearchAssistant
c. 6-3-5 Brainwriting
d. Consumer

32. _____ in organizations and public policy is both the organizational process of creating and maintaining a plan; and the psychological process of thinking about the activities required to create a desired goal on some scale. As such, it is a fundamental property of intelligent behavior. This thought process is essential to the creation and refinement of a plan, or integration of it with other plans, that is, it combines forecasting of developments with the preparation of scenarios of how to react to them.
   a. 180SearchAssistant
   b. 6-3-5 Brainwriting
   c. Planning
   d. Power III

33. _____ is the ongoing process of identifying and articulating market requirements that define a product's feature set.
   a. Brand parity
   b. Product planning
   c. Targeted advertising
   d. Market intelligence

34. Merchandising refers to the methods, practices and operations conducted to promote and sustain certain categories of commercial activity. The term is understood to have different specific meanings depending on the context. _____ is a sale goods at a store

In marketing, one of the definitions of merchandising is the practice in which the brand or image from one product or service is used to sell another.

   a. Merchandising
   b. New Media Strategies
   c. Merchandise
   d. Sales promotion

35. _____ is the equation of personal happiness with consumption and the purchase of material possessions.

The term is often associated with criticisms of consumption starting with Thorstein Veblen.

Veblen's subject of examination, the newly emergent middle class arising at the turn of the twentieth century, comes to full fruition by the end of the twentieth century through the process of globalization.

In economics, _____ refers to economic policies placing emphasis on consumption.

   a. 6-3-5 Brainwriting
   b. Power III
   c. 180SearchAssistant
   d. Consumerism

36. A _____ is a written document that details the necessary actions to achieve one or more marketing objectives. It can be for a product or service, a brand, or a product line. _____s cover between one and five years.
   a. Marketing strategy
   b. Disruptive technology
   c. Prosumer
   d. Marketing plan

64 **Chapter 7. Marketing and the Internet**

37. _____ is a form of intellectual property which gives the creator of an original work exclusive rights for a certain time period in relation to that work, including its publication, distribution and adaptation; after which time the work is said to enter the public domain. _____ applies to any expressible form of an idea or information that is substantive and discrete. Some jurisdictions also recognize 'moral rights' of the creator of a work, such as the right to be credited for the work.
   a. Copyright
   b. Collective mark
   c. Celler-Kefauver Act
   d. Reasonable person standard

38. A _____ is a set of exclusive rights granted by a State to an inventor or his assignee for a limited period of time in exchange for a disclosure of an invention.

The procedure for granting _____s, the requirements placed on the _____ee and the extent of the exclusive rights vary widely between countries according to national laws and international agreements. Typically, however, a _____ application must include one or more claims defining the invention which must be new, inventive, and useful or industrially applicable.

   a. Foreign Corrupt Practices Act
   b. Patent
   c. Reasonable person standard
   d. Product liability

39. _____ is the ability of an individual or group to seclude themselves or information about themselves and thereby reveal themselves selectively. The boundaries and content of what is considered private differ among cultures and individuals, but share basic common themes. _____ is sometimes related to anonymity, the wish to remain unnoticed or unidentified in the public realm.
   a. Power III
   b. 6-3-5 Brainwriting
   c. 180SearchAssistant
   d. Privacy

40. A _____ is a framework for creating economic, social, and/or other forms of value. The term _____ is thus used for a broad range of informal and formal descriptions to represent core aspects of a business, including purpose, offerings, strategies, infrastructure, organizational structures, trading practices, and operational processes and policies.

In the most basic sense, a _____ is the method of doing business by which a company can sustain itself -- that is, generate revenue.

   a. Yield management
   b. Business model
   c. Service provider
   d. Pay to surf

41. _____ is a term used to describe the phenomenon of a marketplace being full or even overcrowded with products. It also refers to the extreme amount of advertising the average American sees in their daily lives. _____ is a major problem for marketers and advertisers.
   a. Procter ' Gamble
   b. Clutter
   c. Consumption Map
   d. Push

42. _____ is a branch of philosophy which seeks to address questions about morality, such as how a moral outcome can be achieved in a specific situation (applied _____), how moral values should be determined (normative _____), what moral values people actually abide by (descriptive _____), what the fundamental semantic, ontological, and epistemic nature of _____ or morality is (meta-_____), and how moral capacity or moral agency develops and what its nature is (moral psychology).

Socrates was one of the first Greek philosophers to encourage both scholars and the common citizen to turn their attention from the outside world to the condition of man. In this view, Knowledge having a bearing on human life was placed highest, all other knowledge being secondary.

a. AMAX
b. ADTECH
c. ACNielsen
d. Ethics

Chapter 8. Final Consumers

1. _____ is a broad label that refers to any individuals or households that use goods and services generated within the economy. The concept of a _____ is used in different contexts, so that the usage and significance of the term may vary.

   A _____ is a person who uses any product or service.

   a. 180SearchAssistant
   b. Consumer
   c. 6-3-5 Brainwriting
   d. Power III

2. In population genetics and population ecology, _____ is the number of individual organisms in a population.

   The effective _____ (N_e) is defined as 'the number of breeding individuals in an idealized population that would show the same amount of dispersion of allele frequencies under random genetic drift or the same amount of inbreeding as the population under consideration.' N_e is usually less than N (the absolute _____) and this has important applications in conservation genetics.

   Small _____ results in increased genetic drift.

   a. 6-3-5 Brainwriting
   b. Power III
   c. Population size
   d. 180SearchAssistant

3. _____ or _____ data refers to selected population characteristics as used in government, marketing or opinion research, or the _____ profiles used in such research. Note the distinction from the term 'demography' Commonly-used _____ include race, age, income, disabilities, mobility (in terms of travel time to work or number of vehicles available), educational attainment, home ownership, employment status, and even location.

   a. Demographic
   b. Albert Einstein
   c. African Americans
   d. AStore

4. The General Agreement on Tariffs and Trade was the outcome of the failure of negotiating governments to create the International Trade Organization (ITO.) _____ was formed in 1947 and lasted until 1994, when it was replaced by the World Trade Organization. The Bretton Woods Conference had introduced the idea for an organization to regulate trade as part of a larger plan for economic recovery after World War II.

   a. Trade pact
   b. General Agreement on Tariffs and Trade
   c. Power III
   d. GATT

5. The _____ or gross domestic income (GDI) is one of the measures of national income and output for a given country's economy. It is the total value of all final goods and services produced in a particular economy; the dollar value of all goods and services produced within a country's borders in a given year. _____ can be defined in three ways, all of which are conceptually identical.

   a. Gross domestic product
   b. Microeconomics
   c. Leading indicator
   d. Macroeconomics

6. The _____ was the outcome of the failure of negotiating governments to create the International Trade Organization (ITO.) GATT was formed in 1947 and lasted until 1994, when it was replaced by the World Trade Organization. The Bretton Woods Conference had introduced the idea for an organization to regulate trade as part of a larger plan for economic recovery after World War II.

a. General Agreement on Trade in Services
b. General Agreement on Tariffs and Trade
c. Trade pact
d. Power III

7. _____ is either an activity of a living being (such as a human), consisting of receiving knowledge of the outside world through the senses, or the recording of data using scientific instruments. The term may also refer to any datum collected during this activity.

The scientific method requires _____s of nature to formulate and test hypotheses.

a. ACNielsen
b. AMAX
c. Observation
d. ADTECH

8. Combining Existing _____ Sources with New Primary Data Sources

Imagine that we could get hold of a good collection of surveys taken in earlier years, such as detailed studies about changes going on in this phase and hopefully additional studies in the years to come. Analyzing this data base over time could give us a good picture of what changes actually have taken place in the orientation of the population and of the extent to which new technical concepts did have an impact on subgroups of the population. Furthermore, data archives can help to prepare studies on change over time by monitoring what questions have been asked in earlier years and alerting principal investigators to important questions which should be repeated in planned research projects.

a. 180SearchAssistant
b. 6-3-5 Brainwriting
c. Secondary data
d. Power III

9. A _____ is a tax imposed on goods when they are moved across a political boundary. They are usually associated with protectionism, the economic policy of restraining trade between nations. For political reasons, _____s are usually imposed on imported goods, although they may also be imposed on exported goods.
a. Monetary policy
b. Tariff
c. Power III
d. Fiscal policy

10. _____ is a form of communication that typically attempts to persuade potential customers to purchase or to consume more of a particular brand of product or service. 'While now central to the contemporary global economy and the reproduction of global production networks, it is only quite recently that _____ has been more than a marginal influence on patterns of sales and production. The formation of modern _____ was intimately bound up with the emergence of new forms of monopoly capitalism around the end of the 19th and beginning of the 20th century as one element in corporate strategies to create, organize and where possible control markets, especially for mass produced consumer goods.
a. Advertising
b. ACNielsen
c. AMAX
d. ADTECH

11. _____ refer to a collection of facts usually collected as the result of experience, observation or experiment or a set of premises. This may consist of numbers, words particularly as measurements or observations of a set of variables. _____ are often viewed as a lowest level of abstraction from which information and knowledge are derived.
a. Pearson product-moment correlation coefficient
b. Sample size
c. Mean
d. Data

12. _____ is a term used to describe a process of preparing and collecting data - for example as part of a process improvement or similar project.

_____ usually takes place early on in an improvement project, and is often formalised through a _____ Plan which often contains the following activity.

1. Pre collection activity - Agree goals, target data, definitions, methods
2. Collection - _____
3. Present Findings - usually involves some form of sorting analysis and/or presentation.

A formal _____ process is necessary as it ensures that data gathered is both defined and accurate and that subsequent decisions based on arguments embodied in the findings are valid . The process provides both a baseline from which to measure from and in certain cases a target on what to improve. Types of _____ 1-By mail questionnaires 2-By personal interview

- Six sigma
- Sampling (statistics)

a. 6-3-5 Brainwriting
c. Data collection
b. Power III
d. 180SearchAssistant

13. _____ is a measure of the strength of a brand, product, service relative to competitive offerings. There is often a geographic element to the competitive landscape. In defining _____, you must see to what extent a product, brand, or firm controls a product category in a given geographic area.
    a. Market system
    b. Productivity
    c. Discretionary spending
    d. Market dominance

14. _____ is defined by the American _____ Association as the activity, set of institutions, and processes for creating, communicating, delivering, and exchanging offerings that have value for customers, clients, partners, and society at large. The term developed from the original meaning which referred literally to going to market, as in shopping, or going to a market to sell goods or services.

_____ practice tends to be seen as a creative industry, which includes advertising, distribution and selling.

a. Marketing
c. Customer acquisition management
b. Product naming
d. Marketing myopia

15. _____s is the social science that studies the production, distribution, and consumption of goods and services. The term _____s comes from the Ancient Greek oá¼°κονομῖα from oá¼¶κος (oikos, 'house') + vῐΌεμος (nomos, 'custom' or 'law'), hence 'rules of the house(hold)'. Current _____ models developed out of the broader field of political economy in the late 19th century, owing to a desire to use an empirical approach more akin to the physical sciences.
    a. Industrial organization
    b. ADTECH
    c. Economic
    d. ACNielsen

Chapter 8. Final Consumers

16. _____ refers to the structured transmission of data between organizations by electronic means. It is used to transfer electronic documents from one computer system to another (ie) from one trading partner to another trading partner. It is more than mere E-mail; for instance, organizations might replace bills of lading and even checks with appropriate _____ messages.

    a. ACNielsen   b. ADTECH
    c. Electronic data interchange   d. AMAX

17. _____ is an advertisement in which a particular product specifically mentions a competitor by name for the express purpose of showing why the competitor is inferior to the product naming it.

This should not be confused with parody advertisements, where a fictional product is being advertised for the purpose of poking fun at the particular advertisement, nor should it be confused with the use of a coined brand name for the purpose of comparing the product without actually naming an actual competitor. ('Wikipedia tastes better and is less filling than the Encyclopedia Galactica.')

In the 1980s, during what has been referred to as the cola wars, soft-drink manufacturer Pepsi ran a series of advertisements where people, caught on hidden camera, in a blind taste test, chose Pepsi over rival Coca-Cola.

    a. Heavy-up   b. Comparative advertising
    c. Cost per conversion   d. GL-70

18. _____ is a mathematical science pertaining to the collection, analysis, interpretation or explanation, and presentation of data. It also provides tools for prediction and forecasting based on data. It is applicable to a wide variety of academic disciplines, from the natural and social sciences to the humanities, government and business.

    a. Null hypothesis   b. Type I error
    c. Statistics   d. Median

19. The _____ is an international organization whose stated aims are to facilitate cooperation in international law, international security, economic development, social progress, human rights and achieving world peace. The _____ was founded in 1945 after World War II to replace the League of Nations, to stop wars between countries and to provide a platform for dialogue.

There are currently 192 member states, including nearly every recognized independent state in the world.

    a. ACNielsen   b. United Nations
    c. ADTECH   d. AMAX

20. In economics, _____ is the desire to own something and the ability to pay for it. The term _____ signifies the ability or the willingness to buy a particular commodity at a given point of time.

    a. Demand   b. Discretionary spending
    c. Market system   d. Market dominance

Chapter 8. Final Consumers

21. _____ is the physical growth of urban areas from rural areas as a result of population immigration to an existing urban area. Effects include change in density and administration services. While the exact definition and population size of urbanized areas varies among different countries, _____ is attributed to growth of cities.

   a. AMAX
   b. Urbanization
   c. ADTECH
   d. ACNielsen

22. A _____ is a measure of the average price of consumer goods and services purchased by households. It is a price index determined by measuring the price of a standard group of goods meant to represent the typical market basket of a typical urban consumer. Related, but different, terms are the _____, the RPI, and the RPIX used in the United Kingdom.

   a. Power III
   b. CPI
   c. Consumer price index
   d. 180SearchAssistant

23. In economics, business, retail, and accounting, a _____ is the value of money that has been used up to produce something, and hence is not available for use anymore. In economics, a _____ is an alternative that is given up as a result of a decision. In business, the _____ may be one of acquisition, in which case the amount of money expended to acquire it is counted as _____.

   a. Variable cost
   b. Fixed costs
   c. Transaction cost
   d. Cost

24. _____ is income after subtracting taxes and normal expenses (such as rent or mortgage and food) to maintain a certain standard of living. It is the amount of an individual's income available for spending after the essentials (such as food, clothing, and shelter) have been taken care of:

   _____ = Gross income - taxes - necessities

Despite the formal definitions above, disposable income is commonly used to denote _____. The meaning should therefore be interpreted from context.

   a. 6-3-5 Brainwriting
   b. 180SearchAssistant
   c. Power III
   d. Discretionary income

25. _____ is gross income minus income tax on that income.

Discretionary income is income after subtracting taxes and normal expenses (such as rent or mortgage and food) to maintain a certain standard of living. It is the amount of an individual's income available for spending after the essentials (such as food, clothing, and shelter) have been taken care of:

   Discretionary income = Gross income - taxes - necessities

Despite the formal definitions above, _____ is commonly used to denote Discretionary income.

   a. 6-3-5 Brainwriting
   b. 180SearchAssistant
   c. Power III
   d. Disposable income

Chapter 8. Final Consumers

26. The _____ is an economic and political union of 27 member states, located primarily in Europe. It was established by the Treaty of Maastricht on 1 November 1993 upon the foundations of the pre-existing European Economic Community. With almost 500 million citizens, the _____ combined generates an estimated 30% share (US$16.8 trillion in 2007) of the nominal gross world product.
   a. Eurozone
   b. European Union
   c. ADTECH
   d. ACNielsen

27. _____ is one of the four aspects of promotional mix. (The other three parts of the promotional mix are advertising, personal selling, and publicity/public relations.) Media and non-media marketing communication are employed for a pre-determined, limited time to increase consumer demand, stimulate market demand or improve product availability.
   a. Merchandise
   b. Marketing communication
   c. New Media Strategies
   d. Sales promotion

28. The U.S. _____ is an independent agency of the United States government which holds primary responsibility for enforcing the federal securities laws and regulating the securities industry, the nation's stock and options exchanges, and other electronic securities markets. The SEC was created by section 4 of the Securities Exchange Act of 1934 (now codified as 15 U.S.C. § 78d and commonly referred to as the 1934 Act.)
   a. 6-3-5 Brainwriting
   b. Power III
   c. 180SearchAssistant
   d. Securities and Exchange Commission

29. A _____ is a type of department store, which sell products at prices lower than those asked by traditional retail outlets. Most discount department stores offer wide assortments of goods; others specialize in such merchandise as jewelry, electronic equipment, or electrical appliances. _____s are not dollar stores, which sell goods at a dollar or less.
   a. Sales per unit area
   b. Discount store
   c. Gruen transfer
   d. Strip mall

30. _____ in economics and business is the result of an exchange and from that trade we assign a numerical monetary value to a good, service or asset. If I trade 4 apples for an orange, the _____ of an orange is 4 - apples. Inversely, the _____ of an apple is 1/4 oranges.
   a. Price
   b. Contribution margin-based pricing
   c. Pricing
   d. Discounts and allowances

31. _____ involves disseminating information about a product, product line, brand, or company. It is one of the four key aspects of the marketing mix. (The other three elements are product marketing, pricing, and distribution). P>_____ is generally sub-divided into two parts:

   - Above the line _____: Promotion in the media (e.g. TV, radio, newspapers, Internet and Mobile Phones) in which the advertiser pays an advertising agency to place the ad
   - Below the line _____: All other _____. Much of this is intended to be subtle enough for the consumer to be unaware that _____ is taking place. E.g. sponsorship, product placement, endorsements, sales _____, merchandising, direct mail, personal selling, public relations, trade shows

   a. Cashmere Agency
   b. Promotion
   c. Davie Brown Index
   d. Bottling lines

Chapter 8. Final Consumers

32. A demographic or _____ is a term used in marketing and broadcasting, to describe a demographic grouping or a market segment. This typically involves age bands (as teenagers do not wish to purchase denture fixant), social class bands (as the rich may want different products than middle and lower classes and may be willing to pay more) and gender (partially because different physical attributes require different hygiene and clothing products, and partially because of the male/female mindsets.)

A _____ can be used to determine when and where advertising should be placed so as to achieve maximum results.

   a. Demographic profile
   b. Cocooning
   c. Shopping Neutral
   d. Diderot effect

33. _____ is difficult to define. For example, in 1952, Alfred Kroeber and Clyde Kluckhohn compiled a list of 164 definitions of '_____' in _____: A Critical Review of Concepts and Definitions. However, the word '_____' is most commonly used in three basic senses:

   - excellence of taste in the fine arts and humanities
   - an integrated pattern of human knowledge, belief, and behavior that depends upon the capacity for symbolic thought and social learning
   - the set of shared attitudes, values, goals, and practices that characterizes an institution, organization or group.

When the concept first emerged in eighteenth- and nineteenth-century Europe, it connoted a process of cultivation or improvement, as in agriculture or horticulture. In the nineteenth century, it came to refer first to the betterment or refinement of the individual, especially through education, and then to the fulfillment of national aspirations or ideals.

   a. Albert Einstein
   b. Culture
   c. AStore
   d. African Americans

34. A _____ is a subgroup of people or organizations sharing one or more characteristics that cause them to have similar product and/or service needs. A true _____ meets all of the following criteria: it is distinct from other segments (different segments have different needs), it is homogeneous within the segment (exhibits common needs); it responds similarly to a market stimulus, and it can be reached by a market intervention. The term is also used when consumers with identical product and/or service needs are divided up into groups so they can be charged different amounts.
   a. Production orientation
   b. Customer insight
   c. Commercial planning
   d. Market segment

35. _____ is a concept that arose out of the theory of two-step flow of communication propounded by Paul Lazarsfeld and Elihu Katz. This theory is one of several models that try to explain the diffusion of innovations, ideas, or commercial products.

The opinion leader is the agent who is an active media user and who interprets the meaning of media messages or content for lower-end media users.

Chapter 8. Final Consumers

a. ACNielsen
b. Opinion leadership
c. Elasticity
d. Intellectual property

36. _____ is the subjective judgment that people make about the characteristics and severity of a risk. The phrase is most commonly used in reference to natural hazards and threats to the environment or health, such as nuclear power. Several theories have been proposed to explain why different people make different estimates of the dangerousness of risks.

a. Risk perception
b. 6-3-5 Brainwriting
c. Power III
d. 180SearchAssistant

37. A _____ is a sociological concept referring to a group to which an individual or another group is compared.

_____s are used in order to evaluate and determine the nature of a given individual or other group's characteristics and sociological attributes. It is the group to which the individual relates or aspires relate himself or self psychologically.

a. Minority
b. Power III
c. Mociology
d. Reference group

38. _____ was originally coined by Austrian psychologist Alfred Adler in 1929. The current broader sense of the word dates from 1961.

In sociology, a _____ is the way a person lives.

a. 180SearchAssistant
b. 6-3-5 Brainwriting
c. Power III
d. Lifestyle

39. _____ is a concept that denotes the precise probability of specific eventualities. Technically, the notion of _____ is independent from the notion of value and, as such, eventualities may have both beneficial and adverse consequences. However, in general usage the convention is to focus only on potential negative impact to some characteristic of value that may arise from a future event.

a. 6-3-5 Brainwriting
b. Power III
c. Risk
d. 180SearchAssistant

40. _____ is a branch of philosophy which seeks to address questions about morality, such as how a moral outcome can be achieved in a specific situation (applied _____), how moral values should be determined (normative _____), what moral values people actually abide by (descriptive _____), what the fundamental semantic, ontological, and epistemic nature of _____ or morality is (meta-_____), and how moral capacity or moral agency develops and what its nature is (moral psychology.)

Socrates was one of the first Greek philosophers to encourage both scholars and the common citizen to turn their attention from the outside world to the condition of man. In this view, Knowledge having a bearing on human life was placed highest, all other knowledge being secondary.

Chapter 8. Final Consumers

a. ADTECH
b. ACNielsen
c. AMAX
d. Ethics

41. _____ is the set of reasons that determines one to engage in a particular behavior. The term is generally used for human _____ but, theoretically, it can be used to describe the causes for animal behavior as well
   a. 180SearchAssistant
   b. Role playing
   c. Power III
   d. Motivation

42. _____ is the examining of goods or services from retailers with the intent to purchase at that time. _____ is an activity of selection and/or purchase. In some contexts it is considered a leisure activity as well as an economic one.
   a. Hawkers
   b. Discount store
   c. Khodebshchik
   d. Shopping

43. _____ is a lifestyle characterized by minimizing the 'more is better' pursuit of wealth and consumption. Adherents may choose _____ for a variety of personal reasons, such as spirituality, health, increase in 'quality time' for family and friends, stress reduction, personal taste or frugality. E. F. Schumacher put it best by saying, 'Any intelligent fool can make things bigger, more complex, and more violent.
   a. Sustainable packaging
   b. Power III
   c. Sustainable development
   d. Simple living

44. A personal and cultural _____ is a relative ethic _____, an assumption upon which implementation can be extrapolated. A _____ system is a set of consistent _____s and measures that is soo not true. A principle _____ is a foundation upon which other _____s and measures of integrity are based.
   a. Supreme Court of the United States
   b. Package-on-Package
   c. Perceptual maps
   d. Value

45. _____ is an American magazine published monthly by Consumers Union. It publishes reviews and comparisons of consumer products and services based on reporting and results from its in-house testing laboratory. It also publishes cleaning and general buying guides.
   a. Power III
   b. Crossing the Chasm
   c. Magalog
   d. Consumer Reports

46. _____ is systematic determination of merit, worth, and significance of something or someone using criteria against a set of standards. _____ often is used to characterize and appraise subjects of interest in a wide range of human enterprises, including the arts, criminal justice, foundations and non-profit organizations, government, health care, and other human services.

Depending on the topic of interest, there are professional groups which look to the quality and rigor of the _____ process.

   a. ACNielsen
   b. AMAX
   c. ADTECH
   d. Evaluation

47. In marketing, _____ has come to mean the process by which marketers try to create an image or identity in the minds of their target market for its product, brand, or organization. It is the 'relative competitive comparison' their product occupies in a given market as perceived by the target market.

Re-_____ involves changing the identity of a product, relative to the identity of competing products, in the collective minds of the target market.

a. GE matrix
b. Containerization
c. Moratorium
d. Positioning

48. Cognition is the scientific term for 'the process of thought.' Its usage varies in different ways in accord with different disciplines: For example, in psychology and _____ science it refers to an information processing view of an individual's psychological functions. Other interpretations of the meaning of cognition link it to the development of concepts; individual minds, groups, organizations, and even larger coalitions of entities, can be modelled as 'societies' (Society of Mind), which cooperate to form concepts.

The autonomous elements of each 'society' would have the opportunity to demonstrate emergent behavior in the face of some crisis or opportunity.

a. 180SearchAssistant
b. Cognitive
c. Power III
d. 6-3-5 Brainwriting

49. _____ is an uncomfortable feeling caused by holding two contradictory ideas simultaneously. The 'ideas' or 'cognitions' in question may include attitudes and beliefs, and also the awareness of one's behavior. The theory of _____ proposes that people have a motivational drive to reduce dissonance by changing their attitudes, beliefs, and behaviors, or by justifying or rationalizing their attitudes, beliefs, and behaviors.

a. 180SearchAssistant
b. Power III
c. Perception
d. Cognitive dissonance

50. _____ can be regarded as an outcome of mental processes (cognitive process) leading to the selection of a course of action among several alternatives. Every _____ process produces a final choice. The output can be an action or an opinion of choice.

a. 180SearchAssistant
b. 6-3-5 Brainwriting
c. Power III
d. Decision making

51. A _____ is a collection of symbols, experiences and associations connected with a product, a service, a person or any other artifact or entity.

_____s have become increasingly important components of culture and the economy, now being described as 'cultural accessories and personal philosophies'.

Some people distinguish the psychological aspect of a _____ from the experiential aspect.

a. Brandable software
b. Store brand
c. Brand
d. Brand equity

Chapter 8. Final Consumers

52. _____, in marketing, consists of a consumer's commitment to repurchase the brand and can be demonstrated by repeated buying of a product or service or other positive behaviors such as word of mouth advocacy. True _____ implies that the consumer is willing, at least on occasion, to put aside their own desires in the interest of the brand. _____ has been proclaimed by some to be the ultimate goal of marketing.

   a. Brand awareness
   b. Trade Symbols
   c. Brand implementation
   d. Brand loyalty

53. _____ of consumer products (often supermarket goods) are distinguished by the absence of a brand name. They are identifed more by product characterstics.

   They may be manufactured by less [prominent companies], or manufactured on the same production line as a 'named' brand. _____ are usually priced below those products sold by supermarkets under their own brand (frequently referred to as 'store brands' or 'own brands'.)

   a. Gross Margin Return on Inventory Investment
   b. Micro ads
   c. Generic brands
   d. M80

54. _____ is the study of when, why, how, where and what people do or do not buy products. It blends elements from psychology, sociology, social psychology, anthropology and economics. It attempts to understand the buyer decision making process, both individually and in groups. It studies characteristics of individual consumers such as demographics and behavioural variables in an attempt to understand people's wants. It also tries to assess influences on the consumer from groups such as family, friends, reference groups, and society in general.

   a. Consumer confidence
   b. Multidimensional scaling
   c. Consumer behavior
   d. Communal marketing

55. _____ refers to a business or organization attempting to acquire goods or services to accomplish the goals of the enterprise. Though there are several organizations that attempt to set standards in the _____ process, processes can vary greatly between organizations. Typically the word '_____' is not used interchangeably with the word 'procurement', since procurement typically includes Expediting, Supplier Quality, and Traffic and Logistics (T'L) in addition to _____.

   a. Purchasing
   b. Supply network
   c. Drop shipping
   d. Supply chain

Chapter 9. Organizational Consumers

1. _____ is a broad label that refers to any individuals or households that use goods and services generated within the economy. The concept of a _____ is used in different contexts, so that the usage and significance of the term may vary.

A _____ is a person who uses any product or service.

  a. Consumer
  b. 6-3-5 Brainwriting
  c. Power III
  d. 180SearchAssistant

2. _____ is subcontracting a process, such as product design or manufacturing, to a third-party company. The decision to outsource is often made in the interest of lowering cost or making better use of time and energy costs, redirecting or conserving energy directed at the competencies of a particular business, or to make more efficient use of land, labor, capital, (information) technology and resources. _____ became part of the business lexicon during the 1980s.
  a. In-house
  b. Intangible assets
  c. ACNielsen
  d. Outsourcing

3. In economics, _____ is the desire to own something and the ability to pay for it. The term _____ signifies the ability or the willingness to buy a particular commodity at a given point of time .

  a. Discretionary spending
  b. Market dominance
  c. Market system
  d. Demand

4. _____ is an advertisement in which a particular product specifically mentions a competitor by name for the express purpose of showing why the competitor is inferior to the product naming it.

This should not be confused with parody advertisements, where a fictional product is being advertised for the purpose of poking fun at the particular advertisement, nor should it be confused with the use of a coined brand name for the purpose of comparing the product without actually naming an actual competitor. ('Wikipedia tastes better and is less filling than the Encyclopedia Galactica.')

In the 1980s, during what has been referred to as the cola wars, soft-drink manufacturer Pepsi ran a series of advertisements where people, caught on hidden camera, in a blind taste test, chose Pepsi over rival Coca-Cola.

  a. GL-70
  b. Heavy-up
  c. Cost per conversion
  d. Comparative advertising

5. _____ is difficult to define. For example, in 1952, Alfred Kroeber and Clyde Kluckhohn compiled a list of 164 definitions of '_____' in _____: A Critical Review of Concepts and Definitions. However, the word '_____' is most commonly used in three basic senses:

- excellence of taste in the fine arts and humanities
- an integrated pattern of human knowledge, belief, and behavior that depends upon the capacity for symbolic thought and social learning
- the set of shared attitudes, values, goals, and practices that characterizes an institution, organization or group.

When the concept first emerged in eighteenth- and nineteenth-century Europe, it connoted a process of cultivation or improvement, as in agriculture or horticulture. In the nineteenth century, it came to refer first to the betterment or refinement of the individual, especially through education, and then to the fulfillment of national aspirations or ideals.

- a. AStore
- b. Albert Einstein
- c. Culture
- d. African Americans

6. _____ is defined by the American _____ Association as the activity, set of institutions, and processes for creating, communicating, delivering, and exchanging offerings that have value for customers, clients, partners, and society at large. The term developed from the original meaning which referred literally to going to market, as in shopping, or going to a market to sell goods or services.

_____ practice tends to be seen as a creative industry, which includes advertising, distribution and selling.

- a. Customer acquisition management
- b. Marketing myopia
- c. Product naming
- d. Marketing

7. Competitiveness is a comparative concept of the ability and performance of a firm, sub-sector or country to sell and supply goods and/or services in a given market. Although widely used in economics and business management, the usefulness of the concept, particularly in the context of national competitiveness, is vigorously disputed by economists, such as Paul Krugman.

The term may also be applied to markets, where it is used to refer to the extent to which the market structure may be regarded as perfectly _____.

- a. Customs union
- b. Geographical pricing
- c. Free trade zone
- d. Competitive

8. _____ is the marketing strategy of giving each product in a product portfolio its own unique brand name. This is contrasted with family branding in which the products in a product line are given the same brand name. The advantage of _____ is that each product has a self image and identity that's unique.
- a. Engagement
- b. Online focus group
- c. Intangibility
- d. Individual branding

9. _____ is one of the four Ps of the marketing mix. The other three aspects are product, promotion, and place. It is also a key variable in microeconomic price allocation theory.
- a. Competitor indexing
- b. Relationship based pricing
- c. Price
- d. Pricing

10. _____ is the study of when, why, how, where and what people do or do not buy products. It blends elements from psychology, sociology, social psychology, anthropology and economics. It attempts to understand the buyer decision making process, both individually and in groups. It studies characteristics of individual consumers such as demographics and behavioural variables in an attempt to understand people's wants. It also tries to assess influences on the consumer from groups such as family, friends, reference groups, and society in general.

Chapter 9. Organizational Consumers

a. Consumer confidence
b. Multidimensional scaling
c. Communal marketing
d. Consumer behavior

11. _____ can be regarded as an outcome of mental processes (cognitive process) leading to the selection of a course of action among several alternatives. Every _____ process produces a final choice. The output can be an action or an opinion of choice.
a. 6-3-5 Brainwriting
b. Decision making
c. Power III
d. 180SearchAssistant

12. A _____ is a plan of action designed to achieve a particular goal.

_____ is different from tactics. In military terms, tactics is concerned with the conduct of an engagement while _____ is concerned with how different engagements are linked.

a. 6-3-5 Brainwriting
b. Power III
c. Strategy
d. 180SearchAssistant

13. _____ is a term in economics, where demand for one good or service occurs as a result of demand for another. This may occur as the former is a part of production of the second. For example, demand for coal leads to _____ for mining, as coal must be mined for coal to be consumed.
a. 180SearchAssistant
b. Derived demand
c. 6-3-5 Brainwriting
d. Power III

14. A personal and cultural _____ is a relative ethic _____, an assumption upon which implementation can be extrapolated. A _____ system is a set of consistent _____s and measures that is soo not true. A principle _____ is a foundation upon which other _____s and measures of integrity are based.
a. Package-on-Package
b. Value
c. Supreme Court of the United States
d. Perceptual maps

15.

_____ is a systematic method to improve the 'value' of goods or products and services by using an examination of function. Value, as defined, is the ratio of function to cost. Value can therefore be increased by either improving the function or reducing the cost.

a. 180SearchAssistant
b. Productivity
c. Power III
d. Value engineering

16. _____ is one of the four elements of marketing mix. An organization or set of organizations (go-betweens) involved in the process of making a product or service available for use or consumption by a consumer or business user.

The other three parts of the marketing mix are product, pricing, and promotion.

a. Comparison-Shopping agent
b. Better Living Through Chemistry
c. Distribution
d. Japan Advertising Photographers' Association

Chapter 9. Organizational Consumers

17. _____ is a form of communication that typically attempts to persuade potential customers to purchase or to consume more of a particular brand of product or service. 'While now central to the contemporary global economy and the reproduction of global production networks, it is only quite recently that _____ has been more than a marginal influence on patterns of sales and production. The formation of modern _____ was intimately bound up with the emergence of new forms of monopoly capitalism around the end of the 19th and beginning of the 20th century as one element in corporate strategies to create, organize and where possible control markets, especially for mass produced consumer goods.
   a. ACNielsen
   b. ADTECH
   c. AMAX
   d. Advertising

18. _____ in organizations and public policy is both the organizational process of creating and maintaining a plan; and the psychological process of thinking about the activities required to create a desired goal on some scale. As such, it is a fundamental property of intelligent behavior. This thought process is essential to the creation and refinement of a plan, or integration of it with other plans, that is, it combines forecasting of developments with the preparation of scenarios of how to react to them.
   a. 180SearchAssistant
   b. Planning
   c. Power III
   d. 6-3-5 Brainwriting

19. _____ is a rivalry between individuals, groups, nations for territory, a niche, or allocation of resources. It arises whenever two or more parties strive for a goal which cannot be shared. _____ occurs naturally between living organisms which co-exist in the same environment.
   a. Competition
   b. Non-price competition
   c. Price fixing
   d. Price competition

20. _____ is a form of government regulation which protects the interests of consumers. For example, a government may require businesses to disclose detailed information about products--particularly in areas where safety or public health is an issue, such as food. _____ is linked to the idea of consumer rights (that consumers have various rights as consumers), and to the formation of consumer organizations which help consumers make better choices in the marketplace.
   a. Sound trademark
   b. Trademark dilution
   c. Federal Bureau of Investigation
   d. Consumer Protection

21. In economics, business, retail, and accounting, a _____ is the value of money that has been used up to produce something, and hence is not available for use anymore. In economics, a _____ is an alternative that is given up as a result of a decision. In business, the _____ may be one of acquisition, in which case the amount of money expended to acquire it is counted as _____.
   a. Variable cost
   b. Cost
   c. Transaction cost
   d. Fixed costs

22. _____ is exchanging goods or services that are paid for, in whole or part, with other goods or services.

Chapter 9. Organizational Consumers 81

There are five main variants of _____:

- Barter: Exchange of goods or services directly for other goods or services without the use of money as means of purchase or payment.
- Switch trading: Practice in which one company sells to another its obligation to make a purchase in a given country.
- Counter purchase: Sale of goods and services to a country by a company that promises to make a future purchase of a specific product from the country.
- Buyback: occurs when a firm builds a plant in a country - or supplies technology, equipment, training, or other services to the country and agrees to take a certain percentage of the plant's output as partial payment for the contract.
- Offset: Agreement that a company will offset a hard - currency purchase of an unspecified product from that nation in the future. Agreement by one nation to buy a product from another, subject to the purchase of some or all of the components and raw materials from the buyer of the finished product, or the assembly of such product in the buyer nation.

a. Retail loss prevention
b. Merchant
c. RFM
d. Countertrade

23. A _____ is a written document that details the necessary actions to achieve one or more marketing objectives. It can be for a product or service, a brand, or a product line. _____s cover between one and five years.
a. Marketing strategy
b. Marketing plan
c. Disruptive technology
d. Prosumer

24. _____ or _____ data refers to selected population characteristics as used in government, marketing or opinion research, or the _____ profiles used in such research. Note the distinction from the term 'demography' Commonly-used _____ include race, age, income, disabilities, mobility (in terms of travel time to work or number of vehicles available), educational attainment, home ownership, employment status, and even location.
a. AStore
b. Albert Einstein
c. African Americans
d. Demographic

25. _____ is a measure of the strength of a brand, product, service relative to competitive offerings. There is often a geographic element to the competitive landscape. In defining _____, you must see to what extent a product, brand, or firm controls a product category in a given geographic area.
a. Productivity
b. Market system
c. Market dominance
d. Discretionary spending

26. _____ in economics and business is the result of an exchange and from that trade we assign a numerical monetary value to a good, service or asset. If I trade 4 apples for an orange, the _____ of an orange is 4 - apples. Inversely, the _____ of an apple is 1/4 oranges.
a. Pricing
b. Discounts and allowances
c. Contribution margin-based pricing
d. Price

27. _____ is an agreement between business competitors to sell the same product or service at the same price. In general, it is an agreement intended to ultimately push the price of a product as high as possible, leading to profits for all the sellers. _____ can also involve any agreement to fix, peg, discount or stabilize prices.

a. Price competition
b. Non-price competition
c. Direct competition
d. Price fixing

28. An _____ is the manufacturing of a good or service within a category. Although _____ is a broad term for any kind of economic production, in economics and urban planning _____ is a synonym for the secondary sector, which is a type of economic activity involved in the manufacturing of raw materials into goods and products.

There are four key industrial economic sectors: the primary sector, largely raw material extraction industries such as mining and farming; the secondary sector, involving refining, construction, and manufacturing; the tertiary sector, which deals with services (such as law and medicine) and distribution of manufactured goods; and the quaternary sector, a relatively new type of knowledge _____ focusing on technological research, design and development such as computer programming, and biochemistry.

a. ACNielsen
b. ADTECH
c. Industry
d. AMAX

29. A _____ is a type of wholesale merchant business that buys goods and bulk products from importers, other wholesalers and then sells to retailers. _____s can deal in any commodity destined for the retail market. Typical categories are food, lumber, hardware, fuel, and textiles.

a. Jobbing house
b. Refusal to deal
c. Tacit collusion
d. Chief privacy officer

30. The _____ or _____ is used by business and government to classify and measure economic activity in Canada, Mexico and the United States. It has largely replaced the older Standard Industrial Classification system; however, certain government departments and agencies, such as the U.S. Securities and Exchange Commission (SEC), still use the SIC codes.

The _____ numbering system is a six-digit code.

a. Power III
b. 6-3-5 Brainwriting
c. 180SearchAssistant
d. North American Industry Classification System

31. _____ consists of the sale of goods or merchandise from a fixed location, such as a department store or kiosk in small or individual lots for direct consumption by the purchaser. _____ may include subordinated services, such as delivery. Purchasers may be individuals or businesses.

a. Thrifting
b. Charity shop
c. Warehouse store
d. Retailing

32. The United States _____ is the Cabinet department of the United States government concerned with promoting economic growth. It was originally created as the United States _____ and Labor on February 14, 1903. It was subsequently renamed to the _____ on March 4, 1913, and its bureaus and agencies specializing in labor were transferred to the new Department of Labor.

a. 180SearchAssistant
b. 6-3-5 Brainwriting
c. Department of Commerce
d. Power III

33. The _____ is the Cabinet department of the United States government concerned with promoting economic growth. It was originally created as the _____ and Labor on February 14, 1903. It was subsequently renamed to the Department of Commerce on March 4, 1913, and its bureaus and agencies specializing in labor were transferred to the new Department of Labor.
  a. ADTECH
  b. AMAX
  c. United States Department of Commerce
  d. ACNielsen

34. _____ is the process of estimation in unknown situations. Prediction is a similar, but more general term. Both can refer to estimation of time series, cross-sectional or longitudinal data.
  a. Forecasting
  b. 180SearchAssistant
  c. 6-3-5 Brainwriting
  d. Power III

35. _____ refers to the methods of practicing and using another person's philosophy of business. The franchisor grants the independent operator the right to distribute its products, techniques, and trademarks for a percentage of gross monthly sales and a royalty fee. Various tangibles and intangibles such as national or international advertising, training, and other support services are commonly made available by the franchisor.
  a. 180SearchAssistant
  b. Franchising
  c. Franchise fee
  d. Power III

36. A _____ is the price one pays as remuneration for services, especially the honorarium paid to a doctor, lawyer, consultant, or other member of a learned profession. _____s usually allow for overhead, wages, costs, and markup.

Traditionally, professionals in Great Britain received a _____ in contradistinction to a payment, salary, or wage, and would often use guineas rather than pounds as units of account.

  a. Transfer pricing
  b. Price shading
  c. Fee
  d. Price war

37. A _____ is a business that is independently owned and operated, with a small number of employees and relatively low volume of sales. The legal definition of 'small' often varies by country and industry, but is generally under 100 employees in the United States and under 50 employees in the European Union. In comparison, the definition of mid-sized business by the number of employees is generally under 500 in the U.S. and 250 for the European Union.
  a. Time to market
  b. Customer centricity
  c. Product support
  d. Small Business

38. _____ is a list for goods and materials held available in stock by a business. It is also used for a list of the contents of a household and for a list for testamentary purposes of the possessions of someone who has died. In accounting _____ is considered an asset.
  a. Inventory
  b. ADTECH
  c. ACNielsen
  d. Ending Inventory

39. _____ describes the situation when output from (or information about the result of) an event or phenomenon in the past will influence the same event/phenomenon in the present or future. When an event is part of a chain of cause-and-effect that forms a circuit or loop, then the event is said to 'feed back' into itself.

_____ is also a synonym for:

- _____ Signal; the information about the initial event that is the basis for subsequent modification of the event.
- _____ Loop; the causal path that leads from the initial generation of the _____ signal to the subsequent modification of the event.

_____ is a mechanism, process or signal that is looped back to control a system within itself. Such a loop is called a _____ loop.

a. 180SearchAssistant
b. Power III
c. 6-3-5 Brainwriting
d. Feedback

40. _____ is a form of social influence. It is the process of guiding people toward the adoption of an idea, attitude, or action by rational and symbolic (though not always logical) means. It is strategy of problem-solving relying on 'appeals' rather than coercion.

a. Persuasion
b. 6-3-5 Brainwriting
c. Power III
d. 180SearchAssistant

41. _____ refers to a business or organization attempting to acquire goods or services to accomplish the goals of the enterprise. Though there are several organizations that attempt to set standards in the _____ process, processes can vary greatly between organizations. Typically the word '_____' is not used interchangeably with the word 'procurement', since procurement typically includes Expediting, Supplier Quality, and Traffic and Logistics (T'L) in addition to _____.

a. Drop shipping
b. Supply network
c. Purchasing
d. Supply chain

Chapter 10. Developing a Target Market Strategy

1. _____ is defined by the American _____ Association as the activity, set of institutions, and processes for creating, communicating, delivering, and exchanging offerings that have value for customers, clients, partners, and society at large. The term developed from the original meaning which referred literally to going to market, as in shopping, or going to a market to sell goods or services.

_____ practice tends to be seen as a creative industry, which includes advertising, distribution and selling.

a. Product naming
c. Customer acquisition management
b. Marketing
d. Marketing myopia

2. _____ is a broad label that refers to any individuals or households that use goods and services generated within the economy. The concept of a _____ is used in different contexts, so that the usage and significance of the term may vary.

A _____ is a person who uses any product or service.

a. 6-3-5 Brainwriting
c. Power III
b. 180SearchAssistant
d. Consumer

3. A _____ is a subgroup of people or organizations sharing one or more characteristics that cause them to have similar product and/or service needs. A true _____ meets all of the following criteria: it is distinct from other segments (different segments have different needs), it is homogeneous within the segment (exhibits common needs); it responds similarly to a market stimulus, and it can be reached by a market intervention. The term is also used when consumers with identical product and/or service needs are divided up into groups so they can be charged different amounts.

a. Customer insight
c. Commercial planning
b. Production orientation
d. Market segment

4. In marketing, _____ is the process of distinguishing the differences of a product or offering from others, to make it more attractive to a particular target market. This involves differentiating it from competitors' products as well as one's own product offerings.

Differentiation is a source of competitive advantage.

a. Packshot
c. Marketing myopia
b. Corporate image
d. Product differentiation

5. _____ consists of the sale of goods or merchandise from a fixed location, such as a department store or kiosk in small or individual lots for direct consumption by the purchaser. _____ may include subordinated services, such as delivery. Purchasers may be individuals or businesses.

a. Charity shop
c. Warehouse store
b. Thrifting
d. Retailing

6. _____ or _____ data refers to selected population characteristics as used in government, marketing or opinion research, or the _____ profiles used in such research. Note the distinction from the term 'demography' Commonly-used _____ include race, age, income, disabilities, mobility (in terms of travel time to work or number of vehicles available), educational attainment, home ownership, employment status, and even location.

a. African Americans
b. Demographic
c. AStore
d. Albert Einstein

7. _____ was originally coined by Austrian psychologist Alfred Adler in 1929. The current broader sense of the word dates from 1961.

In sociology, a _____ is the way a person lives.

a. 180SearchAssistant
b. Power III
c. 6-3-5 Brainwriting
d. Lifestyle

8. A _____ is a process that can allow an organization to concentrate its limited resources on the greatest opportunities to increase sales and achieve a sustainable competitive advantage. A _____ should be centered around the key concept that customer satisfaction is the main goal.

A _____ is most effective when it is an integral component of corporate strategy, defining how the organization will successfully engage customers, prospects, and competitors in the market arena.

a. Marketing strategy
b. Cyberdoc
c. Psychographic
d. Societal marketing

9. A _____ is a plan of action designed to achieve a particular goal.

_____ is different from tactics. In military terms, tactics is concerned with the conduct of an engagement while _____ is concerned with how different engagements are linked.

a. Power III
b. 180SearchAssistant
c. Strategy
d. 6-3-5 Brainwriting

10. In economics, _____ is the desire to own something and the ability to pay for it. The term _____ signifies the ability or the willingness to buy a particular commodity at a given point of time .

a. Market dominance
b. Discretionary spending
c. Market system
d. Demand

11. The _____ is an economic and political union of 27 member states, located primarily in Europe. It was established by the Treaty of Maastricht on 1 November 1993 upon the foundations of the pre-existing European Economic Community. With almost 500 million citizens, the _____ combined generates an estimated 30% share (US$16.8 trillion in 2007) of the nominal gross world product.

a. ACNielsen
b. Eurozone
c. ADTECH
d. European Union

12. _____ is the study of the Earth and its lands, features, inhabitants, and phenomena. A literal translation would be 'to describe or write about the Earth'. The first person to use the word '_____' was Eratosthenes .

Chapter 10. Developing a Target Market Strategy

a. Power III
b. 6-3-5 Brainwriting
c. 180SearchAssistant
d. Geography

13. _____ is the state or fact of exclusive rights and control over property, which may be an object, land/real estate, or some other kind of property (like government-granted monopolies collectively referred to as intellectual property.) It is embodied in an _____ right also referred to as title.

_____ is the key building block in the development of the capitalist socio-economic system.

a. Ownership
b. AMAX
c. ACNielsen
d. ADTECH

14. _____ refers to the methods of practicing and using another person's philosophy of business. The franchisor grants the independent operator the right to distribute its products, techniques, and trademarks for a percentage of gross monthly sales and a royalty fee. Various tangibles and intangibles such as national or international advertising, training, and other support services are commonly made available by the franchisor.

a. 180SearchAssistant
b. Franchise fee
c. Power III
d. Franchising

15. The United States _____ is the Cabinet department of the United States government concerned with promoting economic growth. It was originally created as the United States _____ and Labor on February 14, 1903. It was subsequently renamed to the _____ on March 4, 1913, and its bureaus and agencies specializing in labor were transferred to the new Department of Labor.

a. 180SearchAssistant
b. 6-3-5 Brainwriting
c. Power III
d. Department of Commerce

16. An _____ is the manufacturing of a good or service within a category. Although _____ is a broad term for any kind of economic production, in economics and urban planning _____ is a synonym for the secondary sector, which is a type of economic activity involved in the manufacturing of raw materials into goods and products.

There are four key industrial economic sectors: the primary sector, largely raw material extraction industries such as mining and farming; the secondary sector, involving refining, construction, and manufacturing; the tertiary sector, which deals with services (such as law and medicine) and distribution of manufactured goods; and the quaternary sector, a relatively new type of knowledge _____ focusing on technological research, design and development such as computer programming, and biochemistry.

a. Industry
b. AMAX
c. ACNielsen
d. ADTECH

17. _____ is exchange of capital, goods, and services across international borders or territories. In most countries, it represents a significant share of gross domestic product (GDP.) While _____ has been present throughout much of history, its economic, social, and political importance has been on the rise in recent centuries.

a. ADTECH
b. Incoterms
c. ACNielsen
d. International Trade

18. The _____ or _____ is used by business and government to classify and measure economic activity in Canada, Mexico and the United States. It has largely replaced the older Standard Industrial Classification system; however, certain government departments and agencies, such as the U.S. Securities and Exchange Commission (SEC), still use the SIC codes.

The _____ numbering system is a six-digit code.

   a. 6-3-5 Brainwriting
   b. 180SearchAssistant
   c. Power III
   d. North American Industry Classification System

19. The _____ is the Cabinet department of the United States government concerned with promoting economic growth. It was originally created as the _____ and Labor on February 14, 1903. It was subsequently renamed to the Department of Commerce on March 4, 1913, and its bureaus and agencies specializing in labor were transferred to the new Department of Labor.

   a. AMAX
   b. ACNielsen
   c. United States Department of Commerce
   d. ADTECH

20. The acronym _____, is a psychographic segmentation. It was developed in the 1970s to explain changing U.S. values and lifestyles. It has since been reworked to enhance its ability to predict consumer behavior.

According to the _____ Framework, groups of people are arranged in a rectangle and are based on two dimensions. The vertical dimension segments people based on the degree to which they are innovative and have resources such as income, education, self-confidence, intelligence, leadership skills, and energy.

   a. 180SearchAssistant
   b. VALS
   c. 6-3-5 Brainwriting
   d. Power III

21. In marketing, _____ has come to mean the process by which marketers try to create an image or identity in the minds of their target market for its product, brand, or organization. It is the 'relative competitive comparison' their product occupies in a given market as perceived by the target market.

Re-_____ involves changing the identity of a product, relative to the identity of competing products, in the collective minds of the target market.

   a. GE matrix
   b. Moratorium
   c. Containerization
   d. Positioning

22. Competitiveness is a comparative concept of the ability and performance of a firm, sub-sector or country to sell and supply goods and/or services in a given market. Although widely used in economics and business management, the usefulness of the concept, particularly in the context of national competitiveness, is vigorously disputed by economists, such as Paul Krugman .

The term may also be applied to markets, where it is used to refer to the extent to which the market structure may be regarded as perfectly _____.

Chapter 10. Developing a Target Market Strategy

a. Customs union
c. Competitive
b. Geographical pricing
d. Free trade zone

23. _____ is the process by which a new idea or new product is accepted by the market. The rate of _____ is the speed that the new idea spreads from one consumer to the next. Adoption is similar to _____ except that it deals with the psychological processes an individual goes through, rather than an aggregate market process.

a. Perceptual maps
c. Market development
b. Kano model
d. Diffusion

24. In probability theory, a branch of mathematics, a _____ is a solution to a stochastic differential equation. It is a continuous-time Markov process with continuous sample paths.

A sample path of a _____ mimics the trajectory of a molecule, which is embedded in a flowing fluid and at the same time subjected to random displacements due to collisions with other molecules, i.e. Brownian motion.

a. 180SearchAssistant
c. 6-3-5 Brainwriting
b. Power III
d. Diffusion process

25. _____ of consumer products (often supermarket goods) are distinguished by the absence of a brand name. They are identifed more by product characterstics.

They may be manufactured by less [prominent companies], or manufactured on the same production line as a 'named' brand. _____ are usually priced below those products sold by supermarkets under their own brand (frequently referred to as 'store brands' or 'own brands'.)

a. Gross Margin Return on Inventory Investment
c. M80
b. Micro ads
d. Generic brands

26. A _____ is a collection of symbols, experiences and associations connected with a product, a service, a person or any other artifact or entity.

_____s have become increasingly important components of culture and the economy, now being described as 'cultural accessories and personal philosophies'.

Some people distinguish the psychological aspect of a _____ from the experiential aspect.

a. Brandable software
c. Brand equity
b. Store brand
d. Brand

27. _____ is when a large distribution channel member (usually a retailer), buys from a manufacturer in bulk and puts its own name on the product. This strategy is only practical when the retailer does very high levels of volume. The advantages to the retailer are:

- more freedom and flexibility in pricing
- more control over product attributes and quality
- higher margins (or lower selling price)
- eliminates much of the manufacturer's promotional costs

The advantages to the manufacturer are:

- reduced promotional costs
- stability of sales volume (at least while the contract is operative)

- Kumar, Nirmalya; Steenkamp, Jan-Benedict E.M., Private Label Strategy - How to Meet the Store Brand Challenge. Harvard Business Press 2007

- private label
- brand management
- brand
- product management
- marketing

    a. Private branding   b. Promotion
    c. Customization   d. Rural market

28. The _____ is generally accepted as the use and specification of the four p's describing the strategic position of a product in the marketplace. One version of the origins of the _____ starts in 1948 when James Culliton said that a marketing decision should be a result of something similar to a recipe. This version continued in 1953 when Neil Borden, in his American Marketing Association presidential address, took the recipe idea one step further and coined the term 'Marketing-Mix'.
    a. 6-3-5 Brainwriting   b. Power III
    c. 180SearchAssistant   d. Marketing mix

29. The U.S. _____ is an independent agency of the United States government which holds primary responsibility for enforcing the federal securities laws and regulating the securities industry, the nation's stock and options exchanges, and other electronic securities markets. The SEC was created by section 4 of the Securities Exchange Act of 1934 (now codified as 15 U.S.C. Â§ 78d and commonly referred to as the 1934 Act.)
    a. 180SearchAssistant   b. Power III
    c. 6-3-5 Brainwriting   d. Securities and Exchange Commission

30. _____ refer to a collection of facts usually collected as the result of experience, observation or experiment or a set of premises. This may consist of numbers, words particularly as measurements or observations of a set of variables. _____ are often viewed as a lowest level of abstraction from which information and knowledge are derived.

Chapter 10. Developing a Target Market Strategy 91

a. Sample size
b. Mean
c. Pearson product-moment correlation coefficient
d. Data

31. _____ is a term used to describe a process of preparing and collecting data - for example as part of a process improvement or similar project.

_____ usually takes place early on in an improvement project, and is often formalised through a _____ Plan which often contains the following activity.

1. Pre collection activity - Agree goals, target data, definitions, methods
2. Collection - _____
3. Present Findings - usually involves some form of sorting analysis and/or presentation.

A formal _____ process is necessary as it ensures that data gathered is both defined and accurate and that subsequent decisions based on arguments embodied in the findings are valid . The process provides both a baseline from which to measure from and in certain cases a target on what to improve. Types of _____ 1-By mail questionnaires 2-By personal interview

- Six sigma
- Sampling (statistics)

a. 180SearchAssistant
b. Data collection
c. Power III
d. 6-3-5 Brainwriting

32. _____ is the process of estimation in unknown situations. Prediction is a similar, but more general term. Both can refer to estimation of time series, cross-sectional or longitudinal data.

a. 180SearchAssistant
b. Power III
c. 6-3-5 Brainwriting
d. Forecasting

33. Combining Existing _____ Sources with New Primary Data Sources

Imagine that we could get hold of a good collection of surveys taken in earlier years, such as detailed studies about changes going on in this phase and hopefully additional studies in the years to come. Analyzing this data base over time could give us a good picture of what changes actually have taken place in the orientation of the population and of the extent to which new technical concepts did have an impact on subgroups of the population. Furthermore, data archives can help to prepare studies on change over time by monitoring what questions have been asked in earlier years and alerting principal investigators to important questions which should be repeated in planned research projects.

a. Secondary data
b. Power III
c. 6-3-5 Brainwriting
d. 180SearchAssistant

34. _____, in strategic management and marketing, is the percentage or proportion of the total available market or market segment that is being serviced by a company. It can be expressed as a company's sales revenue (from that market) divided by the total sales revenue available in that market. It can also be expressed as a company's unit sales volume (in a market) divided by the total volume of units sold in that market.

   a. Cyberdoc
   b. Market share
   c. Customer relationship management
   d. Demand generation

35. A _____, in the field of business and marketing, is a geographic region or demographic group used to gauge the viability of a product or service in the mass market prior to a wide scale roll-out. The criteria used to judge the acceptability of a _____ region or group include:

1. a population that is demographically similar to the proposed target market; and
2. relative isolation from densely populated media markets so that advertising to the test audience can be efficient and economical.

The _____ ideally aims to duplicate 'everything' - promotion and distribution as well as `product' - on a smaller scale. The technique replicates, typically in one area, what is planned to occur in a national launch; and the results are very carefully monitored, so that they can be extrapolated to projected national results. The `area' may be any one of the following:

- Television area
- Test town
- Residential neighborhood
- Test site

A number of decisions have to be taken about any _____:

- Which _____?
- What is to be tested?
- How long a test?
- What are the success criteria?

The simple go or no-go decision, together with the related reduction of risk, is normally the main justification for the expense of _____s. At the same time, however, such _____s can be used to test specific elements of a new product's marketing mix; possibly the version of the product itself, the promotional message and media spend, the distribution channels and the price.

   a. 180SearchAssistant
   b. Power III
   c. Preadolescence
   d. Test market

36. _____ in organizations and public policy is both the organizational process of creating and maintaining a plan; and the psychological process of thinking about the activities required to create a desired goal on some scale. As such, it is a fundamental property of intelligent behavior. This thought process is essential to the creation and refinement of a plan, or integration of it with other plans, that is, it combines forecasting of developments with the preparation of scenarios of how to react to them.

a. 180SearchAssistant
c. Planning
b. Power III
d. 6-3-5 Brainwriting

37. In probability theory and statistics, _____ indicates the strength and direction of a linear relationship between two random variables. That is in contrast with the usage of the term in colloquial speech, denoting any relationship, not necessarily linear. In general statistical usage, _____ or co-relation refers to the departure of two random variables from independence.
   a. Frequency distribution
   b. Probability
   c. Mean
   d. Correlation

38. _____ is the imitation of some real thing, state of affairs, or process. The act of simulating something generally entails representing certain key characteristics or behaviors of a selected physical or abstract system.

   _____ is used in many contexts, including the modeling of natural systems or human systems in order to gain insight into their functioning.

   a. Simulation
   b. 180SearchAssistant
   c. Power III
   d. 6-3-5 Brainwriting

39. _____ is the ongoing process of identifying and articulating market requirements that define a product's feature set.
   a. Product planning
   b. Market intelligence
   c. Targeted advertising
   d. Brand parity

Chapter 11. Basic Concepts in Product Planning

1. A _____ is a collection of symbols, experiences and associations connected with a product, a service, a person or any other artifact or entity.

   _____s have become increasingly important components of culture and the economy, now being described as 'cultural accessories and personal philosophies'.

   Some people distinguish the psychological aspect of a _____ from the experiential aspect.

   a. Brandable software
   c. Brand equity
   b. Store brand
   d. Brand

2. _____ or brand stretching is a marketing strategy in which a firm marketing a product with a well-developed image uses the same brand name in a different product category. Organizations use this strategy to increase and leverage brand equity (definition: the net worth and long-term sustainability just from the renowned name.) An example of a _____ is Jello-gelatin creating Jello pudding pops.

   a. Web 2.0
   c. Brand awareness
   b. Brand extension
   d. Brand orientation

3. In marketing, a _____ is a generic product augmented by everything that is needed for the customer to have a compelling reason to buy. The generic product is what is usually shipped to the customer. The _____ typically augments the generic product with training and support, manuals, cables, additional software or hardware, installation instructions, professional services, etc.

   a. Jobbing house
   c. Teaser rate
   b. Mass market
   d. Whole product

4. _____ is defined by the American _____ Association as the activity, set of institutions, and processes for creating, communicating, delivering, and exchanging offerings that have value for customers, clients, partners, and society at large. The term developed from the original meaning which referred literally to going to market, as in shopping, or going to a market to sell goods or services.

   _____ practice tends to be seen as a creative industry, which includes advertising, distribution and selling.

   a. Marketing myopia
   c. Customer acquisition management
   b. Product naming
   d. Marketing

5. A _____ is a written document that details the necessary actions to achieve one or more marketing objectives. It can be for a product or service, a brand, or a product line. _____s cover between one and five years.

   a. Disruptive technology
   c. Marketing strategy
   b. Prosumer
   d. Marketing plan

6. _____ is a form of communication that typically attempts to persuade potential customers to purchase or to consume more of a particular brand of product or service. 'While now central to the contemporary global economy and the reproduction of global production networks, it is only quite recently that _____ has been more than a marginal influence on patterns of sales and production. The formation of modern _____ was intimately bound up with the emergence of new forms of monopoly capitalism around the end of the 19th and beginning of the 20th century as one element in corporate strategies to create, organize and where possible control markets, especially for mass produced consumer goods.

a. ADTECH
b. ACNielsen
c. AMAX
d. Advertising

7. _____ is a measure of the strength of a brand, product, service relative to competitive offerings. There is often a geographic element to the competitive landscape. In defining _____, you must see to what extent a product, brand, or firm controls a product category in a given geographic area.
a. Market dominance
b. Discretionary spending
c. Productivity
d. Market system

8. _____ in organizations and public policy is both the organizational process of creating and maintaining a plan; and the psychological process of thinking about the activities required to create a desired goal on some scale. As such, it is a fundamental property of intelligent behavior. This thought process is essential to the creation and refinement of a plan, or integration of it with other plans, that is, it combines forecasting of developments with the preparation of scenarios of how to react to them.
a. Planning
b. 180SearchAssistant
c. Power III
d. 6-3-5 Brainwriting

9. _____ is the ongoing process of identifying and articulating market requirements that define a product's feature set.
a. Product planning
b. Market intelligence
c. Brand parity
d. Targeted advertising

10. _____ is an advertisement in which a particular product specifically mentions a competitor by name for the express purpose of showing why the competitor is inferior to the product naming it.

This should not be confused with parody advertisements, where a fictional product is being advertised for the purpose of poking fun at the particular advertisement, nor should it be confused with the use of a coined brand name for the purpose of comparing the product without actually naming an actual competitor. ('Wikipedia tastes better and is less filling than the Encyclopedia Galactica.')

In the 1980s, during what has been referred to as the cola wars, soft-drink manufacturer Pepsi ran a series of advertisements where people, caught on hidden camera, in a blind taste test, chose Pepsi over rival Coca-Cola.

a. GL-70
b. Heavy-up
c. Cost per conversion
d. Comparative advertising

11. _____ is a broad label that refers to any individuals or households that use goods and services generated within the economy. The concept of a _____ is used in different contexts, so that the usage and significance of the term may vary.

A _____ is a person who uses any product or service.

a. Power III
b. Consumer
c. 6-3-5 Brainwriting
d. 180SearchAssistant

12. _____ or _____ data refers to selected population characteristics as used in government, marketing or opinion research, or the _____ profiles used in such research. Note the distinction from the term 'demography' Commonly-used _____ include race, age, income, disabilities, mobility (in terms of travel time to work or number of vehicles available), educational attainment, home ownership, employment status, and even location.
- a. AStore
- b. African Americans
- c. Demographic
- d. Albert Einstein

13. _____ is anything that is intended to save time, energy or frustration. A _____ store at a petrol station, for example, sells items that have nothing to do with gasoline/petrol, but it saves the consumer from having to go to a grocery store. '_____' is a very relative term and its meaning tends to change over time.
- a. MaxDiff
- b. Demographic profile
- c. Marketing buzz
- d. Convenience

14. _____ of consumer products (often supermarket goods) are distinguished by the absence of a brand name. They are identifed more by product characterstics.

They may be manufactured by less [prominent companies], or manufactured on the same production line as a 'named' brand. _____ are usually priced below those products sold by supermarkets under their own brand (frequently referred to as 'store brands' or 'own brands'.)

- a. M80
- b. Micro ads
- c. Gross Margin Return on Inventory Investment
- d. Generic brands

15. An _____ is an unplanned or otherwise spontaneous purchase. One who tends to make such purchases is referred to as an impulse purchaser or impulse buyer.

Marketers and retailers tend to exploit these impulses which are tied to the basic want for instant gratification.

- a. AMAX
- b. ADTECH
- c. ACNielsen
- d. Impulse purchase

16. A _____ is a subgroup of people or organizations sharing one or more characteristics that cause them to have similar product and/or service needs. A true _____ meets all of the following criteria: it is distinct from other segments (different segments have different needs), it is homogeneous within the segment (exhibits common needs); it responds similarly to a market stimulus, and it can be reached by a market intervention. The term is also used when consumers with identical product and/or service needs are divided up into groups so they can be charged different amounts.
- a. Production orientation
- b. Customer insight
- c. Commercial planning
- d. Market segment

17. _____ is the examining of goods or services from retailers with the intent to purchase at that time. _____ is an activity of selection and/or purchase. In some contexts it is considered a leisure activity as well as an economic one.
- a. Shopping
- b. Khodebshchik
- c. Discount store
- d. Hawkers

Chapter 11. Basic Concepts in Product Planning

18. _____ is a way of expressing knowledge or belief that an event will occur or has occurred. In mathematics the concept has been given an exact meaning in _____ theory, that is used extensively in such areas of study as mathematics, statistics, finance, gambling, science, and philosophy to draw conclusions about the likelihood of potential events and the underlying mechanics of complex systems.

 a. Heteroskedastic
 b. Data
 c. Linear regression
 d. Probability

19. A sample is a subject chosen from a population for investigation. A _____ is one chosen by a method involving an unpredictable component. Random sampling can also refer to taking a number of independent observations from the same probability distribution, without involving any real population.

 a. Selection bias
 b. Random sample
 c. 180SearchAssistant
 d. Power III

20. In marketing, _____ has come to mean the process by which marketers try to create an image or identity in the minds of their target market for its product, brand, or organization. It is the 'relative competitive comparison' their product occupies in a given market as perceived by the target market.

Re-_____ involves changing the identity of a product, relative to the identity of competing products, in the collective minds of the target market.

 a. Containerization
 b. Moratorium
 c. Positioning
 d. GE matrix

21. A _____ is something that is acted upon or used by or by human labour or industry, for use as a building material to create some product or structure. Often the term is used to denote material that came from nature and is in an unprocessed or minimally processed state. Iron ore, logs, and crude oil, would be examples.

 a. 6-3-5 Brainwriting
 b. 180SearchAssistant
 c. Power III
 d. Raw material

22. _____s are structured marketing efforts that reward, and therefore encourage, loyal buying behaviour -- behaviour which is potentially of benefit to the firm.

In marketing generally and in retailing more specifically, a loyalty card, rewards card, points card, advantage card, or club card is a plastic or paper card, visually similar to a credit card or debit card, that identifies the card holder as a member in a _____. Loyalty cards are a system of the loyalty business model.

 a. 180SearchAssistant
 b. 6-3-5 Brainwriting
 c. Power III
 d. Loyalty program

23. _____ Management is the succession of strategies used by management as a product goes through its _____. The conditions in which a product is sold changes over time and must be managed as it moves through its succession of stages.

The _____ goes through many phases, involves many professional disciplines, and requires many skills, tools and processes.

a. Customer satisfaction
b. Supplier diversity
c. Chain stores
d. Product life cycle

24. There are many important decisions about product and service development and marketing. In the process of product development and marketing we should focus on strategic decisions about product attributes, product branding, product packaging, product labeling and product support services. But product strategy also calls for building a _____.
a. Technology acceptance model
b. Pinstorm
c. Macromarketing
d. Product line

25. A _____ researches, selects, develops, and places a company's products.

A _____ considers numerous factors such as target demographic, the products offered by the competition, and how well the product fits in with the company's business model. Generally, a _____ manages one or more tangible products.

a. Product manager
b. Promotional mix
c. Pick and pack
d. Power III

26. _____ is an organizational lifecycle function within a company dealing with the planning or marketing of a product or products at all stages of the product lifecycle.

_____ and product marketing (outbound focused) are different yet complementary efforts with the objective of maximizing sales revenues, market share, and profit margins. The role of _____ spans many activities from strategic to tactical and varies based on the organizational structure of the company.

a. Product information management
b. Requirement prioritization
c. Service product management
d. Product management

27. _____ is the set of tasks, knowledge, and techniques required to identify business needs and determine solutions to business problems. Solutions often include a systems development component, but may also consist of process improvement or organizational change. The person who carries out this task is called a business analyst or _____.
a. Fast moving consumer goods
b. Door-to-door
c. Marketing management
d. Business analysis

28. _____ is the practice of individuals including commercial businesses, governments and institutions, facilitating the sale of their products or services to other companies or organizations that in turn resell them, use them as components in products or services they offer _____ is also called business-to-_____ for short. (Note that while marketing to government entities shares some of the same dynamics of organizational marketing, B2G Marketing is meaningfully different.)
a. Mass marketing
b. Disruptive technology
c. Law of disruption
d. Business marketing

Chapter 11. Basic Concepts in Product Planning

29. The phrase _____, according to the Organization for Economic Co-operation and Development, refers to 'creative work undertaken on a systematic basis in order to increase the stock of knowledge, including knowledge of man, culture and society, and the use of this stock of knowledge to devise new applications [sic]' Though it is questionable that an organization is needed for this definition, as it is quite obvious that _____ refers to the _____ of something.

New product design and development is more often than not a crucial factor in the survival of a company. In an industry that is fast changing, firms must continually revise their design and range of products.

a. 180SearchAssistant
b. Power III
c. 6-3-5 Brainwriting
d. Research and development

30. In marketing, _____ is the process of distinguishing the differences of a product or offering from others, to make it more attractive to a particular target market. This involves differentiating it from competitors' products as well as one's own product offerings.

Differentiation is a source of competitive advantage.

a. Corporate image
b. Packshot
c. Product differentiation
d. Marketing myopia

31. Competitiveness is a comparative concept of the ability and performance of a firm, sub-sector or country to sell and supply goods and/or services in a given market. Although widely used in economics and business management, the usefulness of the concept, particularly in the context of national competitiveness, is vigorously disputed by economists, such as Paul Krugman .

The term may also be applied to markets, where it is used to refer to the extent to which the market structure may be regarded as perfectly _____.

a. Free trade zone
b. Customs union
c. Geographical pricing
d. Competitive

32. _____ was originally coined by Austrian psychologist Alfred Adler in 1929. The current broader sense of the word dates from 1961.

In sociology, a _____ is the way a person lives.

a. 180SearchAssistant
b. 6-3-5 Brainwriting
c. Power III
d. Lifestyle

33. In psychology, philosophy, and the cognitive sciences, _____ is the process of attaining awareness or understanding of sensory information. It is a task far more complex than was imagined in the 1950s and 1960s, when it was predicted that building perceiving machines would take about a decade, a goal which is still very far from fruition. The word _____ comes from the Latin words _____, percepio, meaning 'receiving, collecting, action of taking possession, apprehension with the mind or senses.'

_____ is one of the oldest fields in psychology.

a. 180SearchAssistant
b. Power III
c. Groupthink
d. Perception

34. _____ is a branch of philosophy which seeks to address questions about morality, such as how a moral outcome can be achieved in a specific situation (applied _____), how moral values should be determined (normative _____), what moral values people actually abide by (descriptive _____), what the fundamental semantic, ontological, and epistemic nature of _____ or morality is (meta-_____), and how moral capacity or moral agency develops and what its nature is (moral psychology.)

Socrates was one of the first Greek philosophers to encourage both scholars and the common citizen to turn their attention from the outside world to the condition of man. In this view, Knowledge having a bearing on human life was placed highest, all other knowledge being secondary.

a. Ethics
b. ADTECH
c. AMAX
d. ACNielsen

35. _____, in marketing, consists of a consumer's commitment to repurchase the brand and can be demonstrated by repeated buying of a product or service or other positive behaviors such as word of mouth advocacy. True _____ implies that the consumer is willing, at least on occasion, to put aside their own desires in the interest of the brand. _____ has been proclaimed by some to be the ultimate goal of marketing.

a. Brand awareness
b. Trade Symbols
c. Brand implementation
d. Brand loyalty

36. A _____ or trade mark, identified by the symbols ™ (not yet registered) and ® (registered) business organization or other legal entity to identify that the products and/or services to consumers with which the _____ appears originate from a unique source of origin, and to distinguish its products or services from those of other entities. A _____ is a type of intellectual property, and typically a name, word, phrase, logo, symbol, design, image, or a combination of these elements. There is also a range of non-conventional _____s comprising marks which do not fall into these standard categories.

a. Power III
b. Risk management
c. 180SearchAssistant
d. Trademark

37. A brand which is widely known in the marketplace acquires _____. When _____ builds up to a point where a brand enjoys a critical mass of positive sentiment in the marketplace, it is said to have achieved brand franchise. One goal in _____ is the identification of a brand without the name of the company present.

a. Trademark distinctiveness
b. Brand recognition
c. Brand blunder
d. Trade Symbols

38. _____ refers to the marketing effects or outcomes that accrue to a product with its brand name compared with those that would accrue if the same product did not have the brand name . And, at the root of these marketing effects is consumers' knowledge. In other words, consumers' knowledge about a brand makes manufacturers/advertisers respond differently or adopt appropriately adapt measures for the marketing of the brand .

a. Brand aversion
b. Product extension
c. Brand image
d. Brand equity

39. _____ is the marketing strategy of giving each product in a product portfolio its own unique brand name. This is contrasted with family branding in which the products in a product line are given the same brand name. The advantage of _____ is that each product has a self image and identity that's unique.

    a. Online focus group
    b. Individual branding
    c. Intangibility
    d. Engagement

40. _____ is a business discipline which is focused on the practical application of marketing techniques and the management of a firm's marketing resources and activities. Marketing managers are often responsible for influencing the level, timing, and composition of customer demand accepted definition of the term. In part, this is because the role of a marketing manager can vary significantly based on a business' size, corporate culture, and industry context.

    a. Business structure
    b. Marketing management
    c. Door-to-door
    d. Performance-based advertising

41. The U.S. _____ is an agency of the United States Department of Health and Human Services and is responsible for regulating and supervising the safety of foods, dietary supplements, drugs, vaccines, biological medical products, blood products, medical devices, radiation-emitting devices, veterinary products, and cosmetics. The FDA also enforces section 361 of the Public Health Service Act and the associated regulations, including sanitation requirements on interstate travel as well as specific rules for control of disease on products ranging from pet turtles to semen donations for assisted reproductive medicine techniques.

The FDA is an agency within the United States Department of Health and Human Services responsible for protecting and promoting the nation's public health.

    a. 6-3-5 Brainwriting
    b. Food and Drug Administration
    c. Power III
    d. 180SearchAssistant

42. _____, in strategic management and marketing, is the percentage or proportion of the total available market or market segment that is being serviced by a company. It can be expressed as a company's sales revenue (from that market) divided by the total sales revenue available in that market. It can also be expressed as a company's unit sales volume (in a market) divided by the total volume of units sold in that market.

    a. Demand generation
    b. Customer relationship management
    c. Cyberdoc
    d. Market share

43. _____ is when a large distribution channel member (usually a retailer), buys from a manufacturer in bulk and puts its own name on the product. This strategy is only practical when the retailer does very high levels of volume. The advantages to the retailer are:

- more freedom and flexibility in pricing
- more control over product attributes and quality
- higher margins (or lower selling price)
- eliminates much of the manufacturer's promotional costs

Chapter 11. Basic Concepts in Product Planning

The advantages to the manufacturer are:

- reduced promotional costs
- stability of sales volume (at least while the contract is operative)

- Kumar, Nirmalya; Steenkamp, Jan-Benedict E.M., Private Label Strategy - How to Meet the Store Brand Challenge. Harvard Business Press 2007

- private label
- brand management
- brand
- product management
- marketing

a. Rural market
c. Customization
b. Promotion
d. Private branding

44. A _____ is a plan of action designed to achieve a particular goal.

_____ is different from tactics. In military terms, tactics is concerned with the conduct of an engagement while _____ is concerned with how different engagements are linked.

a. Strategy
c. Power III
b. 6-3-5 Brainwriting
d. 180SearchAssistant

45. _____ is a marketing strategy that involves selling several related products under one brand name. It is contrasted with individual branding in which each product in a portfolio is given a unique identity and brand name.

There are often economies of scope associated with _____ since several products can efficiently be promoted with a single advertisement or campaign.

a. 180SearchAssistant
c. Power III
b. Family branding
d. 6-3-5 Brainwriting

46. _____ is one of the four aspects of promotional mix. (The other three parts of the promotional mix are advertising, personal selling, and publicity/public relations.) Media and non-media marketing communication are employed for a pre-determined, limited time to increase consumer demand, stimulate market demand or improve product availability.

a. Merchandise
c. New Media Strategies
b. Sales promotion
d. Marketing communication

Chapter 11. Basic Concepts in Product Planning

47. _____ involves disseminating information about a product, product line, brand, or company. It is one of the four key aspects of the marketing mix. (The other three elements are product marketing, pricing, and distribution). P>_____ is generally sub-divided into two parts:

- Above the line _____: Promotion in the media (e.g. TV, radio, newspapers, Internet and Mobile Phones) in which the advertiser pays an advertising agency to place the ad
- Below the line _____: All other _____. Much of this is intended to be subtle enough for the consumer to be unaware that _____ is taking place. E.g. sponsorship, product placement, endorsements, sales _____, merchandising, direct mail, personal selling, public relations, trade shows

a. Davie Brown Index
c. Bottling lines
b. Cashmere Agency
d. Promotion

48. _____ refers to several different marketing arrangements:

_____ is when two companies form an alliance to work together, creating marketing synergy. As described in _____: The Science of Alliance:

_____ is an arrangement that associates a single product or service with more than one brand name, or otherwise associates a product with someone other than the principal producer. The typical _____ agreement involves two or more companies acting in cooperation to associate any of various logos, color schemes, or brand identifiers to a specific product that is contractually designated for this purpose.

a. Target audience
c. Line extension
b. Co-branding
d. Brand Development Index

49. The verb _____ or grant _____ means to give permission. The noun _____ refers to that permission as well as to the document memorializing that permission. _____ may be granted by a party to another party as an element of an agreement between those parties.

a. 180SearchAssistant
c. 6-3-5 Brainwriting
b. Power III
d. License

50. A _____ is a set of exclusive rights granted by a State to an inventor or his assignee for a limited period of time in exchange for a disclosure of an invention.

The procedure for granting _____s, the requirements placed on the _____ee and the extent of the exclusive rights vary widely between countries according to national laws and international agreements. Typically, however, a _____ application must include one or more claims defining the invention which must be new, inventive, and useful or industrially applicable.

a. Foreign Corrupt Practices Act
c. Reasonable person standard
b. Patent
d. Product liability

51. In some countries, notably the United States, a trademark used to identify a service rather than a product is called a _____ or servicemark. When a _____ is federally registered, the standard registration symbol ® or 'Reg U.S. Pat ' TM Off' may be used (the same symbol is used to mark registered trademarks.) Before it is registered, it is common practice (but has no legal standing) to use the _____ symbol ā„ (a superscript '_____'.)

   a. Service mark   b. Screener
   c. Trespass to land   d. Trademark classification

52. Once trademark rights are established in a particular jurisdiction, these rights are generally only enforceable in that jurisdiction, a quality which is sometimes known as territoriality. However, there is a range of international _____ and systems which facilitate the protection of trademarks in more than one jurisdiction

To avoid conflicts with earlier trademark rights, it is highly recommended to conduct trademark searches before the trademarks office (or 'trademarks registry') of a particular jurisdiction--e.g. US Patent and Trademark Office.

   a. Sigg bottles   b. Supreme Court of the United States
   c. Self branding   d. Trademark laws

53. The _____ is an agency in the United States Department of Commerce that issues patents to inventors and businesses for their inventions, and trademark registration for product and intellectual property identification.

The USPTO is currently based in Alexandria, Virginia, after a 2006 move from the Crystal City area of Arlington, Virginia. The offices under Patents and the Chief Information Officer that remained just outside the southern end of Crystal City completed moving to Randolph Square, a brand new building in Shirlington Village, on 27 April 2009.

   a. United States Patent and Trademark Office   b. Underwriters Laboratories
   c. Access Commerce   d. INVISTA

54. _____ is one of the four elements of marketing mix. An organization or set of organizations (go-betweens) involved in the process of making a product or service available for use or consumption by a consumer or business user.

The other three parts of the marketing mix are product, pricing, and promotion.

   a. Better Living Through Chemistry   b. Comparison-Shopping agent
   c. Japan Advertising Photographers' Association   d. Distribution

55. _____ is the state or fact of exclusive rights and control over property, which may be an object, land/real estate, or some other kind of property (like government-granted monopolies collectively referred to as intellectual property.) It is embodied in an _____ right also referred to as title.

_____ is the key building block in the development of the capitalist socio-economic system.

   a. AMAX   b. ADTECH
   c. ACNielsen   d. Ownership

Chapter 11. Basic Concepts in Product Planning

56. _____ in economics and business is the result of an exchange and from that trade we assign a numerical monetary value to a good, service or asset. If I trade 4 apples for an orange, the _____ of an orange is 4 - apples. Inversely, the _____ of an apple is 1/4 oranges.
   a. Discounts and allowances
   b. Pricing
   c. Contribution margin-based pricing
   d. Price

57. _____ consists of the sale of goods or merchandise from a fixed location, such as a department store or kiosk in small or individual lots for direct consumption by the purchaser. _____ may include subordinated services, such as delivery. Purchasers may be individuals or businesses.
   a. Warehouse store
   b. Charity shop
   c. Retailing
   d. Thrifting

58. In economics, business, retail, and accounting, a _____ is the value of money that has been used up to produce something, and hence is not available for use anymore. In economics, a _____ is an alternative that is given up as a result of a decision. In business, the _____ may be one of acquisition, in which case the amount of money expended to acquire it is counted as _____.
   a. Fixed costs
   b. Variable cost
   c. Transaction cost
   d. Cost

59. A _____ is a list of the general tasks and responsibilities of a position. Typically, it also includes to whom the position reports, specifications such as the qualifications needed by the person in the job, salary range for the position, etc. A _____ is usually developed by conducting a job analysis, which includes examining the tasks and sequences of tasks necessary to perform the job.
   a. 180SearchAssistant
   b. Power III
   c. 6-3-5 Brainwriting
   d. Job description

Chapter 12. Goods Versus Services Planning

1. _____ is defined by the American _____ Association as the activity, set of institutions, and processes for creating, communicating, delivering, and exchanging offerings that have value for customers, clients, partners, and society at large. The term developed from the original meaning which referred literally to going to market, as in shopping, or going to a market to sell goods or services.

_____ practice tends to be seen as a creative industry, which includes advertising, distribution and selling.

   a. Marketing myopia
   b. Customer acquisition management
   c. Product naming
   d. Marketing

2. In economics, a _____ or a hard good is a good which does not quickly wear out it yields services or utility over time rather than being completely used up when used once. Most goods are therefore _____s to a certain degree. These are goods that can last for a relatively long time, such as refrigerators, cars, and DVD players.
   a. Free good
   b. Power III
   c. Durable good
   d. Luxury good

3. _____ is an advertisement in which a particular product specifically mentions a competitor by name for the express purpose of showing why the competitor is inferior to the product naming it.

This should not be confused with parody advertisements, where a fictional product is being advertised for the purpose of poking fun at the particular advertisement, nor should it be confused with the use of a coined brand name for the purpose of comparing the product without actually naming an actual competitor. ('Wikipedia tastes better and is less filling than the Encyclopedia Galactica.')

In the 1980s, during what has been referred to as the cola wars, soft-drink manufacturer Pepsi ran a series of advertisements where people, caught on hidden camera, in a blind taste test, chose Pepsi over rival Coca-Cola.

   a. Cost per conversion
   b. GL-70
   c. Heavy-up
   d. Comparative advertising

4. _____ is a broad label that refers to any individuals or households that use goods and services generated within the economy. The concept of a _____ is used in different contexts, so that the usage and significance of the term may vary.

A _____ is a person who uses any product or service.

   a. 180SearchAssistant
   b. 6-3-5 Brainwriting
   c. Power III
   d. Consumer

5. _____ is a contract between two parties, one being the employer and the other being the employee. An employee may be defined as: 'A person in the service of another under any contract of hire, express or implied, oral or written, where the employer has the power or right to control and direct the employee in the material details of how the work is to be performed.' Black's Law Dictionary page 471 (5th ed. 1979.)
   a. ADTECH
   b. ACNielsen
   c. AMAX
   d. Employment

6. The _____ is one of the three economic sectors, the others being the secondary sector and the primary sector The general definition of the Tertiary sector is producing a service instead of just a end product, in the case of the secondary sector. Sometimes an additional sector, the 'quaternary sector', is defined for the sharing of information

   a. 180SearchAssistant   b. 6-3-5 Brainwriting
   c. Power III   d. Tertiary sector of economy

7. A _____ is the central part of a telecom network that provides various services to customers who are connected by the access network.

_____s typically providing the following functionality:

1. Aggregation: The highest level of aggregation in a service provider network. The next level in the hierarchy under the core nodes is the distribution networks and then the edge networks. Customer Premise Equipment (CPE) do not normally connect to the _____s of a large service provider.
2. Authentication: The function to decide whether the user requesting a service from the telecom network is authorized to do so within this network or not.
3. Call Control/Switching: Call control or switching functionality decides the future course of call based on the call signalling processing. E.g. switching functionality may decide based on the 'called number' that the call be routed towards a subscriber within this operator's network or with Number Portability more prevalent to another operator's network.
4. Charging: This functionality handles the collation and processing of charging data generated by various network nodes. Two common types of charging mechanisms found in present day networks are prepaid charging and postpaid charging. See Automatic Message Accounting
5. Service Invocation: _____ performs the task of service invocation for its subscribers. Service invocation may happen based on some explicit action (e.g. call transfer) by user or implicitly (call waiting.) Its important to note however that service 'execution' may or may not be a _____ functionality as third party network/nodes may take part in actual service execution.
6. Gateways: Gateways shall be present in the _____ to access other networks. Gateway functionality is dependent on the type of network it interfaces with.

Physically, one or more of these logical functionalities may simultaneously exist in a given _____ node.

Besides above mentioned functionalities, following also form part of a _____:

- O'M: Operations ' Maintenance centre or Operations Support Systems to configure and provision the _____ nodes. Number of subscribers, peak hour call rate, nature of services, geographical preferences are some of the factors which impact the configuration. Network statistics collection, alarm monitoring and logging of various network nodes actions also happens in the O'M centre. These stats, alarms and traces form important tools for a network operator to monitor the network health and performance and improvise on the same.
- Subscriber Database: _____ also hosts the subscribers database (e.g. HLR in GSM systems.) Subscriber database is accessed by _____ nodes for functions like authentication, service invocation etc.

a. Power III
b. Core network
c. 6-3-5 Brainwriting
d. 180SearchAssistant

8. _____ refers to the additional value of a commodity over the cost of commodities used to produce it from the previous stage of production. An example is the price of gasoline at the pump over the price of the oil in it. In national accounts used in macroeconomics, it refers to the contribution of the factors of production, i.e., land, labor, and capital goods, to raising the value of a product and corresponds to the incomes received by the owners of these factors. The factors of production provide 'services' which raise the unit price of a product (X) relative to the cost per unit of intermediate goods used up in the production of X. _____ is shared between the factors of production (capital, labor, also human capital), giving rise to issues of distribution.
   a. Power III
   b. Consumer spending
   c. Deregulation
   d. Value added

9. _____ is one of the four elements of marketing mix. An organization or set of organizations (go-betweens) involved in the process of making a product or service available for use or consumption by a consumer or business user.

The other three parts of the marketing mix are product, pricing, and promotion.

   a. Comparison-Shopping agent
   b. Japan Advertising Photographers' Association
   c. Better Living Through Chemistry
   d. Distribution

10. _____ is a form of communication that typically attempts to persuade potential customers to purchase or to consume more of a particular brand of product or service. 'While now central to the contemporary global economy and the reproduction of global production networks, it is only quite recently that _____ has been more than a marginal influence on patterns of sales and production. The formation of modern _____ was intimately bound up with the emergence of new forms of monopoly capitalism around the end of the 19th and beginning of the 20th century as one element in corporate strategies to create, organize and where possible control markets, especially for mass produced consumer goods.
   a. Advertising
   b. AMAX
   c. ACNielsen
   d. ADTECH

11. The term _____ is used to describe countries that have a high level of development according to some criteria. Which criteria, and which countries are classified as being developed, is a contentious issue and there is fierce debate about this. Economic criteria have tended to dominate discussions.
   a. Brando
   b. Developed country
   c. Bringin' Home the Oil
   d. Completely randomized designs

12. _____ in organizations and public policy is both the organizational process of creating and maintaining a plan; and the psychological process of thinking about the activities required to create a desired goal on some scale. As such, it is a fundamental property of intelligent behavior. This thought process is essential to the creation and refinement of a plan, or integration of it with other plans, that is, it combines forecasting of developments with the preparation of scenarios of how to react to them.
   a. 180SearchAssistant
   b. 6-3-5 Brainwriting
   c. Power III
   d. Planning

Chapter 12. Goods Versus Services Planning

13. _____ is used in marketing to describe a key quality of services as distinct from goods. _____ is the characteristic that a service has which renders it impossible to divorce the supply or production of the service from its consumption.

Other key characteristics of services include perishability, intangibility and variability.

a. Engagement
c. Individual branding
b. Online focus group
d. Inseparability

14. _____ is used in marketing to describe the inability to assess the value gained from engaging in an activity using any tangible evidence. It is often used to describe services where there isn't a tangible product that the customer can purchase, that can be seen, tasted or touched.

Other key characteristics of services include perishability, inseparability and variability.

a. Individual branding
c. Intangibility
b. Inseparability
d. Automated surveys

15. _____ is used in marketing to describe the way in which service capacity cannot be stored for sale in the future. It is a key concept of services marketing.

Other key characteristics of services include intangibility, inseparability and variability.

a. National brand
c. Specialty catalogs
b. Demonstrator model
d. Perishability

16. _____ is the study of when, why, how, where and what people do or do not buy products. It blends elements from psychology, sociology, social psychology, anthropology and economics. It attempts to understand the buyer decision making process, both individually and in groups. It studies characteristics of individual consumers such as demographics and behavioural variables in an attempt to understand people's wants. It also tries to assess influences on the consumer from groups such as family, friends, reference groups, and society in general.

a. Communal marketing
c. Multidimensional scaling
b. Consumer confidence
d. Consumer behavior

17. _____ is a list for goods and materials held available in stock by a business. It is also used for a list of the contents of a household and for a list for testamentary purposes of the possessions of someone who has died. In accounting _____ is considered an asset.

a. Ending Inventory
c. ADTECH
b. Inventory
d. ACNielsen

18. In marketing, _____ has come to mean the process by which marketers try to create an image or identity in the minds of their target market for its product, brand, or organization. It is the 'relative competitive comparison' their product occupies in a given market as perceived by the target market.

Re-_____ involves changing the identity of a product, relative to the identity of competing products, in the collective minds of the target market.

Chapter 12. Goods Versus Services Planning

a. Moratorium
b. Containerization
c. GE matrix
d. Positioning

19. A _____ is a plan of action designed to achieve a particular goal.

_____ is different from tactics. In military terms, tactics is concerned with the conduct of an engagement while _____ is concerned with how different engagements are linked.

a. Power III
b. 180SearchAssistant
c. 6-3-5 Brainwriting
d. Strategy

20. In economics, _____ is the desire to own something and the ability to pay for it. The term _____ signifies the ability or the willingness to buy a particular commodity at a given point of time .

a. Market dominance
b. Demand
c. Discretionary spending
d. Market system

21. _____ is a form of marketing developed from direct response marketing campaigns conducted in the 1970's and 1980's which emphasizes customer retention and satisfaction, rather than a dominant focus on 'point of sale' transactions.

_____ differs from other forms of marketing in that it recognizes the long term value to the firm of keeping customers, as opposed to direct or 'Intrusion' marketing, which focuses upon acquisition of new clients by targeting majority demographics based upon prospective client lists.

_____ refers to long-term and mutually beneficial arrangement wherein both buyer and seller focus on value enhancement through the certain of more satisfying exchange.This approach attempts to transcend the simple purchase exchange process with customer to make more meaningful and richer contact by providing a more holistic, personalized purchase, and use orn consumption experience to create stronger ties.

a. Relationship marketing
b. Diversity marketing
c. Global marketing
d. Guerrilla Marketing

22. An _____ is the manufacturing of a good or service within a category. Although _____ is a broad term for any kind of economic production, in economics and urban planning _____ is a synonym for the secondary sector, which is a type of economic activity involved in the manufacturing of raw materials into goods and products.

There are four key industrial economic sectors: the primary sector, largely raw material extraction industries such as mining and farming; the secondary sector, involving refining, construction, and manufacturing; the tertiary sector, which deals with services (such as law and medicine) and distribution of manufactured goods; and the quaternary sector, a relatively new type of knowledge _____ focusing on technological research, design and development such as computer programming, and biochemistry.

Chapter 12. Goods Versus Services Planning

a. Industry
c. ACNielsen
b. AMAX
d. ADTECH

23. _____ is a measure of the strength of a brand, product, service relative to competitive offerings. There is often a geographic element to the competitive landscape. In defining _____, you must see to what extent a product, brand, or firm controls a product category in a given geographic area.

a. Discretionary spending
c. Productivity
b. Market system
d. Market dominance

24. The _____ is an international organization designed to supervise and liberalize international trade. The _____ came into being on 1 January 1995, and is the successor to the General Agreement on Tariffs and Trade (GATT), which was created in 1947, and continued to operate for almost five decades as a de facto international organization.

The _____ deals with the rules of trade between nations at a near-global level; it is responsible for negotiating and implementing new trade agreements, and is in charge of policing member countries' adherence to all the _____ agreements, signed by the majority of the world's trading nations and ratified in their parliaments.

a. BSI Group
c. World Trade Organization
b. Population Reference Bureau
d. Merchandise Mart

25. _____ is the systematic application of marketing along with other concepts and techniques to achieve specific behavioral goals for a social good. _____ can be applied to promote, for example, merit goods, make the society avoid demerit goods and thus to promote that considers society's well being as a whole. This may include asking people not to smoke in public areas, for example, ask them to use seat belts, prompting to make them follow speed limits.

a. Marketing strategy
c. Psychographic
b. Market development
d. Social marketing

26. _____ was originally coined by Austrian psychologist Alfred Adler in 1929. The current broader sense of the word dates from 1961.

In sociology, a _____ is the way a person lives.

a. 180SearchAssistant
c. Power III
b. 6-3-5 Brainwriting
d. Lifestyle

27. A _____ is defined by the International Co-operative Alliance's Statement on the Co-operative Identity as an autonomous association of persons united voluntarily to meet their common economic, social, and cultural needs and aspirations through a jointly-owned and democratically-controlled enterprise. It is a business organization owned and operated by a group of individuals for their mutual benefit. A _____ may also be defined as a business owned and controlled equally by the people who use its services or who work at it.

a. Cooperative
c. 180SearchAssistant
b. 6-3-5 Brainwriting
d. Power III

28. _____ is the practice of individuals including commercial businesses, governments and institutions, facilitating the sale of their products or services to other companies or organizations that in turn resell them, use them as components in products or services they offer _____ is also called business-to-_____ for short. (Note that while marketing to government entities shares some of the same dynamics of organizational marketing, B2G Marketing is meaningfully different.)

a. Mass marketing
b. Disruptive technology
c. Law of disruption
d. Business marketing

Chapter 13. Conceiving, Developing, and Managing Products

1. _____ Management is the succession of strategies used by management as a product goes through its _____. The conditions in which a product is sold changes over time and must be managed as it moves through its succession of stages.

The _____ goes through many phases, involves many professional disciplines, and requires many skills, tools and processes.

 a. Supplier diversity
 b. Customer satisfaction
 c. Product life cycle
 d. Chain stores

2. In economics, _____ is the desire to own something and the ability to pay for it. The term _____ signifies the ability or the willingness to buy a particular commodity at a given point of time.

 a. Market dominance
 b. Market system
 c. Demand
 d. Discretionary spending

3. The term _____ is used to describe countries that have a high level of development according to some criteria. Which criteria, and which countries are classified as being developed, is a contentious issue and there is fierce debate about this. Economic criteria have tended to dominate discussions.

 a. Completely randomized designs
 b. Bringin' Home the Oil
 c. Brando
 d. Developed country

4. A craze is a product, idea, cultural movement, or model that gains popularity among a small section of the populace then quickly migrates to the mainstream. Crazes are characterized by their lightning fast adoption and swift departure from public awareness. Crazes and _____s are also characterized by their unusually high interest and sales figures relative to the time they are active in the marketplace, as compared with other similar products, ideas, cultural movements or models.

 a. 6-3-5 Brainwriting
 b. Fad
 c. Power III
 d. 180SearchAssistant

5. _____ is defined by the American _____ Association as the activity, set of institutions, and processes for creating, communicating, delivering, and exchanging offerings that have value for customers, clients, partners, and society at large. The term developed from the original meaning which referred literally to going to market, as in shopping, or going to a market to sell goods or services.

_____ practice tends to be seen as a creative industry, which includes advertising, distribution and selling.

 a. Marketing myopia
 b. Marketing
 c. Customer acquisition management
 d. Product naming

6. _____ in economics and business is the result of an exchange and from that trade we assign a numerical monetary value to a good, service or asset. If I trade 4 apples for an orange, the _____ of an orange is 4 - apples. Inversely, the _____ of an apple is 1/4 oranges.

 a. Pricing
 b. Discounts and allowances
 c. Contribution margin-based pricing
 d. Price

7. _____ is a term used by project managers and project management (PM) organizations to describe methods for analyzing and collectively managing a group of current or proposed projects based on numerous key characteristics. The fundamental objective of the _____ process is to determine the optimal mix and sequencing of proposed projects to best achieve the organization's overall goals - typically expressed in terms of hard economic measures, business strategy goals, or technical strategy goals - while honoring constraints imposed by management or external real-world factors. Typical attributes of projects being analyzed in a _____ process include each project's total expected cost, consumption of scarce resources (human or otherwise) expected timeline and schedule of investment, expected nature, magnitude and timing of benefits to be realized, and relationship or inter-dependencies with other projects in the portfolio.

   a. Pop-up ads
   b. Power III
   c. Customer intelligence
   d. Project Portfolio Management

8. _____ is an advertisement in which a particular product specifically mentions a competitor by name for the express purpose of showing why the competitor is inferior to the product naming it.

This should not be confused with parody advertisements, where a fictional product is being advertised for the purpose of poking fun at the particular advertisement, nor should it be confused with the use of a coined brand name for the purpose of comparing the product without actually naming an actual competitor. ('Wikipedia tastes better and is less filling than the Encyclopedia Galactica.')

In the 1980s, during what has been referred to as the cola wars, soft-drink manufacturer Pepsi ran a series of advertisements where people, caught on hidden camera, in a blind taste test, chose Pepsi over rival Coca-Cola.

   a. Heavy-up
   b. Comparative advertising
   c. Cost per conversion
   d. GL-70

9. _____ is the process by which a new idea or new product is accepted by the market. The rate of _____ is the speed that the new idea spreads from one consumer to the next. Adoption is similar to _____ except that it deals with the psychological processes an individual goes through, rather than an aggregate market process.

   a. Market development
   b. Perceptual maps
   c. Kano model
   d. Diffusion

10. In probability theory, a branch of mathematics, a _____ is a solution to a stochastic differential equation. It is a continuous-time Markov process with continuous sample paths.

A sample path of a _____ mimics the trajectory of a molecule, which is embedded in a flowing fluid and at the same time subjected to random displacements due to collisions with other molecules, i.e. Brownian motion.

   a. 6-3-5 Brainwriting
   b. 180SearchAssistant
   c. Power III
   d. Diffusion process

11. _____ is a broad label that refers to any individuals or households that use goods and services generated within the economy. The concept of a _____ is used in different contexts, so that the usage and significance of the term may vary.

A _____ is a person who uses any product or service.

Chapter 13. Conceiving, Developing, and Managing Products

a. 6-3-5 Brainwriting
c. Power III
b. 180SearchAssistant
d. Consumer

12. A _____ is a type of wholesale merchant business that buys goods and bulk products from importers, other wholesalers and then sells to retailers. _____s can deal in any commodity destined for the retail market. Typical categories are food, lumber, hardware, fuel, and textiles.
   a. Chief privacy officer
   c. Tacit collusion
   b. Refusal to deal
   d. Jobbing house

13. _____ was originally coined by Austrian psychologist Alfred Adler in 1929. The current broader sense of the word dates from 1961.

In sociology, a _____ is the way a person lives.

   a. 180SearchAssistant
   c. Power III
   b. Lifestyle
   d. 6-3-5 Brainwriting

14. _____ involves disseminating information about a product, product line, brand, or company. It is one of the four key aspects of the marketing mix. (The other three elements are product marketing, pricing, and distribution). P>_____ is generally sub-divided into two parts:

   - Above the line _____: Promotion in the media (e.g. TV, radio, newspapers, Internet and Mobile Phones) in which the advertiser pays an advertising agency to place the ad
   - Below the line _____: All other _____. Much of this is intended to be subtle enough for the consumer to be unaware that _____ is taking place. E.g. sponsorship, product placement, endorsements, sales _____, merchandising, direct mail, personal selling, public relations, trade shows

   a. Davie Brown Index
   c. Cashmere Agency
   b. Bottling lines
   d. Promotion

15. _____ or _____ data refers to selected population characteristics as used in government, marketing or opinion research, or the _____ profiles used in such research. Note the distinction from the term 'demography' Commonly-used _____ include race, age, income, disabilities, mobility (in terms of travel time to work or number of vehicles available), educational attainment, home ownership, employment status, and even location.
   a. African Americans
   c. Albert Einstein
   b. AStore
   d. Demographic

16. In business and engineering, new _____ is the term used to describe the complete process of bringing a new product or service to market. There are two parallel paths involved in the Nproduct development process: one involves the idea generation, product design, and detail engineering; the other involves market research and marketing analysis. Companies typically see new _____ as the first stage in generating and commercializing new products within the overall strategic process of product life cycle management used to maintain or grow their market share.
   a. New product screening
   c. New product development
   b. Specification tree
   d. Product development

Chapter 13. Conceiving, Developing, and Managing Products

17. _____ is a branch of philosophy which seeks to address questions about morality, such as how a moral outcome can be achieved in a specific situation (applied _____), how moral values should be determined (normative _____), what moral values people actually abide by (descriptive _____), what the fundamental semantic, ontological, and epistemic nature of _____ or morality is (meta-_____), and how moral capacity or moral agency develops and what its nature is (moral psychology.)

Socrates was one of the first Greek philosophers to encourage both scholars and the common citizen to turn their attention from the outside world to the condition of man. In this view, Knowledge having a bearing on human life was placed highest, all other knowledge being secondary.

- a. ADTECH
- b. ACNielsen
- c. AMAX
- d. Ethics

18. _____ in organizations and public policy is both the organizational process of creating and maintaining a plan; and the psychological process of thinking about the activities required to create a desired goal on some scale. As such, it is a fundamental property of intelligent behavior. This thought process is essential to the creation and refinement of a plan, or integration of it with other plans, that is, it combines forecasting of developments with the preparation of scenarios of how to react to them.

- a. 180SearchAssistant
- b. 6-3-5 Brainwriting
- c. Power III
- d. Planning

19. _____ is the ongoing process of identifying and articulating market requirements that define a product's feature set.

- a. Market intelligence
- b. Targeted advertising
- c. Brand parity
- d. Product planning

20. _____ is the set of tasks, knowledge, and techniques required to identify business needs and determine solutions to business problems. Solutions often include a systems development component, but may also consist of process improvement or organizational change. The person who carries out this task is called a business analyst or _____.

- a. Business analysis
- b. Fast moving consumer goods
- c. Marketing management
- d. Door-to-door

21. _____ is the process or cycle of introducing a new product into the market. The actual launch of a new product is the final stage of new product development, and the one where the most money will have to be spent for advertising, sales promotion, and other marketing efforts. In the case of a new consumer packaged good, costs will be at least $ 10 million, but can reach up to $ 200 million.

- a. Commercialization
- b. Confusion marketing
- c. Sweepstakes
- d. Customer Interaction Tracker

Chapter 13. Conceiving, Developing, and Managing Products

22. _____ is the process of using quantitative methods and qualitative methods to evaluate consumer response to a product idea prior to the introduction of a product to the market. It can also be used to generate communication designed to alter consumer attitudes toward existing products. These methods involve the evaluation by consumers of product concepts having certain rational benefits, such as 'a detergent that removes stains but is gentle on fabrics,' or non-rational benefits, such as 'a shampoo that lets you be yourself.' Such methods are commonly referred to as _____ and have been performed using field surveys, personal interviews and focus groups, in combination with various quantitative methods, to generate and evaluate product concepts.

   a. Logit analysis
   b. Market analysis
   c. Cross tabulation
   d. Concept testing

23. The phrase _____, according to the Organization for Economic Co-operation and Development, refers to 'creative work undertaken on a systematic basis in order to increase the stock of knowledge, including knowledge of man, culture and society, and the use of this stock of knowledge to devise new applications [sic]' Though it is questionable that an organization is needed for this definition, as it is quite obvious that _____ refers to the _____ of something.

   New product design and development is more often than not a crucial factor in the survival of a company. In an industry that is fast changing, firms must continually revise their design and range of products.

   a. 180SearchAssistant
   b. Power III
   c. 6-3-5 Brainwriting
   d. Research and development

24. A _____, in the field of business and marketing, is a geographic region or demographic group used to gauge the viability of a product or service in the mass market prior to a wide scale roll-out. The criteria used to judge the acceptability of a _____ region or group include:

   1. a population that is demographically similar to the proposed target market; and
   2. relative isolation from densely populated media markets so that advertising to the test audience can be efficient and economical.

   The _____ ideally aims to duplicate 'everything' - promotion and distribution as well as `product' - on a smaller scale. The technique replicates, typically in one area, what is planned to occur in a national launch; and the results are very carefully monitored, so that they can be extrapolated to projected national results. The `area' may be any one of the following:

   - Television area
   - Test town
   - Residential neighborhood
   - Test site

118 *Chapter 13. Conceiving, Developing, and Managing Products*

A number of decisions have to be taken about any _____:

- Which _____?
- What is to be tested?
- How long a test?
- What are the success criteria?

The simple go or no-go decision, together with the related reduction of risk, is normally the main justification for the expense of _____s. At the same time, however, such _____s can be used to test specific elements of a new product's marketing mix; possibly the version of the product itself, the promotional message and media spend, the distribution channels and the price.

a. Preadolescence
c. 180SearchAssistant
b. Power III
d. Test market

25. _____ is a group creativity technique designed to generate a large number of ideas for the solution of a problem. The method was first popularized in the late 1930s by Alex Faickney Osborn in a book called Applied Imagination. Osborn proposed that groups could double their creative output with _____.

a. African Americans
c. Brainstorming
b. AStore
d. Albert Einstein

26. In the Mediterranean Basin and the Near East, a _____ is a small, separated garden pavilion open on some or all sides. _____s were common in Persia, India, Pakistan, and in the Ottoman Empire from the 13th century onward. Today, there are many _____s in and around the TopkapÄ± Palace in Istanbul, and they are still a relatively common sight in Greece.

a. 6-3-5 Brainwriting
c. Power III
b. 180SearchAssistant
d. Kiosk

27. The verb _____ or grant _____ means to give permission. The noun _____ refers to that permission as well as to the document memorializing that permission. _____ may be granted by a party to another party as an element of an agreement between those parties.

a. Power III
c. License
b. 180SearchAssistant
d. 6-3-5 Brainwriting

28. A _____ is a set of exclusive rights granted by a State to an inventor or his assignee for a limited period of time in exchange for a disclosure of an invention.

The procedure for granting _____s, the requirements placed on the _____ee and the extent of the exclusive rights vary widely between countries according to national laws and international agreements. Typically, however, a _____ application must include one or more claims defining the invention which must be new, inventive, and useful or industrially applicable.

Chapter 13. Conceiving, Developing, and Managing Products

a. Foreign Corrupt Practices Act
b. Product liability
c. Reasonable person standard
d. Patent

29. A _____ or trade mark, identified by the symbols ™ (not yet registered) and ® (registered) business organization or other legal entity to identify that the products and/or services to consumers with which the _____ appears originate from a unique source of origin, and to distinguish its products or services from those of other entities. A _____ is a type of intellectual property, and typically a name, word, phrase, logo, symbol, design, image, or a combination of these elements. There is also a range of non-conventional _____s comprising marks which do not fall into these standard categories.

a. 180SearchAssistant
b. Power III
c. Risk management
d. Trademark

30. The _____ is an agency in the United States Department of Commerce that issues patents to inventors and businesses for their inventions, and trademark registration for product and intellectual property identification.

The USPTO is currently based in Alexandria, Virginia, after a 2006 move from the Crystal City area of Arlington, Virginia. The offices under Patents and the Chief Information Officer that remained just outside the southern end of Crystal City completed moving to Randolph Square, a brand new building in Shirlington Village, on 27 April 2009.

a. Access Commerce
b. Underwriters Laboratories
c. INVISTA
d. United States Patent and Trademark Office

31. The _____ is an international organization designed to supervise and liberalize international trade. The _____ came into being on 1 January 1995, and is the successor to the General Agreement on Tariffs and Trade (GATT), which was created in 1947, and continued to operate for almost five decades as a de facto international organization.

The _____ deals with the rules of trade between nations at a near-global level; it is responsible for negotiating and implementing new trade agreements, and is in charge of policing member countries' adherence to all the _____ agreements, signed by the majority of the world's trading nations and ratified in their parliaments.

a. World Trade Organization
b. Merchandise Mart
c. BSI Group
d. Population Reference Bureau

32. _____ of consumer products (often supermarket goods) are distinguished by the absence of a brand name. They are identifed more by product characterstics.

They may be manufactured by less [prominent companies], or manufactured on the same production line as a 'named' brand. _____ are usually priced below those products sold by supermarkets under their own brand (frequently referred to as 'store brands' or 'own brands'.)

a. Micro ads
b. Generic brands
c. Gross Margin Return on Inventory Investment
d. M80

Chapter 13. Conceiving, Developing, and Managing Products

33. In marketing, _____ has come to mean the process by which marketers try to create an image or identity in the minds of their target market for its product, brand, or organization. It is the 'relative competitive comparison' their product occupies in a given market as perceived by the target market.

Re-_____ involves changing the identity of a product, relative to the identity of competing products, in the collective minds of the target market.

   a. Moratorium
   c. GE matrix
   b. Containerization
   d. Positioning

34. A _____ is a collection of symbols, experiences and associations connected with a product, a service, a person or any other artifact or entity.

_____s have become increasingly important components of culture and the economy, now being described as 'cultural accessories and personal philosophies'.

Some people distinguish the psychological aspect of a _____ from the experiential aspect.

   a. Brand
   c. Store brand
   b. Brand equity
   d. Brandable software

35. A _____ is a plan of action designed to achieve a particular goal.

_____ is different from tactics. In military terms, tactics is concerned with the conduct of an engagement while _____ is concerned with how different engagements are linked.

   a. 6-3-5 Brainwriting
   c. Power III
   b. Strategy
   d. 180SearchAssistant

36. _____ is one of the four elements of marketing mix. An organization or set of organizations (go-betweens) involved in the process of making a product or service available for use or consumption by a consumer or business user.

The other three parts of the marketing mix are product, pricing, and promotion.

   a. Better Living Through Chemistry
   c. Comparison-Shopping agent
   b. Japan Advertising Photographers' Association
   d. Distribution

37. A _____ is a written document that details the necessary actions to achieve one or more marketing objectives. It can be for a product or service, a brand, or a product line. _____s cover between one and five years.
   a. Prosumer
   c. Disruptive technology
   b. Marketing strategy
   d. Marketing plan

Chapter 13. Conceiving, Developing, and Managing Products

38. _____ is an organization's process of defining its strategy and making decisions on allocating its resources to pursue this strategy, including its capital and people. Various business analysis techniques can be used in _____, including SWOT analysis (Strengths, Weaknesses, Opportunities, and Threats) and PEST analysis (Political, Economic, Social, and Technological analysis) or STEER analysis involving Socio-cultural, Technological, Economic, Ecological, and Regulatory factors and EPISTEL (Environment, Political, Informatic, Social, Technological, Economic and Legal)

_____ is the formal consideration of an organization's future course. All _____ deals with at least one of three key questions:

1. 'What do we do?'
2. 'For whom do we do it?'
3. 'How do we excel?'

In business _____, the third question is better phrased 'How can we beat or avoid competition?'. (Bradford and Duncan, page 1.)

a. Power III
b. 180SearchAssistant
c. 6-3-5 Brainwriting
d. Strategic planning

39. _____ is the process of comparing the cost, cycle time, productivity, or quality of a specific process or method to another that is widely considered to be an industry standard or best practice. The result is often a business case for making changes in order to make improvements. The term _____ was first used by cobblers to measure ones feet for shoes.
a. Business strategy
b. Benchmarking
c. Switching cost
d. Strategic group

40. The U.S. _____ is an agency of the United States Department of Health and Human Services and is responsible for regulating and supervising the safety of foods, dietary supplements, drugs, vaccines, biological medical products, blood products, medical devices, radiation-emitting devices, veterinary products, and cosmetics. The FDA also enforces section 361 of the Public Health Service Act and the associated regulations, including sanitation requirements on interstate travel as well as specific rules for control of disease on products ranging from pet turtles to semen donations for assisted reproductive medicine techniques.

The FDA is an agency within the United States Department of Health and Human Services responsible for protecting and promoting the nation's public health.

a. Power III
b. 180SearchAssistant
c. 6-3-5 Brainwriting
d. Food and Drug Administration

41. The _____ is an economic and political union of 27 member states, located primarily in Europe. It was established by the Treaty of Maastricht on 1 November 1993 upon the foundations of the pre-existing European Economic Community. With almost 500 million citizens, the _____ combined generates an estimated 30% share (US$16.8 trillion in 2007) of the nominal gross world product.
a. ADTECH
b. ACNielsen
c. Eurozone
d. European Union

122 *Chapter 13. Conceiving, Developing, and Managing Products*

42. _____ is when a large distribution channel member (usually a retailer), buys from a manufacturer in bulk and puts its own name on the product. This strategy is only practical when the retailer does very high levels of volume. The advantages to the retailer are:

- more freedom and flexibility in pricing
- more control over product attributes and quality
- higher margins (or lower selling price)
- eliminates much of the manufacturer's promotional costs

The advantages to the manufacturer are:

- reduced promotional costs
- stability of sales volume (at least while the contract is operative)

- Kumar, Nirmalya; Steenkamp, Jan-Benedict E.M., Private Label Strategy - How to Meet the Store Brand Challenge. Harvard Business Press 2007

- private label
- brand management
- brand
- product management
- marketing

a. Promotion
c. Rural market
b. Customization
d. Private branding

43. A personal and cultural _____ is a relative ethic _____, an assumption upon which implementation can be extrapolated. A _____ system is a set of consistent _____s and measures that is soo not true. A principle _____ is a foundation upon which other _____s and measures of integrity are based.
a. Package-on-Package
b. Supreme Court of the United States
c. Perceptual maps
d. Value

44. _____s function as professionals who deal with trade, dealing in commodities that they do not produce themselves, in order to produce profit.

_____s can be of two types:

1. A wholesale _____ operates in the chain between producer and retail _____. Some wholesale _____s only organize the movement of goods rather than move the goods themselves.
2. A retail _____ or retailer, sells commodities to consumers (including businesses.) A shop owner is a retail _____.

Chapter 13. Conceiving, Developing, and Managing Products 123

A _____ class characterizes many pre-modern societies. Its status can range from high (even achieving titles like that of _____ prince or nabob) to low, such as in Chinese culture, due to the soiling capabilities of profiting from 'mere' trade, rather than from the labor of others reflected in agricultural produce, craftsmanship, and tribute.

In the United States, '_____' is defined (under the Uniform Commercial Code) as any person while engaged in a business or profession or a seller who deals regularly in the type of goods sold.

   a. Trade credit   b. RFM
   c. Retail loss prevention   d. Merchant

45. _____ is one of the four Ps of the marketing mix. The other three aspects are product, promotion, and place. It is also a key variable in microeconomic price allocation theory.
   a. Price   b. Competitor indexing
   c. Pricing   d. Relationship based pricing

46. The acronym _____, is a psychographic segmentation. It was developed in the 1970s to explain changing U.S. values and lifestyles. It has since been reworked to enhance its ability to predict consumer behavior.

According to the _____ Framework, groups of people are arranged in a rectangle and are based on two dimensions. The vertical dimension segments people based on the degree to which they are innovative and have resources such as income, education, self-confidence, intelligence, leadership skills, and energy.

   a. Power III   b. 6-3-5 Brainwriting
   c. VALS   d. 180SearchAssistant

47. The _____ is a concept from business management that was first described and popularized by Michael Porter in his 1985 best-seller, Competitive Advantage: Creating and Sustaining Superior Performance.

A _____ is a chain of activities. Products pass through all activities of the chain in order and at each activity the product gains some value.

   a. Relationship management   b. Business-to-business
   c. Mass marketing   d. Value chain

Chapter 14. Value Chain Management and Logistics

1. _____ is one of the four elements of marketing mix. An organization or set of organizations (go-betweens) involved in the process of making a product or service available for use or consumption by a consumer or business user.

The other three parts of the marketing mix are product, pricing, and promotion.

   a. Comparison-Shopping agent
   b. Better Living Through Chemistry
   c. Japan Advertising Photographers' Association
   d. Distribution

2. _____ in organizations and public policy is both the organizational process of creating and maintaining a plan; and the psychological process of thinking about the activities required to create a desired goal on some scale. As such, it is a fundamental property of intelligent behavior. This thought process is essential to the creation and refinement of a plan, or integration of it with other plans, that is, it combines forecasting of developments with the preparation of scenarios of how to react to them.

   a. 6-3-5 Brainwriting
   b. Power III
   c. 180SearchAssistant
   d. Planning

3. A personal and cultural _____ is a relative ethic _____, an assumption upon which implementation can be extrapolated. A _____ system is a set of consistent _____s and measures that is soo not true. A principle _____ is a foundation upon which other _____s and measures of integrity are based.

   a. Package-on-Package
   b. Supreme Court of the United States
   c. Perceptual maps
   d. Value

4. The _____ is a concept from business management that was first described and popularized by Michael Porter in his 1985 best-seller, Competitive Advantage: Creating and Sustaining Superior Performance.

A _____ is a chain of activities. Products pass through all activities of the chain in order and at each activity the product gains some value.

   a. Relationship management
   b. Mass marketing
   c. Value chain
   d. Business-to-business

5. A _____ is a collection of symbols, experiences and associations connected with a product, a service, a person or any other artifact or entity.

_____s have become increasingly important components of culture and the economy, now being described as 'cultural accessories and personal philosophies'.

Some people distinguish the psychological aspect of a _____ from the experiential aspect.

   a. Brandable software
   b. Brand equity
   c. Store brand
   d. Brand

6. _____ is a broad label that refers to any individuals or households that use goods and services generated within the economy. The concept of a _____ is used in different contexts, so that the usage and significance of the term may vary.

A _____ is a person who uses any product or service.

a. 6-3-5 Brainwriting
c. Power III
b. Consumer
d. 180SearchAssistant

7. _____ is the equation of personal happiness with consumption and the purchase of material possessions.

The term is often associated with criticisms of consumption starting with Thorstein Veblen.

Veblen's subject of examination, the newly emergent middle class arising at the turn of the twentieth century, comes to full fruition by the end of the twentieth century through the process of globalization.

In economics, _____ refers to economic policies placing emphasis on consumption.

a. 180SearchAssistant
c. 6-3-5 Brainwriting
b. Power III
d. Consumerism

8. A _____ is a type of wholesale merchant business that buys goods and bulk products from importers, other wholesalers and then sells to retailers. _____s can deal in any commodity destined for the retail market. Typical categories are food, lumber, hardware, fuel, and textiles.
a. Refusal to deal
c. Tacit collusion
b. Chief privacy officer
d. Jobbing house

9. _____ is a form of communication that typically attempts to persuade potential customers to purchase or to consume more of a particular brand of product or service. 'While now central to the contemporary global economy and the reproduction of global production networks, it is only quite recently that _____ has been more than a marginal influence on patterns of sales and production. The formation of modern _____ was intimately bound up with the emergence of new forms of monopoly capitalism around the end of the 19th and beginning of the 20th century as one element in corporate strategies to create, organize and where possible control markets, especially for mass produced consumer goods.
a. Advertising
c. AMAX
b. ADTECH
d. ACNielsen

10. _____ describes the situation when output from (or information about the result of) an event or phenomenon in the past will influence the same event/phenomenon in the present or future. When an event is part of a chain of cause-and-effect that forms a circuit or loop, then the event is said to 'feed back' into itself.

_____ is also a synonym for:

- _____ Signal; the information about the initial event that is the basis for subsequent modification of the event.
- _____ Loop; the causal path that leads from the initial generation of the _____ signal to the subsequent modification of the event.

_____ is a mechanism, process or signal that is looped back to control a system within itself. Such a loop is called a _____ loop.

Chapter 14. Value Chain Management and Logistics

a. 6-3-5 Brainwriting
b. 180SearchAssistant
c. Power III
d. Feedback

11. A supply chain is the system of organizations, people, technology, activities, information and resources involved in moving a product or service from _____ to customer. Supply chain activities transform natural resources, raw materials and components into a finished product that is delivered to the end customer. In sophisticated supply chain systems, used products may re-enter the supply chain at any point where residual value is recyclable.
   a. Product line extension
   b. Bringin' Home the Oil
   c. Rebate
   d. Supplier

12. _____ is the management of the flow of goods, information and other resources, including energy and people, between the point of origin and the point of consumption in order to meet the requirements of consumers (frequently, and originally, military organizations.) _____ involves the integration of information, transportation, inventory, warehousing, material-handling, and packaging. _____ is a channel of the supply chain which adds the value of time and place utility.
   a. Power III
   b. 180SearchAssistant
   c. Logistics
   d. 6-3-5 Brainwriting

13. _____ is defined by the American _____ Association as the activity, set of institutions, and processes for creating, communicating, delivering, and exchanging offerings that have value for customers, clients, partners, and society at large. The term developed from the original meaning which referred literally to going to market, as in shopping, or going to a market to sell goods or services.

_____ practice tends to be seen as a creative industry, which includes advertising, distribution and selling.

   a. Marketing myopia
   b. Marketing
   c. Product naming
   d. Customer acquisition management

14. A _____ is a written document that details the necessary actions to achieve one or more marketing objectives. It can be for a product or service, a brand, or a product line. _____s cover between one and five years.
   a. Marketing plan
   b. Disruptive technology
   c. Prosumer
   d. Marketing strategy

15. In economics, _____ is the desire to own something and the ability to pay for it. The term _____ signifies the ability or the willingness to buy a particular commodity at a given point of time .

   a. Discretionary spending
   b. Market dominance
   c. Demand
   d. Market system

16. _____ is a measure of the strength of a brand, product, service relative to competitive offerings. There is often a geographic element to the competitive landscape. In defining _____, you must see to what extent a product, brand, or firm controls a product category in a given geographic area.
   a. Market system
   b. Productivity
   c. Discretionary spending
   d. Market dominance

Chapter 14. Value Chain Management and Logistics

17. _____ is a list for goods and materials held available in stock by a business. It is also used for a list of the contents of a household and for a list for testamentary purposes of the possessions of someone who has died. In accounting _____ is considered an asset.
   a. Ending Inventory
   b. Inventory
   c. ADTECH
   d. ACNielsen

18. In economics, business, retail, and accounting, a _____ is the value of money that has been used up to produce something, and hence is not available for use anymore. In economics, a _____ is an alternative that is given up as a result of a decision. In business, the _____ may be one of acquisition, in which case the amount of money expended to acquire it is counted as _____.
   a. Variable cost
   b. Fixed costs
   c. Transaction cost
   d. Cost

19. _____ is a form of marketing developed from direct response marketing campaigns conducted in the 1970's and 1980's which emphasizes customer retention and satisfaction, rather than a dominant focus on 'point of sale' transactions.

   _____ differs from other forms of marketing in that it recognizes the long term value to the firm of keeping customers, as opposed to direct or 'Intrusion' marketing, which focuses upon acquisition of new clients by targeting majority demographics based upon prospective client lists.

   _____ refers to long-term and mutually beneficial arrangement wherein both buyer and seller focus on value enhancement through the certain of more satisfying exchange. This approach attempts to transcend the simple purchase exchange process with customer to make more meaningful and richer contact by providing a more holistic, personalized purchase, and use orn consumption experience to create stronger ties.

   a. Guerrilla Marketing
   b. Global marketing
   c. Relationship marketing
   d. Diversity marketing

20. _____ is the provision of service to customers before, during and after a purchase.

   According to Turban et al., '_____ is a series of activities designed to enhance the level of customer satisfaction - that is, the feeling that a product or service has met the customer expectation.'

   Its importance varies by product, industry and customer.

   a. Facing
   b. COPC Inc.
   c. Customer experience
   d. Customer service

21. _____ is one of the four Ps of the marketing mix. The other three aspects are product, promotion, and place. It is also a key variable in microeconomic price allocation theory.
   a. Pricing
   b. Competitor indexing
   c. Price
   d. Relationship based pricing

Chapter 14. Value Chain Management and Logistics

22. A _____ is a list of the general tasks and responsibilities of a position. Typically, it also includes to whom the position reports, specifications such as the qualifications needed by the person in the job, salary range for the position, etc. A _____ is usually developed by conducting a job analysis, which includes examining the tasks and sequences of tasks necessary to perform the job.
    a. Job description
    b. 6-3-5 Brainwriting
    c. Power III
    d. 180SearchAssistant

23. _____ is an advertisement in which a particular product specifically mentions a competitor by name for the express purpose of showing why the competitor is inferior to the product naming it.

This should not be confused with parody advertisements, where a fictional product is being advertised for the purpose of poking fun at the particular advertisement, nor should it be confused with the use of a coined brand name for the purpose of comparing the product without actually naming an actual competitor. ('Wikipedia tastes better and is less filling than the Encyclopedia Galactica.')

In the 1980s, during what has been referred to as the cola wars, soft-drink manufacturer Pepsi ran a series of advertisements where people, caught on hidden camera, in a blind taste test, chose Pepsi over rival Coca-Cola.

   a. GL-70
   b. Cost per conversion
   c. Heavy-up
   d. Comparative advertising

24. A _____ is a plan of action designed to achieve a particular goal.

_____ is different from tactics. In military terms, tactics is concerned with the conduct of an engagement while _____ is concerned with how different engagements are linked.

   a. 180SearchAssistant
   b. 6-3-5 Brainwriting
   c. Power III
   d. Strategy

25. _____ is used in marketing to describe the way in which service capacity cannot be stored for sale in the future. It is a key concept of services marketing.

Other key characteristics of services include intangibility, inseparability and variability.

   a. National brand
   b. Perishability
   c. Specialty catalogs
   d. Demonstrator model

26. The most important feature of a contract is that one party makes an _____ for an arrangement that another accepts. This can be called a 'concurrence of wills' or 'ad idem' (meeting of the minds) of two or more parties. The concept is somewhat contested.
    a. ADTECH
    b. AMAX
    c. ACNielsen
    d. Offer

Chapter 14. Value Chain Management and Logistics

27. _____ involves disseminating information about a product, product line, brand, or company. It is one of the four key aspects of the marketing mix. (The other three elements are product marketing, pricing, and distribution). P>_____ is generally sub-divided into two parts:

- Above the line _____: Promotion in the media (e.g. TV, radio, newspapers, Internet and Mobile Phones) in which the advertiser pays an advertising agency to place the ad
- Below the line _____: All other _____. Much of this is intended to be subtle enough for the consumer to be unaware that _____ is taking place. E.g. sponsorship, product placement, endorsements, sales _____, merchandising, direct mail, personal selling, public relations, trade shows

   a. Davie Brown Index   b. Cashmere Agency
   c. Bottling lines   d. Promotion

28. _____ , according to The American Marketing Association, is 'a planning process designed to assure that all brand contacts received by a customer or prospect for a product, service, or organization are relevant to that person and consistent over time.' (Marketing Power Dictionary)

_____ is a term used to describe a holistic approach to marketing. It aims to ensure consistency of message and the complementary use of media. The concept includes online and offline marketing channels.

   a. ADTECH   b. ACNielsen
   c. Integrated marketing communications   d. AMAX

29. _____ consists of the sale of goods or merchandise from a fixed location, such as a department store or kiosk in small or individual lots for direct consumption by the purchaser. _____ may include subordinated services, such as delivery. Purchasers may be individuals or businesses.
   a. Retailing   b. Warehouse store
   c. Thrifting   d. Charity shop

30. In the Mediterranean Basin and the Near East, a _____ is a small, separated garden pavilion open on some or all sides. _____s were common in Persia, India, Pakistan, and in the Ottoman Empire from the 13th century onward. Today, there are many _____s in and around the Topkapı Palace in Istanbul, and they are still a relatively common sight in Greece.
   a. Power III   b. 180SearchAssistant
   c. 6-3-5 Brainwriting   d. Kiosk

31. _____ in economics and business is the result of an exchange and from that trade we assign a numerical monetary value to a good, service or asset. If I trade 4 apples for an orange, the _____ of an orange is 4 - apples. Inversely, the _____ of an apple is 1/4 oranges.
   a. Pricing   b. Price
   c. Contribution margin-based pricing d. Discounts and allowances

32. _____ occurs when manufacturers (brands) disintermediate their channel partners, such as distributors, retailers, dealers, and sales representatives, by selling their products direct to consumers through general marketing methods and/or over the internet through eCommerce.

Some manufacturers want their brands to capture the power of the internet but do not want to create conflict with their other distribution channels, as these partners are necessary and viable for any manufacturer to maintain and gain success. The Census Bureau of the U.S. Department of Commerce reported that online sales in 2005 grew 24.6 percent over 2004 to reach 86.3 billion dollars.

a. Trade Symbols
c. Store brand
b. Retail design
d. Channel conflict

33. _____ is a branch of philosophy which seeks to address questions about morality, such as how a moral outcome can be achieved in a specific situation (applied _____), how moral values should be determined (normative _____), what moral values people actually abide by (descriptive _____), what the fundamental semantic, ontological, and epistemic nature of _____ or morality is (meta-_____), and how moral capacity or moral agency develops and what its nature is (moral psychology.)

Socrates was one of the first Greek philosophers to encourage both scholars and the common citizen to turn their attention from the outside world to the condition of man. In this view, Knowledge having a bearing on human life was placed highest, all other knowledge being secondary.

a. ACNielsen
c. Ethics
b. ADTECH
d. AMAX

34. _____ is when a large distribution channel member (usually a retailer), buys from a manufacturer in bulk and puts its own name on the product. This strategy is only practical when the retailer does very high levels of volume. The advantages to the retailer are:

- more freedom and flexibility in pricing
- more control over product attributes and quality
- higher margins (or lower selling price)
- eliminates much of the manufacturer's promotional costs

Chapter 14. Value Chain Management and Logistics

The advantages to the manufacturer are:

- reduced promotional costs
- stability of sales volume (at least while the contract is operative)

- Kumar, Nirmalya; Steenkamp, Jan-Benedict E.M., Private Label Strategy - How to Meet the Store Brand Challenge. Harvard Business Press 2007

- private label
- brand management
- brand
- product management
- marketing

a. Rural market
b. Customization
c. Promotion
d. Private branding

35. The United States _____ is the Cabinet department of the United States government concerned with promoting economic growth. It was originally created as the United States _____ and Labor on February 14, 1903. It was subsequently renamed to the _____ on March 4, 1913, and its bureaus and agencies specializing in labor were transferred to the new Department of Labor.
a. 6-3-5 Brainwriting
b. Power III
c. Department of Commerce
d. 180SearchAssistant

36. The _____ is an economic and political union of 27 member states, located primarily in Europe. It was established by the Treaty of Maastricht on 1 November 1993 upon the foundations of the pre-existing European Economic Community. With almost 500 million citizens, the _____ combined generates an estimated 30% share (US$16.8 trillion in 2007) of the nominal gross world product.
a. European Union
b. ACNielsen
c. ADTECH
d. Eurozone

37. A _____ is a set of companies with interlocking business relationships and shareholdings. It is a type of business group.

The prototypical _____ are those which appeared in Japan during the 'economic miracle' following World War II.

a. 180SearchAssistant
b. Keiretsu
c. 6-3-5 Brainwriting
d. Power III

Chapter 14. Value Chain Management and Logistics

38. The _____ is the Cabinet department of the United States government concerned with promoting economic growth. It was originally created as the _____ and Labor on February 14, 1903. It was subsequently renamed to the Department of Commerce on March 4, 1913, and its bureaus and agencies specializing in labor were transferred to the new Department of Labor.

   a. ADTECH
   b. United States Department of Commerce
   c. AMAX
   d. ACNielsen

39. An _____ is the manufacturing of a good or service within a category. Although _____ is a broad term for any kind of economic production, in economics and urban planning _____ is a synonym for the secondary sector, which is a type of economic activity involved in the manufacturing of raw materials into goods and products.

   There are four key industrial economic sectors: the primary sector, largely raw material extraction industries such as mining and farming; the secondary sector, involving refining, construction, and manufacturing; the tertiary sector, which deals with services (such as law and medicine) and distribution of manufactured goods; and the quaternary sector, a relatively new type of knowledge _____ focusing on technological research, design and development such as computer programming, and biochemistry.

   a. AMAX
   b. ACNielsen
   c. Industry
   d. ADTECH

40. A _____ or logistics network is the system of organizations, people, technology, activities, information and resources involved in moving a product or service from supplier to customer. _____ activities transform natural resources, raw materials and components into a finished product that is delivered to the end customer. In sophisticated _____ systems, used products may re-enter the _____ at any point where residual value is recyclable.

   a. Supply chain network
   b. Purchasing
   c. Demand chain management
   d. Supply chain

41. _____ is an organization's process of defining its strategy and making decisions on allocating its resources to pursue this strategy, including its capital and people. Various business analysis techniques can be used in _____, including SWOT analysis (Strengths, Weaknesses, Opportunities, and Threats) and PEST analysis (Political, Economic, Social, and Technological analysis) or STEER analysis involving Socio-cultural, Technological, Economic, Ecological, and Regulatory factors and EPISTEL (Environment, Political, Informatic, Social, Technological, Economic and Legal)

   _____ is the formal consideration of an organization's future course. All _____ deals with at least one of three key questions:

   1. 'What do we do?'
   2. 'For whom do we do it?'
   3. 'How do we excel?'

   In business _____, the third question is better phrased 'How can we beat or avoid competition?'. (Bradford and Duncan, page 1.)

   a. Strategic planning
   b. 6-3-5 Brainwriting
   c. Power III
   d. 180SearchAssistant

Chapter 14. Value Chain Management and Logistics

42. _____ is the process of comparing the cost, cycle time, productivity, or quality of a specific process or method to another that is widely considered to be an industry standard or best practice. The result is often a business case for making changes in order to make improvements. The term _____ was first used by cobblers to measure ones feet for shoes.
   a. Strategic group
   b. Benchmarking
   c. Switching cost
   d. Business strategy

43. _____ is a process by which government's control over businesses and individuals is reduced or eliminated. It is the removal of some governmental controls over a market. _____ does not mean elimination of laws against fraud, but eliminating or reducing government control of how business is done, thereby moving toward a more free market.
   a. Power III
   b. Consumer spending
   c. Value added
   d. Deregulation

44. _____ is a rivalry between individuals, groups, nations for territory, a niche, or allocation of resources. It arises whenever two or more parties strive for a goal which cannot be shared. _____ occurs naturally between living organisms which co-exist in the same environment.
   a. Price competition
   b. Non-price competition
   c. Price fixing
   d. Competition

45. Competitiveness is a comparative concept of the ability and performance of a firm, sub-sector or country to sell and supply goods and/or services in a given market. Although widely used in economics and business management, the usefulness of the concept, particularly in the context of national competitiveness, is vigorously disputed by economists, such as Paul Krugman .

The term may also be applied to markets, where it is used to refer to the extent to which the market structure may be regarded as perfectly _____.

   a. Customs union
   b. Geographical pricing
   c. Free trade zone
   d. Competitive

46. A _____ is a retail establishment which specializes in selling a wide range of products without a single predominant merchandise line. _____s usually sell products including apparel, furniture, appliances, electronics, and additionally select other lines of products such as paint, hardware, toiletries, cosmetics, photographic equipment, jewelery, toys, and sporting goods. Certain _____s are further classified as discount _____s.
   a. 6-3-5 Brainwriting
   b. Power III
   c. Department store
   d. 180SearchAssistant

47. _____ is a system of intermodal freight transport using standard intermodal containers that are standardised by the International Organization for Standardization (ISO.) These can be loaded and sealed intact onto container ships, railroad cars, planes, and trucks.
   a. BeyondROI
   b. Containerization
   c. Scientific controls
   d. Rebate

48. _____ refers to the structured transmission of data between organizations by electronic means. It is used to transfer electronic documents from one computer system to another (ie) from one trading partner to another trading partner. It is more than mere E-mail; for instance, organizations might replace bills of lading and even checks with appropriate _____ messages.

a. ADTECH
b. Electronic data interchange
c. ACNielsen
d. AMAX

49. _____ is an inventory strategy implemented to improve the return on investment of a business by reducing in-process inventory and its associated carrying costs. In order to achieve JIT the process must have signals of what is going on elsewhere within the process. This means that the process is often driven by a series of signals, which can be Kanban , that tell production processes when to make the next part.
   a. Personalization
   b. Promotion
   c. Clutter
   d. Just-in-time

50. _____ refer to a collection of facts usually collected as the result of experience, observation or experiment or a set of premises. This may consist of numbers, words particularly as measurements or observations of a set of variables. _____ are often viewed as a lowest level of abstraction from which information and knowledge are derived.
   a. Mean
   b. Pearson product-moment correlation coefficient
   c. Sample size
   d. Data

51. The _____ is the level of inventory when a fresh order should be made with suppliers to bring the inventory up by the Economic order quantity (EOQ.)

The _____ for replenishment of stock occurs when the level of inventory drops down to zero. In view of instantaneous replenishment of stock the level of inventory jumps to the original level from zero level.

   a. Stock forecast
   b. Stock obsolescence
   c. Reorder point
   d. Net realisable value

52. _____s is the social science that studies the production, distribution, and consumption of goods and services. The term _____s comes from the Ancient Greek oá¼°κονομῑα from oá¼¶κος (oikos, 'house') + vÍŒµος (nomos, 'custom' or 'law'), hence 'rules of the house(hold)'. Current _____ models developed out of the broader field of political economy in the late 19th century, owing to a desire to use an empirical approach more akin to the physical sciences.
   a. ACNielsen
   b. Industrial organization
   c. ADTECH
   d. Economic

53. _____ is a term used by inventory specialists to describe a level of stock that is maintained below the cycle stock to buffer against stockouts. _____ exists to counter uncertainties in supply and demand. _____ is defined as extra units of inventory carried as protection against possible stockouts.
   a. Price-weighted
   b. Safety stock
   c. Cross-docking
   d. Product support

54. _____ is the level of inventory that minimizes the total inventory holding costs and ordering costs. The framework used to determine this order quantity is also known as Wilson _____ Model. The model was developed by F. W. Harris in 1913.
   a. AMAX
   b. ADTECH
   c. ACNielsen
   d. Economic order quantity

55. A _____ is a commercial building for storage of goods. _____s are used by manufacturers, importers, exporters, wholesalers, transport businesses, customs, etc. They are usually large plain buildings in industrial areas of cities and towns.
   a. 6-3-5 Brainwriting
   b. 180SearchAssistant
   c. Power III
   d. Warehouse

Chapter 15. Wholesaling

1. _____ is one of the four elements of marketing mix. An organization or set of organizations (go-betweens) involved in the process of making a product or service available for use or consumption by a consumer or business user.

The other three parts of the marketing mix are product, pricing, and promotion.

   a. Distribution
   b. Comparison-Shopping agent
   c. Japan Advertising Photographers' Association
   d. Better Living Through Chemistry

2. A _____ is a type of wholesale merchant business that buys goods and bulk products from importers, other wholesalers and then sells to retailers. _____s can deal in any commodity destined for the retail market. Typical categories are food, lumber, hardware, fuel, and textiles.

   a. Refusal to deal
   b. Chief privacy officer
   c. Tacit collusion
   d. Jobbing house

3. The acronym _____, is a psychographic segmentation. It was developed in the 1970s to explain changing U.S. values and lifestyles. It has since been reworked to enhance its ability to predict consumer behavior.

According to the _____ Framework, groups of people are arranged in a rectangle and are based on two dimensions. The vertical dimension segments people based on the degree to which they are innovative and have resources such as income, education, self-confidence, intelligence, leadership skills, and energy.

   a. 180SearchAssistant
   b. 6-3-5 Brainwriting
   c. Power III
   d. VALS

4. _____ is a broad label that refers to any individuals or households that use goods and services generated within the economy. The concept of a _____ is used in different contexts, so that the usage and significance of the term may vary.

A _____ is a person who uses any product or service.

   a. 180SearchAssistant
   b. Power III
   c. Consumer
   d. 6-3-5 Brainwriting

5. _____ is defined by the American _____ Association as the activity, set of institutions, and processes for creating, communicating, delivering, and exchanging offerings that have value for customers, clients, partners, and society at large. The term developed from the original meaning which referred literally to going to market, as in shopping, or going to a market to sell goods or services.

_____ practice tends to be seen as a creative industry, which includes advertising, distribution and selling.

   a. Product naming
   b. Marketing
   c. Customer acquisition management
   d. Marketing myopia

6. _____ consists of the sale of goods or merchandise from a fixed location, such as a department store or kiosk in small or individual lots for direct consumption by the purchaser. _____ may include subordinated services, such as delivery. Purchasers may be individuals or businesses.

Chapter 15. Wholesaling

a. Retailing
b. Warehouse store
c. Charity shop
d. Thrifting

7. A _____ is a list of the general tasks and responsibilities of a position. Typically, it also includes to whom the position reports, specifications such as the qualifications needed by the person in the job, salary range for the position, etc. A _____ is usually developed by conducting a job analysis, which includes examining the tasks and sequences of tasks necessary to perform the job.
a. 180SearchAssistant
b. 6-3-5 Brainwriting
c. Power III
d. Job description

8. A supply chain is the system of organizations, people, technology, activities, information and resources involved in moving a product or service from _____ to customer. Supply chain activities transform natural resources, raw materials and components into a finished product that is delivered to the end customer. In sophisticated supply chain systems, used products may re-enter the supply chain at any point where residual value is recyclable.
a. Bringin' Home the Oil
b. Product line extension
c. Rebate
d. Supplier

9. A _____ is a party that mediates between a buyer and a seller. A _____ who also acts as a seller or as a buyer becomes a principal party to the deal. Distinguish agent: one who acts on behalf of a principal.
a. Broker
b. Spokesperson
c. 180SearchAssistant
d. Power III

10. _____s function as professionals who deal with trade, dealing in commodities that they do not produce themselves, in order to produce profit.

_____s can be of two types:

1. A wholesale _____ operates in the chain between producer and retail _____. Some wholesale _____s only organize the movement of goods rather than move the goods themselves.
2. A retail _____ or retailer, sells commodities to consumers (including businesses.) A shop owner is a retail _____.

A _____ class characterizes many pre-modern societies. Its status can range from high (even achieving titles like that of _____ prince or nabob) to low, such as in Chinese culture, due to the soiling capabilities of profiting from 'mere' trade, rather than from the labor of others reflected in agricultural produce, craftsmanship, and tribute.

In the United States, '_____' is defined (under the Uniform Commercial Code) as any person while engaged in a business or profession or a seller who deals regularly in the type of goods sold.

a. Retail loss prevention
b. Merchant
c. RFM
d. Trade credit

11. A _____ is defined by the International Co-operative Alliance's Statement on the Co-operative Identity as an autonomous association of persons united voluntarily to meet their common economic, social, and cultural needs and aspirations through a jointly-owned and democratically-controlled enterprise. It is a business organization owned and operated by a group of individuals for their mutual benefit. A _____ may also be defined as a business owned and controlled equally by the people who use its services or who work at it.
   a. 6-3-5 Brainwriting
   b. Power III
   c. 180SearchAssistant
   d. Cooperative

12. Wholesaling, historically called jobbing, is the sale of goods or merchandise to retailers, to industrial, commercial, institutional or to other wholesalers and related subordinated services.

   According to the United Nations Statistics Division, '_____' is the resale (sale without transformation) of new and used goods to retailers, to industrial, commercial, institutional or professional users or involves acting as an agent or broker in buying merchandise for such persons or companies. Wholesalers frequently physically assemble, sort and grade goods in large lots, break bulk, repack and redistribute in smaller lots.

   a. Supply chain network
   b. Wholesale
   c. Purchasing
   d. Supply network

13. _____ is an inventory strategy implemented to improve the return on investment of a business by reducing in-process inventory and its associated carrying costs. In order to achieve JIT the process must have signals of what is going on elsewhere within the process. This means that the process is often driven by a series of signals, which can be Kanban , that tell production processes when to make the next part.
   a. Clutter
   b. Promotion
   c. Just-in-time
   d. Personalization

14. _____ is a form of communication that typically attempts to persuade potential customers to purchase or to consume more of a particular brand of product or service. 'While now central to the contemporary global economy and the reproduction of global production networks, it is only quite recently that _____ has been more than a marginal influence on patterns of sales and production. The formation of modern _____ was intimately bound up with the emergence of new forms of monopoly capitalism around the end of the 19th and beginning of the 20th century as one element in corporate strategies to create, organize and where possible control markets, especially for mass produced consumer goods.
   a. ADTECH
   b. Advertising
   c. AMAX
   d. ACNielsen

15. _____ is a list for goods and materials held available in stock by a business. It is also used for a list of the contents of a household and for a list for testamentary purposes of the possessions of someone who has died. In accounting _____ is considered an asset.
   a. ACNielsen
   b. Ending Inventory
   c. ADTECH
   d. Inventory

16. Merchandising refers to the methods, practices and operations conducted to promote and sustain certain categories of commercial activity. The term is understood to have different specific meanings depending on the context. _____ is a sale goods at a store

Chapter 15. Wholesaling

In marketing, one of the definitions of merchandising is the practice in which the brand or image from one product or service is used to sell another.

a. Merchandising
b. New Media Strategies
c. Sales promotion
d. Merchandise

17. _____ is a sub-discipline and type of marketing. There are two main definitional characteristics which distinguish it from other types of marketing. The first is that it attempts to send its messages directly to consumers, without the use of intervening media.

a. Power III
b. Direct Marketing Associations
c. Direct marketing
d. Database marketing

18. In economics, _____ is the desire to own something and the ability to pay for it. The term _____ signifies the ability or the willingness to buy a particular commodity at a given point of time.

a. Market dominance
b. Market system
c. Discretionary spending
d. Demand

19. An _____ is the manufacturing of a good or service within a category. Although _____ is a broad term for any kind of economic production, in economics and urban planning _____ is a synonym for the secondary sector, which is a type of economic activity involved in the manufacturing of raw materials into goods and products.

There are four key industrial economic sectors: the primary sector, largely raw material extraction industries such as mining and farming; the secondary sector, involving refining, construction, and manufacturing; the tertiary sector, which deals with services (such as law and medicine) and distribution of manufactured goods; and the quaternary sector, a relatively new type of knowledge _____ focusing on technological research, design and development such as computer programming, and biochemistry.

a. Industry
b. ACNielsen
c. AMAX
d. ADTECH

20. The phrase _____ refers to the aspect of corporate strategy, corporate finance and management dealing with the buying, selling and combining of different companies that can aid, finance, or help a growing company in a given industry grow rapidly without having to create another business entity.

An acquisition, also known as a takeover or a buyout, is the buying of one company (the 'target') by another. An acquisition may be friendly or hostile.

a. Power III
b. 180SearchAssistant
c. 6-3-5 Brainwriting
d. Mergers and acquisitions

21. _____ is one of the four Ps of the marketing mix. The other three aspects are product, promotion, and place. It is also a key variable in microeconomic price allocation theory.

Chapter 15. Wholesaling

a. Price
b. Competitor indexing
c. Relationship based pricing
d. Pricing

22. _____ is the provision of service to customers before, during and after a purchase.

According to Turban et al., '_____ is a series of activities designed to enhance the level of customer satisfaction - that is, the feeling that a product or service has met the customer expectation.'

Its importance varies by product, industry and customer.

a. Facing
b. Customer experience
c. COPC Inc.
d. Customer service

23. _____ in economics refers to metrics and measures of output from production processes, per unit of input. Labor _____, for example, is typically measured as a ratio of output per labor-hour, an input. _____ may be conceived of as a metrics of the technical or engineering efficiency of production.

a. 180SearchAssistant
b. Productivity
c. Power III
d. Value engineering

24. _____ is an advertisement in which a particular product specifically mentions a competitor by name for the express purpose of showing why the competitor is inferior to the product naming it.

This should not be confused with parody advertisements, where a fictional product is being advertised for the purpose of poking fun at the particular advertisement, nor should it be confused with the use of a coined brand name for the purpose of comparing the product without actually naming an actual competitor. ('Wikipedia tastes better and is less filling than the Encyclopedia Galactica.')

In the 1980s, during what has been referred to as the cola wars, soft-drink manufacturer Pepsi ran a series of advertisements where people, caught on hidden camera, in a blind taste test, chose Pepsi over rival Coca-Cola.

a. GL-70
b. Heavy-up
c. Cost per conversion
d. Comparative advertising

Chapter 16. Retailing

1. An _____ is a person who has possession of an enterprise and assumes significant accountability for the inherent risks and the outcome. It is an ambitious leader who combines land, labour, and capital to create and market new goods or services. The term is a loanword from French and was first defined by the Irish economist Richard Cantillon.
    a. AMAX
    b. Entrepreneur
    c. ACNielsen
    d. ADTECH

2. _____ consists of the sale of goods or merchandise from a fixed location, such as a department store or kiosk in small or individual lots for direct consumption by the purchaser. _____ may include subordinated services, such as delivery. Purchasers may be individuals or businesses.
    a. Charity shop
    b. Warehouse store
    c. Thrifting
    d. Retailing

3. _____ is one of the four elements of marketing mix. An organization or set of organizations (go-betweens) involved in the process of making a product or service available for use or consumption by a consumer or business user.

    The other three parts of the marketing mix are product, pricing, and promotion.

    a. Comparison-Shopping agent
    b. Japan Advertising Photographers' Association
    c. Distribution
    d. Better Living Through Chemistry

4. _____ refers to the methods of practicing and using another person's philosophy of business. The franchisor grants the independent operator the right to distribute its products, techniques, and trademarks for a percentage of gross monthly sales and a royalty fee. Various tangibles and intangibles such as national or international advertising, training, and other support services are commonly made available by the franchisor.
    a. 180SearchAssistant
    b. Power III
    c. Franchise fee
    d. Franchising

5. The _____, a unit of the United States Department of Labor, is the principal fact-finding agency for the U.S. government in the broad field of labor economics and statistics. The BLS is an independent national statistical agency that collects, processes, analyzes, and disseminates essential statistical data to the American public, the U.S. Congress, other Federal agencies, State and local governments, business, and labor representatives. The BLS also serves as a statistical resource to the Department of Labor.
    a. Gross national product
    b. Consumer Expenditure Survey
    c. Power III
    d. Bureau of Labor Statistics

6. _____ is anything that is intended to save time, energy or frustration. A _____ store at a petrol station, for example, sells items that have nothing to do with gasoline/petrol, but it saves the consumer from having to go to a grocery store. '_____' is a very relative term and its meaning tends to change over time.
    a. Marketing buzz
    b. Demographic profile
    c. Convenience
    d. MaxDiff

7. A _____ is a small store or shop that sells candy, ice-cream, soft drinks, lottery tickets, newspapers and magazines, along with a small selection of food and grocery supplies. Stores that are part of gas stations may also sell motor oil, windshield washer fluid, radiator fluid, and maps. Often toiletries and other hygiene products are stocked, and some of these stores also offer money orders and wire transfer services or liquor products.

Chapter 16. Retailing

a. 180SearchAssistant
b. Power III
c. 6-3-5 Brainwriting
d. Convenience store

8. _____ is a mathematical science pertaining to the collection, analysis, interpretation or explanation, and presentation of data. It also provides tools for prediction and forecasting based on data. It is applicable to a wide variety of academic disciplines, from the natural and social sciences to the humanities, government and business.
   a. Median
   b. Null hypothesis
   c. Type I error
   d. Statistics

9. _____ is defined by the American _____ Association as the activity, set of institutions, and processes for creating, communicating, delivering, and exchanging offerings that have value for customers, clients, partners, and society at large. The term developed from the original meaning which referred literally to going to market, as in shopping, or going to a market to sell goods or services.

_____ practice tends to be seen as a creative industry, which includes advertising, distribution and selling.

   a. Product naming
   b. Marketing
   c. Customer acquisition management
   d. Marketing myopia

10. _____ is a broad label that refers to any individuals or households that use goods and services generated within the economy. The concept of a _____ is used in different contexts, so that the usage and significance of the term may vary.

A _____ is a person who uses any product or service.

   a. 6-3-5 Brainwriting
   b. Power III
   c. 180SearchAssistant
   d. Consumer

11. In economics, _____ is the desire to own something and the ability to pay for it. The term _____ signifies the ability or the willingness to buy a particular commodity at a given point of time .

   a. Discretionary spending
   b. Demand
   c. Market dominance
   d. Market system

12. A _____ is a list of the general tasks and responsibilities of a position. Typically, it also includes to whom the position reports, specifications such as the qualifications needed by the person in the job, salary range for the position, etc. A _____ is usually developed by conducting a job analysis, which includes examining the tasks and sequences of tasks necessary to perform the job.
   a. Power III
   b. 180SearchAssistant
   c. Job description
   d. 6-3-5 Brainwriting

13. _____ was originally coined by Austrian psychologist Alfred Adler in 1929. The current broader sense of the word dates from 1961.

In sociology, a _____ is the way a person lives.

Chapter 16. Retailing

a. Power III
c. 180SearchAssistant
b. 6-3-5 Brainwriting
d. Lifestyle

14. _____ is an advertisement in which a particular product specifically mentions a competitor by name for the express purpose of showing why the competitor is inferior to the product naming it.

This should not be confused with parody advertisements, where a fictional product is being advertised for the purpose of poking fun at the particular advertisement, nor should it be confused with the use of a coined brand name for the purpose of comparing the product without actually naming an actual competitor. ('Wikipedia tastes better and is less filling than the Encyclopedia Galactica.')

In the 1980s, during what has been referred to as the cola wars, soft-drink manufacturer Pepsi ran a series of advertisements where people, caught on hidden camera, in a blind taste test, chose Pepsi over rival Coca-Cola.

a. GL-70
c. Cost per conversion
b. Heavy-up
d. Comparative advertising

15. A supply chain is the system of organizations, people, technology, activities, information and resources involved in moving a product or service from _____ to customer. Supply chain activities transform natural resources, raw materials and components into a finished product that is delivered to the end customer. In sophisticated supply chain systems, used products may re-enter the supply chain at any point where residual value is recyclable.

a. Product line extension
c. Rebate
b. Supplier
d. Bringin' Home the Oil

16. A _____ is a business that is independently owned and operated, with a small number of employees and relatively low volume of sales. The legal definition of 'small' often varies by country and industry, but is generally under 100 employees in the United States and under 50 employees in the European Union. In comparison, the definition of mid-sized business by the number of employees is generally under 500 in the U.S. and 250 for the European Union.

a. Customer centricity
c. Small Business
b. Time to market
d. Product support

17. The _____ is a United States government agency that provides support to small businesses.

The mission of the _____ is 'to maintain and strengthen the nation's economy by enabling the establishment and viability of small businesses and by assisting in the economic recovery of communities after disasters.'

The _____ makes loans directly to businesses and acts as a guarantor on bank loans. In some circumstances it also makes loans to victims of natural disasters, works to get government procurement contracts for small businesses, and assists businesses with management, technical and training issues.

a. 6-3-5 Brainwriting
c. Small Business Administration
b. Power III
d. 180SearchAssistant

18. _____ is the state or fact of exclusive rights and control over property, which may be an object, land/real estate, or some other kind of property (like government-granted monopolies collectively referred to as intellectual property.) It is embodied in an _____ right also referred to as title.

Chapter 16. Retailing

_____ is the key building block in the development of the capitalist socio-economic system.

a. AMAX
b. ADTECH
c. ACNielsen
d. Ownership

19. A _____ is a retail establishment which specializes in selling a wide range of products without a single predominant merchandise line. _____s usually sell products including apparel, furniture, appliances, electronics, and additionally select other lines of products such as paint, hardware, toiletries, cosmetics, photographic equipment, jewelery, toys, and sporting goods. Certain _____s are further classified as discount _____s.
a. 180SearchAssistant
b. 6-3-5 Brainwriting
c. Power III
d. Department store

20. _____ is a sub-discipline and type of marketing. There are two main definitional characteristics which distinguish it from other types of marketing. The first is that it attempts to send its messages directly to consumers, without the use of intervening media.
a. Database marketing
b. Direct Marketing Associations
c. Power III
d. Direct marketing

21. _____ is a retail channel for the distribution of goods and services. At a basic level it may be defined as marketing and selling products, direct to consumers away from a fixed retail location. Sales are typically made through party plan, one to one demonstrations, and other personal contact arrangements.
a. Power III
b. 180SearchAssistant
c. 6-3-5 Brainwriting
d. Direct selling

22. A _____ is a type of department store, which sell products at prices lower than those asked by traditional retail outlets. Most discount department stores offer wide assortments of goods; others specialize in such merchandise as jewelry, electronic equipment, or electrical appliances. _____s are not dollar stores, which sell goods at a dollar or less.
a. Discount store
b. Strip mall
c. Gruen transfer
d. Sales per unit area

23. _____ are small stores which specialize in a specific range of merchandise and related items. Most stores have an extensive width and depth of stock in the item that they specify in and provide high levels of service and expertise. The pricing policy is generally in the medium to high range, depending on factors like the type and exclusivity of merchandise and ownership, that is, whether they are owner operated or a chain operation which has the advantage of bulk purchasing and centralized warehousing system.
a. Catalog merchant
b. Brick and mortar business
c. Wardrobing
d. Specialty stores

24. A _____ is a plan of action designed to achieve a particular goal.

_____ is different from tactics. In military terms, tactics is concerned with the conduct of an engagement while _____ is concerned with how different engagements are linked.

a. 6-3-5 Brainwriting
c. 180SearchAssistant
b. Power III
d. Strategy

25. A _____ is a commercial building for storage of goods. _____s are used by manufacturers, importers, exporters, wholesalers, transport businesses, customs, etc. They are usually large plain buildings in industrial areas of cities and towns.
   a. Power III
   b. 180SearchAssistant
   c. 6-3-5 Brainwriting
   d. Warehouse

26. A _____ is a retail store, usually selling a wide variety of merchandise, in which customers pay annual membership fees in order to shop. The clubs are able to keep prices low due to the no-frills format of the stores. In addition, customers are required to buy large, wholesale quantities of the store's products, which makes these clubs attractive to both bargain hunters and small business owners.
   a. Consignment
   b. Warehouse club
   c. Self service
   d. Power centre

27. _____ is a form of communication that typically attempts to persuade potential customers to purchase or to consume more of a particular brand of product or service. 'While now central to the contemporary global economy and the reproduction of global production networks, it is only quite recently that _____ has been more than a marginal influence on patterns of sales and production. The formation of modern _____ was intimately bound up with the emergence of new forms of monopoly capitalism around the end of the 19th century and beginning of the 20th century as one element in corporate strategies to create, organize and where possible control markets, especially for mass produced consumer goods.
   a. ACNielsen
   b. ADTECH
   c. Advertising
   d. AMAX

28. In commerce, a _____ is a superstore which combines a supermarket and a department store. The result is a very large retail facility which carries an enormous range of products under one roof, including full lines of groceries and general merchandise. In theory, _____s allow customers to satisfy all their routine weekly shopping needs in one trip.
   a. Power III
   b. 180SearchAssistant
   c. Hypermarket
   d. 6-3-5 Brainwriting

29. _____ is a term used in marketing and strategic management to describe a product, service, brand, or company that has such a distinct sustainable competitive advantage that competing firms find it almost impossible to operate profitably in that industry. The existence of a _____ will eliminate almost all market entities, whether real or virtual. Many existing firms will leave the industry, thereby increasing the industry's concentration ratio.
   a. 180SearchAssistant
   b. 6-3-5 Brainwriting
   c. Power III
   d. Category killer

30. The _____ is an economic and political union of 27 member states, located primarily in Europe. It was established by the Treaty of Maastricht on 1 November 1993 upon the foundations of the pre-existing European Economic Community. With almost 500 million citizens, the _____ combined generates an estimated 30% share (US$16.8 trillion in 2007) of the nominal gross world product.
   a. Eurozone
   b. European Union
   c. ADTECH
   d. ACNielsen

31. _____s function as professionals who deal with trade, dealing in commodities that they do not produce themselves, in order to produce profit.

_____s can be of two types:

1. A wholesale _____ operates in the chain between producer and retail _____. Some wholesale _____s only organize the movement of goods rather than move the goods themselves.
2. A retail _____ or retailer, sells commodities to consumers (including businesses.) A shop owner is a retail _____.

A _____ class characterizes many pre-modern societies. Its status can range from high (even achieving titles like that of _____ prince or nabob) to low, such as in Chinese culture, due to the soiling capabilities of profiting from 'mere' trade, rather than from the labor of others reflected in agricultural produce, craftsmanship, and tribute.

In the United States, '_____' is defined (under the Uniform Commercial Code) as any person while engaged in a business or profession or a seller who deals regularly in the type of goods sold.

a. Merchant
c. Retail loss prevention
b. Trade credit
d. RFM

32. An _____ or factory outlet or 'Best Saving Outlet' is a retail store in which manufacturers sell their stock directly to the public through their own branded stores. The stores can be brick and mortar or online. Traditionally, a factory outlet was a store, attached to a factory or warehouse.

a. Online ticket brokering
c. Endcap
b. Electronic Shelf Label
d. Outlet store

33. _____ or _____ data refers to selected population characteristics as used in government, marketing or opinion research, or the _____ profiles used in such research. Note the distinction from the term 'demography' Commonly-used _____ include race, age, income, disabilities, mobility (in terms of travel time to work or number of vehicles available), educational attainment, home ownership, employment status, and even location.

a. Albert Einstein
c. AStore
b. African Americans
d. Demographic

34. A _____ is a process that can allow an organization to concentrate its limited resources on the greatest opportunities to increase sales and achieve a sustainable competitive advantage. A _____ should be centered around the key concept that customer satisfaction is the main goal.

A _____ is most effective when it is an integral component of corporate strategy, defining how the organization will successfully engage customers, prospects, and competitors in the market arena.

a. Cyberdoc
c. Marketing strategy
b. Societal marketing
d. Psychographic

Chapter 16. Retailing

35. _____ involves disseminating information about a product, product line, brand, or company. It is one of the four key aspects of the marketing mix. (The other three elements are product marketing, pricing, and distribution). P>_____ is generally sub-divided into two parts:

- Above the line _____: Promotion in the media (e.g. TV, radio, newspapers, Internet and Mobile Phones) in which the advertiser pays an advertising agency to place the ad
- Below the line _____: All other _____. Much of this is intended to be subtle enough for the consumer to be unaware that _____ is taking place. E.g. sponsorship, product placement, endorsements, sales _____, merchandising, direct mail, personal selling, public relations, trade shows

   a. Cashmere Agency   b. Promotion
   c. Davie Brown Index   d. Bottling lines

36. _____ is a measure of the strength of a brand, product, service relative to competitive offerings. There is often a geographic element to the competitive landscape. In defining _____, you must see to what extent a product, brand, or firm controls a product category in a given geographic area.
   a. Productivity   b. Market system
   c. Discretionary spending   d. Market dominance

37. _____ is the examining of goods or services from retailers with the intent to purchase at that time. _____ is an activity of selection and/or purchase. In some contexts it is considered a leisure activity as well as an economic one.
   a. Shopping   b. Hawkers
   c. Khodebshchik   d. Discount store

38. _____ refers to the methods, practices and operations conducted to promote and sustain certain categories of commercial activity. The term is understood to have different specific meanings depending on the context. Merchandise is a sale goods at a store

In marketing, one of the definitions of _____ is the practice in which the brand or image from one product or service is used to sell another.

   a. Marketing communication   b. Word of mouth
   c. New Media Strategies   d. Merchandising

39. In the Mediterranean Basin and the Near East, a _____ is a small, separated garden pavilion open on some or all sides. _____s were common in Persia, India, Pakistan, and in the Ottoman Empire from the 13th century onward. Today, there are many _____s in and around the TopkapÄ± Palace in Istanbul, and they are still a relatively common sight in Greece.
   a. Kiosk   b. Power III
   c. 6-3-5 Brainwriting   d. 180SearchAssistant

Chapter 16. Retailing

40. _____ is when a large distribution channel member (usually a retailer), buys from a manufacturer in bulk and puts its own name on the product. This strategy is only practical when the retailer does very high levels of volume. The advantages to the retailer are:

- more freedom and flexibility in pricing
- more control over product attributes and quality
- higher margins (or lower selling price)
- eliminates much of the manufacturer's promotional costs

The advantages to the manufacturer are:

- reduced promotional costs
- stability of sales volume (at least while the contract is operative)

- Kumar, Nirmalya; Steenkamp, Jan-Benedict E.M., Private Label Strategy - How to Meet the Store Brand Challenge. Harvard Business Press 2007

- private label
- brand management
- brand
- product management
- marketing

a. Customization
c. Rural market
b. Promotion
d. Private branding

41. A _____ is a collection of symbols, experiences and associations connected with a product, a service, a person or any other artifact or entity.

_____s have become increasingly important components of culture and the economy, now being described as 'cultural accessories and personal philosophies'.

Some people distinguish the psychological aspect of a _____ from the experiential aspect.

a. Store brand
c. Brand
b. Brandable software
d. Brand equity

42. _____ is a rivalry between individuals, groups, nations for territory, a niche, or allocation of resources. It arises whenever two or more parties strive for a goal which cannot be shared. _____ occurs naturally between living organisms which co-exist in the same environment.

a. Price competition
c. Non-price competition
b. Price fixing
d. Competition

Chapter 16. Retailing

43. In economics, business, retail, and accounting, a _____ is the value of money that has been used up to produce something, and hence is not available for use anymore. In economics, a _____ is an alternative that is given up as a result of a decision. In business, the _____ may be one of acquisition, in which case the amount of money expended to acquire it is counted as _____.

   a. Fixed costs
   b. Transaction cost
   c. Cost
   d. Variable cost

44. _____ is a branch of philosophy which seeks to address questions about morality, such as how a moral outcome can be achieved in a specific situation (applied _____), how moral values should be determined (normative _____), what moral values people actually abide by (descriptive _____), what the fundamental semantic, ontological, and epistemic nature of _____ or morality is (meta-_____), and how moral capacity or moral agency develops and what its nature is (moral psychology.)

   Socrates was one of the first Greek philosophers to encourage both scholars and the common citizen to turn their attention from the outside world to the condition of man. In this view, Knowledge having a bearing on human life was placed highest, all other knowledge being secondary.

   a. ACNielsen
   b. AMAX
   c. ADTECH
   d. Ethics

45. _____ is one of the four Ps of the marketing mix. The other three aspects are product, promotion, and place. It is also a key variable in microeconomic price allocation theory.

   a. Price
   b. Relationship based pricing
   c. Competitor indexing
   d. Pricing

46. _____ is the practice of managing the flow of information between an organization and its publics. _____ - often referred to as _____ - gains an organization or individual exposure to their audiences using topics of public interest and news items that do not require direct payment. Because _____ places exposure in credible third-party outlets, it offers a third-party legitimacy that advertising does not have.

   a. Graphic communication
   b. Public relations
   c. Symbolic analysis
   d. Power III

Chapter 17. Integrated Marketing Communications

1. _____ involves disseminating information about a product, product line, brand, or company. It is one of the four key aspects of the marketing mix. (The other three elements are product marketing, pricing, and distribution). P>_____ is generally sub-divided into two parts:

- Above the line _____: Promotion in the media (e.g. TV, radio, newspapers, Internet and Mobile Phones) in which the advertiser pays an advertising agency to place the ad
- Below the line _____: All other _____. Much of this is intended to be subtle enough for the consumer to be unaware that _____ is taking place. E.g. sponsorship, product placement, endorsements, sales _____, merchandising, direct mail, personal selling, public relations, trade shows

a. Cashmere Agency
c. Promotion
b. Davie Brown Index
d. Bottling lines

2. _____ is a form of communication that typically attempts to persuade potential customers to purchase or to consume more of a particular brand of product or service. 'While now central to the contemporary global economy and the reproduction of global production networks, it is only quite recently that _____ has been more than a marginal influence on patterns of sales and production. The formation of modern _____ was intimately bound up with the emergence of new forms of monopoly capitalism around the end of the 19th and beginning of the 20th century as one element in corporate strategies to create, organize and where possible control markets, especially for mass produced consumer goods.

a. ACNielsen
c. ADTECH
b. AMAX
d. Advertising

3. _____ is an advertisement in which a particular product specifically mentions a competitor by name for the express purpose of showing why the competitor is inferior to the product naming it.

This should not be confused with parody advertisements, where a fictional product is being advertised for the purpose of poking fun at the particular advertisement, nor should it be confused with the use of a coined brand name for the purpose of comparing the product without actually naming an actual competitor. ('Wikipedia tastes better and is less filling than the Encyclopedia Galactica.')

In the 1980s, during what has been referred to as the cola wars, soft-drink manufacturer Pepsi ran a series of advertisements where people, caught on hidden camera, in a blind taste test, chose Pepsi over rival Coca-Cola.

a. Comparative advertising
c. GL-70
b. Cost per conversion
d. Heavy-up

4. In economics, _____ is the desire to own something and the ability to pay for it. The term _____ signifies the ability or the willingness to buy a particular commodity at a given point of time .

a. Market dominance
c. Market system
b. Discretionary spending
d. Demand

5. _____ is a measure of the strength of a brand, product, service relative to competitive offerings. There is often a geographic element to the competitive landscape. In defining _____, you must see to what extent a product, brand, or firm controls a product category in a given geographic area.

Chapter 17. Integrated Marketing Communications

a. Discretionary spending
c. Market system

b. Productivity
d. Market dominance

6. _____ , according to The American Marketing Association, is 'a planning process designed to assure that all brand contacts received by a customer or prospect for a product, service, or organization are relevant to that person and consistent over time.' (Marketing Power Dictionary)

_____ is a term used to describe a holistic approach to marketing. It aims to ensure consistency of message and the complementary use of media. The concept includes online and offline marketing channels.

a. ACNielsen
c. AMAX

b. ADTECH
d. Integrated marketing communications

7. _____ is defined by the American _____ Association as the activity, set of institutions, and processes for creating, communicating, delivering, and exchanging offerings that have value for customers, clients, partners, and society at large. The term developed from the original meaning which referred literally to going to market, as in shopping, or going to a market to sell goods or services.

_____ practice tends to be seen as a creative industry, which includes advertising, distribution and selling.

a. Customer acquisition management
c. Marketing myopia

b. Product naming
d. Marketing

8. _____ refers to messages and related media used to communicate with a market. Those who practice advertising, branding, direct marketing, graphic design, marketing, packaging, promotion, publicity, sponsorship, public relations, sales, sales promotion and online marketing are termed marketing communicators, _____ managers, or more briefly as marcom managers.

a. Marketing communication
c. Merchandising

b. Merchandise
d. Sales promotion

9. _____ is the practice of managing the flow of information between an organization and its publics. _____ - often referred to as _____ - gains an organization or individual exposure to their audiences using topics of public interest and news items that do not require direct payment. Because _____ places exposure in credible third-party outlets, it offers a third-party legitimacy that advertising does not have.

a. Power III
c. Symbolic analysis

b. Graphic communication
d. Public relations

10. _____ is the deliberate attempt to manage the public's perception of a subject. The subjects of _____ include people (for example, politicians and performing artists), goods and services, organizations of all kinds, and works of art or entertainment.

From a marketing perspective, _____ is one component of promotion.

a. Pearson's chi-square
c. Little value placed on potential benefits

b. Brando
d. Publicity

Chapter 17. Integrated Marketing Communications

11. _____ is one of the four aspects of promotional mix. (The other three parts of the promotional mix are advertising, personal selling, and publicity/public relations.) Media and non-media marketing communication are employed for a pre-determined, limited time to increase consumer demand, stimulate market demand or improve product availability.

   a. Marketing communication
   b. New Media Strategies
   c. Sales promotion
   d. Merchandise

12. _____ is a search engine marketing product where the search engine company charges fees related to inclusion of websites in their search index. _____ products are provided by most search engine companies, the most notable exception being Google.

   a. Paid inclusion
   b. Hit inflation attack
   c. VoloMedia
   d. Microsoft adCenter

13. The _____ is an economic indicator that measures the satisfaction of consumers across the U.S. economy. It is produced by the National Quality Research Center (NQRC) at the University of Michigan in Ann Arbor, Michigan.

   The _____ interviews about 80,000 Americans annually and asks about their satisfaction with the goods and services they have consumed.

   a. AMAX
   b. ADTECH
   c. American Customer Satisfaction Index
   d. ACNielsen

14. A _____ is a customs union with common policies on product regulation, and freedom of movement of the factors of production (capital and labour) and of enterprise. The goal is that the movement of capital, labour, goods, and services between the members is as easy as within them. This is the fourth stage of economic integration.

   a. Competitive
   b. Monetary union
   c. Customs union
   d. Common Market

15. _____, a business term, is a measure of how products and services supplied by a company meet or surpass customer expectation. It is seen as a key performance indicator within business and is part of the four perspectives of a Balanced Scorecard.

   In a competitive marketplace where businesses compete for customers, _____ is seen as a key differentiator and increasingly has become a key element of business strategy.

   a. Supplier diversity
   b. Customer Satisfaction
   c. Customer base
   d. Psychological pricing

Chapter 17. Integrated Marketing Communications 153

16. _____ is the reverse of encoding, which is the process of transforming information from one format into another. Information about _____ can be found in the following:

- Digital-to-analog converter, the use of analog circuit for _____ operations
- Code, a rule for converting a piece of information into another form or representation
- Code (cryptography), a method used to transform a message into an obscured form
- _____
- _____ methods, methods in communication theory for _____ codewords sent over a noisy channel
- Digital signal processing, the study of signals in a digital representation and the processing methods of these signals
- Word _____, the use of phonics to decipher print patterns and translate them into the sounds of language
- deCODE genetics

a. Power III
b. 180SearchAssistant
c. 6-3-5 Brainwriting
d. Decoding

17. _____ is the process of transforming information from one format into another. The opposite operation is called decoding.

There are a number of more specific meanings that apply in certain contexts:

- _____ is a basic perceptual process of interpreting incoming stimuli; technically speaking, it is a complex, multi-stage process of converting relatively objective sensory input (e.g., light, sound) into subjectively meaningful experience.
- A content format is a specific _____ format for converting a specific type of data to information.
- Character _____ is a code that pairs a set of natural language characters (such as an alphabet or syllabary) with a set of something else, such as numbers or electrical pulses.
- Text _____ uses a markup language to tag the structure and other features of a text to facilitate processing by computers.
- Semantics _____ of formal language A in formal language B is a method of representing all terms (e.g. programs or descriptions) of language A using language B.
- Electronic _____ transforms a signal into a code optimized for transmission or storage, generally done with a codec.
- Neural _____ is the way in which information is represented in neurons.
- Memory _____ is the process of converting sensations into memories.
- Encryption transforms information for secrecy.

a. ACNielsen
b. AMAX
c. Encoding
d. ADTECH

18. The _____ is an economic and political union of 27 member states, located primarily in Europe. It was established by the Treaty of Maastricht on 1 November 1993 upon the foundations of the pre-existing European Economic Community. With almost 500 million citizens, the _____ combined generates an estimated 30% share (US$16.8 trillion in 2007) of the nominal gross world product.
   a. ACNielsen
   c. ADTECH
   b. Eurozone
   d. European Union

19. _____ describes the situation when output from (or information about the result of) an event or phenomenon in the past will influence the same event/phenomenon in the present or future. When an event is part of a chain of cause-and-effect that forms a circuit or loop, then the event is said to 'feed back' into itself.

   _____ is also a synonym for:

   - _____ Signal; the information about the initial event that is the basis for subsequent modification of the event.
   - _____ Loop; the causal path that leads from the initial generation of the _____ signal to the subsequent modification of the event.

   _____ is a mechanism, process or signal that is looped back to control a system within itself. Such a loop is called a _____ loop.

   a. Power III
   c. 180SearchAssistant
   b. Feedback
   d. 6-3-5 Brainwriting

20. The phrase _____ refers to the aspect of corporate strategy, corporate finance and management dealing with the buying, selling and combining of different companies that can aid, finance, or help a growing company in a given industry grow rapidly without having to create another business entity.

   An acquisition, also known as a takeover or a buyout, is the buying of one company (the 'target') by another. An acquisition may be friendly or hostile.

   a. 180SearchAssistant
   c. Mergers and acquisitions
   b. 6-3-5 Brainwriting
   d. Power III

21. _____ consists of the sale of goods or merchandise from a fixed location, such as a department store or kiosk in small or individual lots for direct consumption by the purchaser. _____ may include subordinated services, such as delivery. Purchasers may be individuals or businesses.
   a. Warehouse store
   c. Charity shop
   b. Thrifting
   d. Retailing

22. _____ is a broad label that refers to any individuals or households that use goods and services generated within the economy. The concept of a _____ is used in different contexts, so that the usage and significance of the term may vary.

   A _____ is a person who uses any product or service.

Chapter 17. Integrated Marketing Communications

a. Power III
c. 180SearchAssistant
b. 6-3-5 Brainwriting
d. Consumer

23. _____ is an American magazine published monthly by Consumers Union. It publishes reviews and comparisons of consumer products and services based on reporting and results from its in-house testing laboratory. It also publishes cleaning and general buying guides.

a. Crossing the Chasm
c. Power III
b. Magalog
d. Consumer Reports

24. _____ is a strategic planning method used to evaluate the Strengths, Weaknesses, Opportunities, and Threats involved in a project or in a business venture. It involves specifying the objective of the business venture or project and identifying the internal and external factors that are favorable and unfavorable to achieving that objective. The technique is credited to Albert Humphrey, who led a research project at Stanford University in the 1960s and 1970s using data from Fortune 500 companies.

a. SWOT analysis
c. Market environment
b. Lead scoring
d. Product differentiation

25. _____ is a marketing term, and involves evaluating the situation and trends in a particular company's market. _____ is often called the 'three c's', which refers to the three major elements that must be studied:

- Customers
- Costs
- Competition

The number of 'c's' is sometimes extended to four, five, or even six, with 'Collaboration', 'Company', and 'Competitive advantage'.

- Marketing mix
- SWOT analysis

a. 180SearchAssistant
c. Power III
b. Situation analysis
d. 6-3-5 Brainwriting

26. _____ are uniquely different from the rhetorical appeal to fear. There has been nearly 50 years of research on _____ in various disciplines and these studies have collectively garnered mixed results However, _____ are commonly used in persuasive health campaigns designed to modify behavior.

a. Fear appeals
c. Power III
b. 180SearchAssistant
d. 6-3-5 Brainwriting

27. In grammar, the _____ is the form of an adjective or adverb which denotes the degree or grade by which a person, thing and is used in this context with a subordinating conjunction, such as than, as...as, etc.

The structure of a _____ in English consists normally of the positive form of the adjective or adverb, plus the suffix -er e.g. 'he is taller than his father is', or 'the village is less picturesque than the town nearby'.

a. 6-3-5 Brainwriting
c. Power III
b. 180SearchAssistant
d. Comparative

28. _____ is a form of government regulation which protects the interests of consumers. For example, a government may require businesses to disclose detailed information about products--particularly in areas where safety or public health is an issue, such as food. _____ is linked to the idea of consumer rights (that consumers have various rights as consumers), and to the formation of consumer organizations which help consumers make better choices in the marketplace.
   a. Federal Bureau of Investigation
   b. Trademark dilution
   c. Consumer Protection
   d. Sound trademark

29. A _____ is a collection of symbols, experiences and associations connected with a product, a service, a person or any other artifact or entity.

_____s have become increasingly important components of culture and the economy, now being described as 'cultural accessories and personal philosophies'.

Some people distinguish the psychological aspect of a _____ from the experiential aspect.

   a. Brand equity
   b. Brandable software
   c. Brand
   d. Store brand

30. A _____ is a party that mediates between a buyer and a seller. A _____ who also acts as a seller or as a buyer becomes a principal party to the deal. Distinguish agent: one who acts on behalf of a principal.
   a. Broker
   b. Spokesperson
   c. 180SearchAssistant
   d. Power III

31. _____ is one of the four Ps of the marketing mix. The other three aspects are product, promotion, and place. It is also a key variable in microeconomic price allocation theory.
   a. Relationship based pricing
   b. Price
   c. Pricing
   d. Competitor indexing

32. _____ generally refers to a list of all planned expenses and revenues. It is a plan for saving and spending. A _____ is an important concept in microeconomics, which uses a _____ line to illustrate the trade-offs between two or more goods.
   a. 180SearchAssistant
   b. Power III
   c. 6-3-5 Brainwriting
   d. Budget

33. _____ or _____ data refers to selected population characteristics as used in government, marketing or opinion research, or the _____ profiles used in such research. Note the distinction from the term 'demography' Commonly-used _____ include race, age, income, disabilities, mobility (in terms of travel time to work or number of vehicles available), educational attainment, home ownership, employment status, and even location.
   a. African Americans
   b. Albert Einstein
   c. AStore
   d. Demographic

34. _____ was originally coined by Austrian psychologist Alfred Adler in 1929. The current broader sense of the word dates from 1961.

In sociology, a _____ is the way a person lives.

a. Power III
b. 180SearchAssistant
c. 6-3-5 Brainwriting
d. Lifestyle

35. _____ in organizations and public policy is both the organizational process of creating and maintaining a plan; and the psychological process of thinking about the activities required to create a desired goal on some scale. As such, it is a fundamental property of intelligent behavior. This thought process is essential to the creation and refinement of a plan, or integration of it with other plans, that is, it combines forecasting of developments with the preparation of scenarios of how to react to them.

a. Planning
b. 180SearchAssistant
c. 6-3-5 Brainwriting
d. Power III

36. A _____ is a plan of action designed to achieve a particular goal.

_____ is different from tactics. In military terms, tactics is concerned with the conduct of an engagement while _____ is concerned with how different engagements are linked.

a. 180SearchAssistant
b. Power III
c. 6-3-5 Brainwriting
d. Strategy

37. Competitiveness is a comparative concept of the ability and performance of a firm, sub-sector or country to sell and supply goods and/or services in a given market. Although widely used in economics and business management, the usefulness of the concept, particularly in the context of national competitiveness, is vigorously disputed by economists, such as Paul Krugman .

The term may also be applied to markets, where it is used to refer to the extent to which the market structure may be regarded as perfectly _____.

a. Customs union
b. Geographical pricing
c. Free trade zone
d. Competitive

38. The _____ is an international organization designed to supervise and liberalize international trade. The _____ came into being on 1 January 1995, and is the successor to the General Agreement on Tariffs and Trade (GATT), which was created in 1947, and continued to operate for almost five decades as a de facto international organization.

The _____ deals with the rules of trade between nations at a near-global level; it is responsible for negotiating and implementing new trade agreements, and is in charge of policing member countries' adherence to all the _____ agreements, signed by the majority of the world's trading nations and ratified in their parliaments.

a. Merchandise Mart
b. BSI Group
c. Population Reference Bureau
d. World Trade Organization

Chapter 17. Integrated Marketing Communications

39. _____ is a branch of philosophy which seeks to address questions about morality, such as how a moral outcome can be achieved in a specific situation (applied _____), how moral values should be determined (normative _____), what moral values people actually abide by (descriptive _____), what the fundamental semantic, ontological, and epistemic nature of _____ or morality is (meta-_____), and how moral capacity or moral agency develops and what its nature is (moral psychology.)

Socrates was one of the first Greek philosophers to encourage both scholars and the common citizen to turn their attention from the outside world to the condition of man. In this view, Knowledge having a bearing on human life was placed highest, all other knowledge being secondary.

   a. AMAX
   b. ACNielsen
   c. Ethics
   d. ADTECH

40. False advertising or _____ is the use of false or misleading statements in advertising. As advertising has the potential to persuade people into commercial transactions that they might otherwise avoid, many governments around the world use regulations to control false, deceptive or misleading advertising. Truth in labeling refers to essentially the same concept, that customers have the right to know what they are buying, and that all necessary information should be on the label.
   a. Misleading advertising
   b. Fine print
   c. Power III
   d. Deceptive advertising

41. The U.S. _____ is an agency of the United States Department of Health and Human Services and is responsible for regulating and supervising the safety of foods, dietary supplements, drugs, vaccines, biological medical products, blood products, medical devices, radiation-emitting devices, veterinary products, and cosmetics. The FDA also enforces section 361 of the Public Health Service Act and the associated regulations, including sanitation requirements on interstate travel as well as specific rules for control of disease on products ranging from pet turtles to semen donations for assisted reproductive medicine techniques.

The FDA is an agency within the United States Department of Health and Human Services responsible for protecting and promoting the nation's public health.

   a. 6-3-5 Brainwriting
   b. 180SearchAssistant
   c. Power III
   d. Food and Drug Administration

42. _____ is a sales technique in which a salesperson walks from one door of a house to another trying to sell a product or service to the general public. A variant of this involves cold calling first, when another sales representative attempts to gain agreement that a salesperson should visit. _____ selling is usually conducted in the afternoon hours, when the majority of people are at home.
   a. Fast moving consumer goods
   b. Marketing management
   c. Performance-based advertising
   d. Door-to-door

Chapter 18. Advertising and Public Relations

1. _____ is a form of communication that typically attempts to persuade potential customers to purchase or to consume more of a particular brand of product or service. 'While now central to the contemporary global economy and the reproduction of global production networks, it is only quite recently that _____ has been more than a marginal influence on patterns of sales and production. The formation of modern _____ was intimately bound up with the emergence of new forms of monopoly capitalism around the end of the 19th and beginning of the 20th century as one element in corporate strategies to create, organize and where possible control markets, especially for mass produced consumer goods.
   a. ADTECH
   b. Advertising
   c. AMAX
   d. ACNielsen

2. _____ is the practice of managing the flow of information between an organization and its publics. _____ - often referred to as _____ - gains an organization or individual exposure to their audiences using topics of public interest and news items that do not require direct payment. Because _____ places exposure in credible third-party outlets, it offers a third-party legitimacy that advertising does not have.
   a. Graphic communication
   b. Power III
   c. Public relations
   d. Symbolic analysis

3. _____ Management is the succession of strategies used by management as a product goes through its _____. The conditions in which a product is sold changes over time and must be managed as it moves through its succession of stages.

   The _____ goes through many phases, involves many professional disciplines, and requires many skills, tools and processes.

   a. Supplier diversity
   b. Product life cycle
   c. Chain stores
   d. Customer satisfaction

4. _____ involves disseminating information about a product, product line, brand, or company. It is one of the four key aspects of the marketing mix. (The other three elements are product marketing, pricing, and distribution). P>_____ is generally sub-divided into two parts:

   - Above the line _____: Promotion in the media (e.g. TV, radio, newspapers, Internet and Mobile Phones) in which the advertiser pays an advertising agency to place the ad
   - Below the line _____: All other _____. Much of this is intended to be subtle enough for the consumer to be unaware that _____ is taking place. E.g. sponsorship, product placement, endorsements, sales _____, merchandising, direct mail, personal selling, public relations, trade shows

   a. Bottling lines
   b. Cashmere Agency
   c. Davie Brown Index
   d. Promotion

5. Advertising mail junk mail is the delivery of advertising material to recipients of postal mail. The delivery of advertising mail forms a large and growing service for many postal services, and _____ marketing forms a significant portion of the direct marketing industry. Some organizations attempt to help people opt-out of receiving advertising mail, in many cases motivated by a concern over its negative environmental impact.
   a. Directory Harvest Attack
   b. Direct mail
   c. Phishing
   d. Telemarketing

6. _____ is one of the four aspects of promotional mix. (The other three parts of the promotional mix are advertising, personal selling, and publicity/public relations.) Media and non-media marketing communication are employed for a pre-determined, limited time to increase consumer demand, stimulate market demand or improve product availability.

   a. New Media Strategies   b. Merchandise
   c. Marketing communication   d. Sales promotion

7. The _____ is an international organization designed to supervise and liberalize international trade. The _____ came into being on 1 January 1995, and is the successor to the General Agreement on Tariffs and Trade (GATT), which was created in 1947, and continued to operate for almost five decades as a de facto international organization.

The _____ deals with the rules of trade between nations at a near-global level; it is responsible for negotiating and implementing new trade agreements, and is in charge of policing member countries' adherence to all the _____ agreements, signed by the majority of the world's trading nations and ratified in their parliaments.

   a. Population Reference Bureau   b. BSI Group
   c. World Trade Organization   d. Merchandise Mart

8. In economics, _____ is the desire to own something and the ability to pay for it. The term _____ signifies the ability or the willingness to buy a particular commodity at a given point of time .

   a. Market system   b. Demand
   c. Market dominance   d. Discretionary spending

9. _____ is defined by the American _____ Association as the activity, set of institutions, and processes for creating, communicating, delivering, and exchanging offerings that have value for customers, clients, partners, and society at large. The term developed from the original meaning which referred literally to going to market, as in shopping, or going to a market to sell goods or services.

_____ practice tends to be seen as a creative industry, which includes advertising, distribution and selling.

   a. Product naming   b. Customer acquisition management
   c. Marketing   d. Marketing myopia

10. _____ consists of the sale of goods or merchandise from a fixed location, such as a department store or kiosk in small or individual lots for direct consumption by the purchaser. _____ may include subordinated services, such as delivery. Purchasers may be individuals or businesses.

   a. Warehouse store   b. Thrifting
   c. Charity shop   d. Retailing

11. _____ is the pioneer of the digital video recorder . _____ was introduced in the United States, and is now available in Canada, Mexico, Australia, and Taiwan. Created by _____, Inc..

   a. Power III   b. TiVo
   c. 6-3-5 Brainwriting   d. 180SearchAssistant

Chapter 18. Advertising and Public Relations

12. _____ generally refers to a list of all planned expenses and revenues. It is a plan for saving and spending. A _____ is an important concept in microeconomics, which uses a _____ line to illustrate the trade-offs between two or more goods.

   a. Budget
   b. 6-3-5 Brainwriting
   c. Power III
   d. 180SearchAssistant

13. A _____ is defined by the International Co-operative Alliance's Statement on the Co-operative Identity as an autonomous association of persons united voluntarily to meet their common economic, social, and cultural needs and aspirations through a jointly-owned and democratically-controlled enterprise. It is a business organization owned and operated by a group of individuals for their mutual benefit. A _____ may also be defined as a business owned and controlled equally by the people who use its services or who work at it.

   a. Power III
   b. Cooperative
   c. 6-3-5 Brainwriting
   d. 180SearchAssistant

14. _____ is systematic determination of merit, worth, and significance of something or someone using criteria against a set of standards. _____ often is used to characterize and appraise subjects of interest in a wide range of human enterprises, including the arts, criminal justice, foundations and non-profit organizations, government, health care, and other human services.

Depending on the topic of interest, there are professional groups which look to the quality and rigor of the _____ process.

   a. ADTECH
   b. AMAX
   c. ACNielsen
   d. Evaluation

15. _____ describes the situation when output from (or information about the result of) an event or phenomenon in the past will influence the same event/phenomenon in the present or future. When an event is part of a chain of cause-and-effect that forms a circuit or loop, then the event is said to 'feed back' into itself.

_____ is also a synonym for:

- _____ Signal; the information about the initial event that is the basis for subsequent modification of the event.
- _____ Loop; the causal path that leads from the initial generation of the _____ signal to the subsequent modification of the event.

_____ is a mechanism, process or signal that is looped back to control a system within itself. Such a loop is called a _____ loop.

   a. 180SearchAssistant
   b. 6-3-5 Brainwriting
   c. Power III
   d. Feedback

16. An _____ or ad agency is a service business dedicated to creating, planning and handling advertising (and sometimes other forms of promotion) for its clients. An ad agency is independent from the client and provides an outside point of view to the effort of selling the client's products or services. An agency can also handle overall marketing and branding strategies and sales promotions for its clients.

a. Onsert
b. Advertising agency
c. Advertising research
d. Openad

17. A _____ is a relatively new executive level position at a corporation, company, organization typically reporting directly to the CEO or board of directors. The _____ is responsible for a brand's image, experience, and promise, and propagating it throughout all aspects of the company. The brand officer oversees marketing, advertising, design, public relations and customer service departments.

a. Financial analyst
b. Chief executive officer
c. Power III
d. Chief brand officer

18. In economics, business, retail, and accounting, a _____ is the value of money that has been used up to produce something, and hence is not available for use anymore. In economics, a _____ is an alternative that is given up as a result of a decision. In business, the _____ may be one of acquisition, in which case the amount of money expended to acquire it is counted as _____.

a. Cost
b. Fixed costs
c. Transaction cost
d. Variable cost

19. _____ is a rivalry between individuals, groups, nations for territory, a niche, or allocation of resources. It arises whenever two or more parties strive for a goal which cannot be shared. _____ occurs naturally between living organisms which co-exist in the same environment.

a. Price competition
b. Price fixing
c. Non-price competition
d. Competition

20. _____ is exchange of capital, goods, and services across international borders or territories. In most countries, it represents a significant share of gross domestic product (GDP.) While _____ has been present throughout much of history, its economic, social, and political importance has been on the rise in recent centuries.

a. International trade
b. Incoterms
c. ADTECH
d. ACNielsen

21. An _____ is the manufacturing of a good or service within a category. Although _____ is a broad term for any kind of economic production, in economics and urban planning _____ is a synonym for the secondary sector, which is a type of economic activity involved in the manufacturing of raw materials into goods and products.

There are four key industrial economic sectors: the primary sector, largely raw material extraction industries such as mining and farming; the secondary sector, involving refining, construction, and manufacturing; the tertiary sector, which deals with services (such as law and medicine) and distribution of manufactured goods; and the quaternary sector, a relatively new type of knowledge _____ focusing on technological research, design and development such as computer programming, and biochemistry.

a. Industry
b. AMAX
c. ACNielsen
d. ADTECH

22. _____ has traditionally been understood as the dissemination of information (usually by radio or television) to a narrow audience, not to the general public. Some forms of _____ involve directional signals or use of encryption. In the context of out-of-home advertising, this term often refers to the display of content on a digital signage network.

Chapter 18. Advertising and Public Relations

a. Promotional mix
c. Narrowcasting
b. Wells Fargo ' Co.
d. Chief privacy officer

23. The _____ is a trilateral trade bloc in North America created by the governments of the United States, Canada, and Mexico. It superseded the Canada-United States Free Trade Agreement between the US and Canada.

Following diplomatic negotiations dating back to 1990 between the three nations, the leaders met in San Antonio, Texas on December 17, 1992 to sign _____.

a. Power III
c. 6-3-5 Brainwriting
b. 180SearchAssistant
d. North American Free Trade Agreement

24. The _____ or _____ is used by business and government to classify and measure economic activity in Canada, Mexico and the United States. It has largely replaced the older Standard Industrial Classification system; however, certain government departments and agencies, such as the U.S. Securities and Exchange Commission (SEC), still use the SIC codes.

The _____ numbering system is a six-digit code.

a. Power III
c. 180SearchAssistant
b. 6-3-5 Brainwriting
d. North American Industry Classification System

25. _____ is a form of social influence. It is the process of guiding people toward the adoption of an idea, attitude, or action by rational and symbolic (though not always logical) means. It is strategy of problem-solving relying on 'appeals' rather than coercion.

a. 6-3-5 Brainwriting
c. Power III
b. Persuasion
d. 180SearchAssistant

26. A _____ is a single page leaflet advertising a nightclub, event, service, or other activity. _____s are typically used by individuals or businesses to promote their products or services. They are a form of mass marketing or small scale, community communication.

a. Quantitative
c. Flyer
b. Consumption Map
d. Just-In-Case

27. _____ is a measure of the strength of a brand, product, service relative to competitive offerings. There is often a geographic element to the competitive landscape. In defining _____, you must see to what extent a product, brand, or firm controls a product category in a given geographic area.

a. Productivity
c. Discretionary spending
b. Market dominance
d. Market system

28. An _____ is an advertisement written in the form of an objective opinion editorial, and presented in a printed publication--usually designed to look like a legitimate and independent news story.

_____s differ from traditional advertisements in that they are designed to look like the articles that appear in the publication.

Chapter 18. Advertising and Public Relations

a. ACNielsen
b. Informative advertising
c. ADTECH
d. Advertorial

29. _____ is a term used to describe the phenomenon of a marketplace being full or even overcrowded with products. It also refers to the extreme amount of advertising the average American sees in their daily lives. _____ is a major problem for marketers and advertisers.
   a. Procter ' Gamble
   b. Consumption Map
   c. Push
   d. Clutter

30. A _____ is a type of wholesale merchant business that buys goods and bulk products from importers, other wholesalers and then sells to retailers. _____s can deal in any commodity destined for the retail market. Typical categories are food, lumber, hardware, fuel, and textiles.
   a. Tacit collusion
   b. Chief privacy officer
   c. Refusal to deal
   d. Jobbing house

31. _____ is a broad label that refers to any individuals or households that use goods and services generated within the economy. The concept of a _____ is used in different contexts, so that the usage and significance of the term may vary.

A _____ is a person who uses any product or service.

   a. Power III
   b. 6-3-5 Brainwriting
   c. 180SearchAssistant
   d. Consumer

32. The _____ Awards are advertising awards given yearly by the New York American Marketing Association. _____ appears to be an acronym since it is usually written in capital letters, but it is a pseudo-acronym, since the letters don't stand for individual words. They are from the word effectiveness, a desirable trait in an advertisement.
   a. EFFIE
   b. ADTECH
   c. AMAX
   d. ACNielsen

33. _____ is the deliberate attempt to manage the public's perception of a subject. The subjects of _____ include people (for example, politicians and performing artists), goods and services, organizations of all kinds, and works of art or entertainment.

From a marketing perspective, _____ is one component of promotion.

   a. Pearson's chi-square
   b. Publicity
   c. Little value placed on potential benefits
   d. Brando

34. _____ is an advertisement in which a particular product specifically mentions a competitor by name for the express purpose of showing why the competitor is inferior to the product naming it.

This should not be confused with parody advertisements, where a fictional product is being advertised for the purpose of poking fun at the particular advertisement, nor should it be confused with the use of a coined brand name for the purpose of comparing the product without actually naming an actual competitor. ('Wikipedia tastes better and is less filling than the Encyclopedia Galactica.')

Chapter 18. Advertising and Public Relations

In the 1980s, during what has been referred to as the cola wars, soft-drink manufacturer Pepsi ran a series of advertisements where people, caught on hidden camera, in a blind taste test, chose Pepsi over rival Coca-Cola.

a. Heavy-up
b. GL-70
c. Cost per conversion
d. Comparative advertising

35. The term _____, invented to replace the older gender-based terms, is a typical example of a gender-neutral neologism.

In the present media-sensitive world, many organizations are increasingly likely to employ professionals who have received formal training in journalism, communications, public relations and public affairs in this role in order to ensure that public announcements are made in the most appropriate fashion and through the most appropriate channels to maximize the impact of favorable messages, and to minimize the impact of unfavorable messages. Popular local and national sports stars are often chosen as spokespeople for commercial advertising.

a. Power III
b. Spokesperson
c. Professional services
d. 180SearchAssistant

36. _____ or _____ data refers to selected population characteristics as used in government, marketing or opinion research, or the _____ profiles used in such research. Note the distinction from the term 'demography' Commonly-used _____ include race, age, income, disabilities, mobility (in terms of travel time to work or number of vehicles available), educational attainment, home ownership, employment status, and even location.

a. African Americans
b. Albert Einstein
c. AStore
d. Demographic

37. _____ is a branch of philosophy which seeks to address questions about morality, such as how a moral outcome can be achieved in a specific situation (applied _____), how moral values should be determined (normative _____), what moral values people actually abide by (descriptive _____), what the fundamental semantic, ontological, and epistemic nature of _____ or morality is (meta-_____), and how moral capacity or moral agency develops and what its nature is (moral psychology.)

Socrates was one of the first Greek philosophers to encourage both scholars and the common citizen to turn their attention from the outside world to the condition of man. In this view, Knowledge having a bearing on human life was placed highest, all other knowledge being secondary.

a. Ethics
b. ADTECH
c. ACNielsen
d. AMAX

38. _____ is one of the four elements of marketing mix. An organization or set of organizations (go-betweens) involved in the process of making a product or service available for use or consumption by a consumer or business user.

The other three parts of the marketing mix are product, pricing, and promotion.

a. Distribution
b. Comparison-Shopping agent
c. Better Living Through Chemistry
d. Japan Advertising Photographers' Association

39. A _____ is a video segment created by a PR firm, advertising agency, marketing firm, corporation or government agency and provided to television news stations for the purpose of informing, shaping public opinion commercial products and services.

News reports may incorporate a _____ in whole or part if the news producer feels it contains information appropriate to the story or of interest to viewers.

a. Power III
b. 6-3-5 Brainwriting
c. Video news release
d. 180SearchAssistant

40. The _____ is an English-language international daily newspaper published by Dow Jones ' Company in New York City with Asian and European editions. As of 2007, It has a worldwide daily circulation of more than 2 million, with approximately 931,000 paying online subscribers. It was the largest-circulation newspaper in the United States until November 2003, when it was surpassed by USA Today.

a. 180SearchAssistant
b. 6-3-5 Brainwriting
c. Power III
d. Wall Street Journal

41. _____ in organizations and public policy is both the organizational process of creating and maintaining a plan; and the psychological process of thinking about the activities required to create a desired goal on some scale. As such, it is a fundamental property of intelligent behavior. This thought process is essential to the creation and refinement of a plan, or integration of it with other plans, that is, it combines forecasting of developments with the preparation of scenarios of how to react to them.

a. 6-3-5 Brainwriting
b. Planning
c. Power III
d. 180SearchAssistant

42. _____ is the study of when, why, how, where and what people do or do not buy products. It blends elements from psychology, sociology,social psychology, anthropology and economics. It attempts to understand the buyer decision making process, both individually and in groups. It studies characteristics of individual consumers such as demographics and behavioural variables in an attempt to understand people's wants. It also tries to assess influences on the consumer from groups such as family, friends, reference groups, and society in general.

a. Multidimensional scaling
b. Consumer behavior
c. Consumer confidence
d. Communal marketing

43. _____ is a list for goods and materials held available in stock by a business. It is also used for a list of the contents of a household and for a list for testamentary purposes of the possessions of someone who has died. In accounting _____ is considered an asset.

a. ACNielsen
b. ADTECH
c. Ending Inventory
d. Inventory

Chapter 19. Personal Selling and Sales Promotion

1. _____ is one of the four aspects of promotional mix. (The other three parts of the promotional mix are advertising, personal selling, and publicity/public relations.) Media and non-media marketing communication are employed for a pre-determined, limited time to increase consumer demand, stimulate market demand or improve product availability.
   - a. New Media Strategies
   - b. Marketing communication
   - c. Sales promotion
   - d. Merchandise

2. _____ involves disseminating information about a product, product line, brand, or company. It is one of the four key aspects of the marketing mix. (The other three elements are product marketing, pricing, and distribution). P>_____ is generally sub-divided into two parts:

   - Above the line _____: Promotion in the media (e.g. TV, radio, newspapers, Internet and Mobile Phones) in which the advertiser pays an advertising agency to place the ad
   - Below the line _____: All other _____. Much of this is intended to be subtle enough for the consumer to be unaware that _____ is taking place. E.g. sponsorship, product placement, endorsements, sales _____, merchandising, direct mail, personal selling, public relations, trade shows

   - a. Cashmere Agency
   - b. Davie Brown Index
   - c. Bottling lines
   - d. Promotion

3. _____ is a form of communication that typically attempts to persuade potential customers to purchase or to consume more of a particular brand of product or service. 'While now central to the contemporary global economy and the reproduction of global production networks, it is only quite recently that _____ has been more than a marginal influence on patterns of sales and production. The formation of modern _____ was intimately bound up with the emergence of new forms of monopoly capitalism around the end of the 19th and beginning of the 20th century as one element in corporate strategies to create, organize and where possible control markets, especially for mass produced consumer goods.
   - a. ADTECH
   - b. ACNielsen
   - c. AMAX
   - d. Advertising

4. In marketing a _____ is a ticket or document that can be exchanged for a financial discount or rebate when purchasing a product. Customarily, _____s are issued by manufacturers of consumer packaged goods or by retailers, to be used in retail stores as a part of sales promotions. They are often widely distributed through mail, magazines, newspapers, the Internet, and mobile devices such as cell phones.
   - a. Coupon
   - b. Merchandising
   - c. Marketing communication
   - d. Merchandise

5. In the United States consumer sales promotions known as _____ or simply sweeps (both single and plural) have become associated with marketing promotions targeted toward both generating enthusiasm and providing incentive reactions among customers by enticing consumers to submit free entries into drawings of chance (and not skill) that are tied to product or service awareness wherein the featured prizes are given away by sponsoring companies. Prizes can vary in value from less than one dollar to more than one million U.S. dollars and can be in the form of cash, cars, homes, electronics, etc.

   _____ frequently have eligibility limited by international, national, state, local, or other geographical factors.

   - a. Sweepstakes
   - b. Commercial planning
   - c. Claritas Prizm
   - d. Market segment

Chapter 19. Personal Selling and Sales Promotion

6. _____ is a method of direct marketing in which a salesperson solicits to prospective customers to buy products or services, either over the phone or through a subsequent face to face or Web conferencing appointment scheduled during the call.

_____ can also include recorded sales pitches programmed to be played over the phone via automatic dialing. _____ has come under fire in recent years, being viewed as an annoyance by many.

a. Directory Harvest Attack
b. Joe job
c. Phishing
d. Telemarketing

7. A trade fair (trade show or expo) is an exhibition organized so that companies in a specific industry can showcase and demonstrate their latest products, service, study activities of rivals and examine recent trends and opportunities. Some trade fairs are open to the public, while others can only be attended by company representatives (members of the trade) and members of the press, therefore _____ are classified as either 'Public' or 'Trade Only'. They are held on a continuing basis in virtually all markets and normally attract companies from around the globe.

a. Power III
b. 6-3-5 Brainwriting
c. 180SearchAssistant
d. Trade shows

8. In economics, business, retail, and accounting, a _____ is the value of money that has been used up to produce something, and hence is not available for use anymore. In economics, a _____ is an alternative that is given up as a result of a decision. In business, the _____ may be one of acquisition, in which case the amount of money expended to acquire it is counted as _____.

a. Fixed costs
b. Variable cost
c. Transaction cost
d. Cost

9. _____ is defined by the American _____ Association as the activity, set of institutions, and processes for creating, communicating, delivering, and exchanging offerings that have value for customers, clients, partners, and society at large. The term developed from the original meaning which referred literally to going to market, as in shopping, or going to a market to sell goods or services.

_____ practice tends to be seen as a creative industry, which includes advertising, distribution and selling.

a. Customer acquisition management
b. Marketing
c. Marketing myopia
d. Product naming

10. _____ is an advertisement in which a particular product specifically mentions a competitor by name for the express purpose of showing why the competitor is inferior to the product naming it.

This should not be confused with parody advertisements, where a fictional product is being advertised for the purpose of poking fun at the particular advertisement, nor should it be confused with the use of a coined brand name for the purpose of comparing the product without actually naming an actual competitor. ('Wikipedia tastes better and is less filling than the Encyclopedia Galactica.')

In the 1980s, during what has been referred to as the cola wars, soft-drink manufacturer Pepsi ran a series of advertisements where people, caught on hidden camera, in a blind taste test, chose Pepsi over rival Coca-Cola.

Chapter 19. Personal Selling and Sales Promotion

a. Comparative advertising
c. Heavy-up
b. GL-70
d. Cost per conversion

11. _____ is the provision of service to customers before, during and after a purchase.

According to Turban et al., '_____ is a series of activities designed to enhance the level of customer satisfaction - that is, the feeling that a product or service has met the customer expectation.'

Its importance varies by product, industry and customer.

a. Facing
c. COPC Inc.
b. Customer experience
d. Customer service

12. _____ is a business discipline which is focused on the practical application of marketing techniques and the management of a firm's marketing resources and activities. Marketing managers are often responsible for influencing the level, timing, and composition of customer demand accepted definition of the term. In part, this is because the role of a marketing manager can vary significantly based on a business' size, corporate culture, and industry context.

a. Door-to-door
c. Business structure
b. Marketing Management
d. Performance-based advertising

13. In grammar, the _____ is the form of an adjective or adverb which denotes the degree or grade by which a person, thing and is used in this context with a subordinating conjunction, such as than, as...as, etc.

The structure of a _____ in English consists normally of the positive form of the adjective or adverb, plus the suffix -er e.g. 'he is taller than his father is', or 'the village is less picturesque than the town nearby'.

a. 180SearchAssistant
c. 6-3-5 Brainwriting
b. Power III
d. Comparative

14. A _____ is a party that mediates between a buyer and a seller. A _____ who also acts as a seller or as a buyer becomes a principal party to the deal. Distinguish agent: one who acts on behalf of a principal.

a. Power III
c. Broker
b. Spokesperson
d. 180SearchAssistant

15. _____ generally refers to a list of all planned expenses and revenues. It is a plan for saving and spending. A _____ is an important concept in microeconomics, which uses a _____ line to illustrate the trade-offs between two or more goods.

a. 180SearchAssistant
c. Budget
b. 6-3-5 Brainwriting
d. Power III

16. _____ is a broad label that refers to any individuals or households that use goods and services generated within the economy. The concept of a _____ is used in different contexts, so that the usage and significance of the term may vary.

A _____ is a person who uses any product or service.

a. Power III
b. 180SearchAssistant
c. 6-3-5 Brainwriting
d. Consumer

17. _____ is the equation of personal happiness with consumption and the purchase of material possessions.

The term is often associated with criticisms of consumption starting with Thorstein Veblen.

Veblen's subject of examination, the newly emergent middle class arising at the turn of the twentieth century, comes to full fruition by the end of the twentieth century through the process of globalization.

In economics, _____ refers to economic policies placing emphasis on consumption.

a. Power III
b. 180SearchAssistant
c. Consumerism
d. 6-3-5 Brainwriting

18. The U.S. _____ is an agency of the United States Department of Health and Human Services and is responsible for regulating and supervising the safety of foods, dietary supplements, drugs, vaccines, biological medical products, blood products, medical devices, radiation-emitting devices, veterinary products, and cosmetics. The FDA also enforces section 361 of the Public Health Service Act and the associated regulations, including sanitation requirements on interstate travel as well as specific rules for control of disease on products ranging from pet turtles to semen donations for assisted reproductive medicine techniques.

The FDA is an agency within the United States Department of Health and Human Services responsible for protecting and promoting the nation's public health.

a. 180SearchAssistant
b. Power III
c. 6-3-5 Brainwriting
d. Food and Drug Administration

19. Competitiveness is a comparative concept of the ability and performance of a firm, sub-sector or country to sell and supply goods and/or services in a given market. Although widely used in economics and business management, the usefulness of the concept, particularly in the context of national competitiveness, is vigorously disputed by economists, such as Paul Krugman .

The term may also be applied to markets, where it is used to refer to the extent to which the market structure may be regarded as perfectly _____.

a. Free trade zone
b. Geographical pricing
c. Customs union
d. Competitive

20. _____ is a marketing strategy that involves selling several related products under one brand name. It is contrasted with individual branding in which each product in a portfolio is given a unique identity and brand name.

There are often economies of scope associated with _____ since several products can efficiently be promoted with a single advertisement or campaign.

Chapter 19. Personal Selling and Sales Promotion   171

a. 6-3-5 Brainwriting
c. Power III
b. 180SearchAssistant
d. Family branding

21. _____ is the physical search for minerals, fossils, precious metals or mineral specimens, and is also known as fossicking.

_____ is synonymous in some ways with mineral exploration which is an organised, large scale and at least semi-scientific effort undertaken by mineral resource companies to find commercially viable ore deposits. To actually be considered a prospector you must become registered as a professional prospector.

a. Power III
c. 6-3-5 Brainwriting
b. 180SearchAssistant
d. Prospecting

22. Importance of _____ is critical for any commercial organization. Expanding business is not possible without increasing sales volumes, and effective _____ goal is to organize sales team work in such a manner that ensures a growing flow of regular customers and increasing amount of sales.

The four phase-model of Management Process

1. Conception
2. Planning
3. Execution
4. Control

This model is cyclical, so it is a constant/continuous process.

===_____ is attainment of sales force goals in a effective ' efficient manner through planning, staffing, training, leading ' controlling organizational resources.

a. Hit rate
c. Request for proposal
b. Sales management
d. Sales process

23. _____ is one of the four elements of marketing mix. An organization or set of organizations (go-betweens) involved in the process of making a product or service available for use or consumption by a consumer or business user.

The other three parts of the marketing mix are product, pricing, and promotion.

a. Better Living Through Chemistry
c. Japan Advertising Photographers' Association
b. Distribution
d. Comparison-Shopping agent

24. _____ in economics and business is the result of an exchange and from that trade we assign a numerical monetary value to a good, service or asset. If I trade 4 apples for an orange, the _____ of an orange is 4 - apples. Inversely, the _____ of an apple is 1/4 oranges.

a. Price
b. Discounts and allowances
c. Contribution margin-based pricing
d. Pricing

25. The _____, a unit of the United States Department of Labor, is the principal fact-finding agency for the U.S. government in the broad field of labor economics and statistics. The BLS is an independent national statistical agency that collects, processes, analyzes, and disseminates essential statistical data to the American public, the U.S. Congress, other Federal agencies, State and local governments, business, and labor representatives. The BLS also serves as a statistical resource to the Department of Labor.
   a. Power III
   b. Consumer Expenditure Survey
   c. Gross national product
   d. Bureau of Labor Statistics

26. _____ is the set of reasons that determines one to engage in a particular behavior. The term is generally used for human _____ but, theoretically, it can be used to describe the causes for animal behavior as well
   a. Motivation
   b. 180SearchAssistant
   c. Role playing
   d. Power III

27. _____ is a mathematical science pertaining to the collection, analysis, interpretation or explanation, and presentation of data. It also provides tools for prediction and forecasting based on data. It is applicable to a wide variety of academic disciplines, from the natural and social sciences to the humanities, government and business.
   a. Null hypothesis
   b. Type I error
   c. Statistics
   d. Median

28. Advertising mail junk mail is the delivery of advertising material to recipients of postal mail. The delivery of advertising mail forms a large and growing service for many postal services, and _____ marketing forms a significant portion of the direct marketing industry. Some organizations attempt to help people opt-out of receiving advertising mail, in many cases motivated by a concern over its negative environmental impact.
   a. Phishing
   b. Direct mail
   c. Directory Harvest Attack
   d. Telemarketing

29. _____ is a measure of the strength of a brand, product, service relative to competitive offerings. There is often a geographic element to the competitive landscape. In defining _____, you must see to what extent a product, brand, or firm controls a product category in a given geographic area.
   a. Discretionary spending
   b. Market dominance
   c. Market system
   d. Productivity

30. _____ in organizations and public policy is both the organizational process of creating and maintaining a plan; and the psychological process of thinking about the activities required to create a desired goal on some scale. As such, it is a fundamental property of intelligent behavior. This thought process is essential to the creation and refinement of a plan, or integration of it with other plans, that is, it combines forecasting of developments with the preparation of scenarios of how to react to them.
   a. 6-3-5 Brainwriting
   b. Planning
   c. Power III
   d. 180SearchAssistant

31. A _____ is a collection of symbols, experiences and associations connected with a product, a service, a person or any other artifact or entity.

_____s have become increasingly important components of culture and the economy, now being described as 'cultural accessories and personal philosophies'.

Some people distinguish the psychological aspect of a _____ from the experiential aspect.

a. Brand equity
b. Brandable software
c. Store brand
d. Brand

32. _____, in marketing, consists of a consumer's commitment to repurchase the brand and can be demonstrated by repeated buying of a product or service or other positive behaviors such as word of mouth advocacy. True _____ implies that the consumer is willing, at least on occasion, to put aside their own desires in the interest of the brand. _____ has been proclaimed by some to be the ultimate goal of marketing.

a. Brand awareness
b. Brand implementation
c. Trade Symbols
d. Brand loyalty

33. A _____ is an amount paid by way of reduction, return, or refund on what has already been paid or contributed. It is a type of sales promotion marketers use primarily as incentives or supplements to product sales. The mail-in _____ is the most common.

a. Rebate
b. Lifestyle city
c. Personalization
d. Strand

34. A _____ is defined by the International Co-operative Alliance's Statement on the Co-operative Identity as an autonomous association of persons united voluntarily to meet their common economic, social, and cultural needs and aspirations through a jointly-owned and democratically-controlled enterprise. It is a business organization owned and operated by a group of individuals for their mutual benefit. A _____ may also be defined as a business owned and controlled equally by the people who use its services or who work at it.

a. Power III
b. 180SearchAssistant
c. 6-3-5 Brainwriting
d. Cooperative

35. _____ is systematic determination of merit, worth, and significance of something or someone using criteria against a set of standards. _____ often is used to characterize and appraise subjects of interest in a wide range of human enterprises, including the arts, criminal justice, foundations and non-profit organizations, government, health care, and other human services.

Depending on the topic of interest, there are professional groups which look to the quality and rigor of the _____ process.

a. ADTECH
b. AMAX
c. Evaluation
d. ACNielsen

36. The business terms _____ and pull originated in the logistic and supply chain management, but are also widely used in marketing.

Chapter 19. Personal Selling and Sales Promotion

A _____-pull-system in business describes the move of a product or information between two subjects. On markets the consumers usually 'pulls' the goods or information they demand for their needs, while the offerers or suppliers '_____es' them toward the consumers.

- a. Gold Key Matching Service
- b. Manufacturers' representatives
- c. Completely randomized designs
- d. Push

37. _____ or _____ data refers to selected population characteristics as used in government, marketing or opinion research, or the _____ profiles used in such research. Note the distinction from the term 'demography' Commonly-used _____ include race, age, income, disabilities, mobility (in terms of travel time to work or number of vehicles available), educational attainment, home ownership, employment status, and even location.
- a. AStore
- b. Demographic
- c. Albert Einstein
- d. African Americans

38. _____ refers to the methods of practicing and using another person's philosophy of business. The franchisor grants the independent operator the right to distribute its products, techniques, and trademarks for a percentage of gross monthly sales and a royalty fee. Various tangibles and intangibles such as national or international advertising, training, and other support services are commonly made available by the franchisor.
- a. Franchising
- b. 180SearchAssistant
- c. Franchise fee
- d. Power III

39. Merchandising refers to the methods, practices and operations conducted to promote and sustain certain categories of commercial activity. The term is understood to have different specific meanings depending on the context. _____ is a sale goods at a store

In marketing, one of the definitions of merchandising is the practice in which the brand or image from one product or service is used to sell another.

- a. New Media Strategies
- b. Sales promotion
- c. Merchandise
- d. Merchandising

40. _____ is anything that is generally accepted as payment for goods and services and repayment of debts. The main uses of _____ are as a medium of exchange, a unit of account, and a store of value. Some authors explicitly require _____ to be a standard of deferred payment.
- a. Money
- b. Law of supply
- c. Microeconomics
- d. Leading indicator

41. _____ is a form of advertisement, where branded goods or services are placed in a context usually devoid of ads, such as movies, the story line of television shows Broadcasting ' Cable reported, 'Two thirds of advertisers employ 'branded entertainment'--_____--with the vast majority of that (80%) in commercial TV programming.' The story, based on a survey by the Association of National Advertisers, added, 'Reasons for using in-show plugs varied from 'stronger emotional connection' to better dovetailing with relevant content, to targetting a specific group.'

_____ became common in the 1980s, but can be traced back to the nineteenth century in publishing.

a. 180SearchAssistant
b. 6-3-5 Brainwriting
c. Power III
d. Product placement

42. _____ is a branch of philosophy which seeks to address questions about morality, such as how a moral outcome can be achieved in a specific situation (applied _____), how moral values should be determined (normative _____), what moral values people actually abide by (descriptive _____), what the fundamental semantic, ontological, and epistemic nature of _____ or morality is (meta-_____), and how moral capacity or moral agency develops and what its nature is (moral psychology.)

Socrates was one of the first Greek philosophers to encourage both scholars and the common citizen to turn their attention from the outside world to the condition of man. In this view, Knowledge having a bearing on human life was placed highest, all other knowledge being secondary.

a. ADTECH
b. AMAX
c. ACNielsen
d. Ethics

43. _____ is one of the four Ps of the marketing mix. The other three aspects are product, promotion, and place. It is also a key variable in microeconomic price allocation theory.

a. Price
b. Relationship based pricing
c. Pricing
d. Competitor indexing

Chapter 20. Considerations in Price Planning

1. _____ in economics and business is the result of an exchange and from that trade we assign a numerical monetary value to a good, service or asset. If I trade 4 apples for an orange, the _____ of an orange is 4 - apples. Inversely, the _____ of an apple is 1/4 oranges.
   - a. Price
   - b. Pricing
   - c. Contribution margin-based pricing
   - d. Discounts and allowances

2. _____ is one of the four Ps of the marketing mix. The other three aspects are product, promotion, and place. It is also a key variable in microeconomic price allocation theory.
   - a. Competitor indexing
   - b. Pricing
   - c. Relationship based pricing
   - d. Price

3. _____ in organizations and public policy is both the organizational process of creating and maintaining a plan; and the psychological process of thinking about the activities required to create a desired goal on some scale. As such, it is a fundamental property of intelligent behavior. This thought process is essential to the creation and refinement of a plan, or integration of it with other plans, that is, it combines forecasting of developments with the preparation of scenarios of how to react to them.
   - a. Power III
   - b. Planning
   - c. 180SearchAssistant
   - d. 6-3-5 Brainwriting

4. A personal and cultural _____ is a relative ethic _____, an assumption upon which implementation can be extrapolated. A _____ system is a set of consistent _____s and measures that is soo not true. A principle _____ is a foundation upon which other _____s and measures of integrity are based.
   - a. Value
   - b. Perceptual maps
   - c. Supreme Court of the United States
   - d. Package-on-Package

5. _____ is a form of communication that typically attempts to persuade potential customers to purchase or to consume more of a particular brand of product or service. 'While now central to the contemporary global economy and the reproduction of global production networks, it is only quite recently that _____ has been more than a marginal influence on patterns of sales and production. The formation of modern _____ was intimately bound up with the emergence of new forms of monopoly capitalism around the end of the 19th and beginning of the 20th century as one element in corporate strategies to create, organize and where possible control markets, especially for mass produced consumer goods.
   - a. ADTECH
   - b. ACNielsen
   - c. AMAX
   - d. Advertising

6. _____ is a rivalry between individuals, groups, nations for territory, a niche, or allocation of resources. It arises whenever two or more parties strive for a goal which cannot be shared. _____ occurs naturally between living organisms which co-exist in the same environment.
   - a. Non-price competition
   - b. Price competition
   - c. Price fixing
   - d. Competition

7. _____ is one of the four elements of marketing mix. An organization or set of organizations (go-betweens) involved in the process of making a product or service available for use or consumption by a consumer or business user.

The other three parts of the marketing mix are product, pricing, and promotion.

Chapter 20. Considerations in Price Planning

a. Distribution
b. Japan Advertising Photographers' Association
c. Comparison-Shopping agent
d. Better Living Through Chemistry

8. _____ is a measure of the strength of a brand, product, service relative to competitive offerings. There is often a geographic element to the competitive landscape. In defining _____, you must see to what extent a product, brand, or firm controls a product category in a given geographic area.

a. Discretionary spending
b. Productivity
c. Market dominance
d. Market system

9. _____ is defined by the American _____ Association as the activity, set of institutions, and processes for creating, communicating, delivering, and exchanging offerings that have value for customers, clients, partners, and society at large. The term developed from the original meaning which referred literally to going to market, as in shopping, or going to a market to sell goods or services.

_____ practice tends to be seen as a creative industry, which includes advertising, distribution and selling.

a. Marketing
b. Product naming
c. Customer acquisition management
d. Marketing myopia

10. Non-_____ is a marketing strategy 'in which one firm tries to distinguish its product or service from competing products on the basis of attributes like design and workmanship' (McConnell-Brue, 2002, p. 437-438.) The firm can also distinguish its product offering through quality of service, extensive distribution, customer focus, or any other sustainable competitive advantage other than price.

a. Price fixing
b. Direct competition
c. Non-price competition
d. Price Competition

11. _____ is an advertisement in which a particular product specifically mentions a competitor by name for the express purpose of showing why the competitor is inferior to the product naming it.

This should not be confused with parody advertisements, where a fictional product is being advertised for the purpose of poking fun at the particular advertisement, nor should it be confused with the use of a coined brand name for the purpose of comparing the product without actually naming an actual competitor. ('Wikipedia tastes better and is less filling than the Encyclopedia Galactica.')

In the 1980s, during what has been referred to as the cola wars, soft-drink manufacturer Pepsi ran a series of advertisements where people, caught on hidden camera, in a blind taste test, chose Pepsi over rival Coca-Cola.

a. Heavy-up
b. GL-70
c. Comparative advertising
d. Cost per conversion

12. A _____ is a plan of action designed to achieve a particular goal.

_____ is different from tactics. In military terms, tactics is concerned with the conduct of an engagement while _____ is concerned with how different engagements are linked.

a. Power III
b. Strategy
c. 6-3-5 Brainwriting
d. 180SearchAssistant

13. _____s are used in open sentences. For instance, in the formula x + 1 = 5, x is a _____ which represents an 'unknown' number. _____s are often represented by letters of the Roman alphabet, or those of other alphabets, such as Greek, and use other special symbols.
   a. Variable
   b. Book of business
   c. Quantitative
   d. Personalization

14. In economics, _____ is the desire to own something and the ability to pay for it. The term _____ signifies the ability or the willingness to buy a particular commodity at a given point of time .

   a. Demand
   b. Market system
   c. Market dominance
   d. Discretionary spending

15. _____ is an economic model based on price, utility and quantity in a market. It concludes that in a competitive market, price will function to equalize the quantity demanded by consumers, and the quantity supplied by producers, resulting in an economic equilibrium of price and quantity. Similarly, an increase in the number of workers tends to result in lower wages and vice-versa.
   a. 180SearchAssistant
   b. Power III
   c. 6-3-5 Brainwriting
   d. Supply and demand

16. In economics, _____ describes demand that is not very sensitive to a change in price.
   a. AMAX
   b. ACNielsen
   c. ADTECH
   d. Inelastic

17. In economics, the _____ is an economic law that states that consumers buy more of a good when its price decreases and less when its price increases.

   - Supply and Demand

as there is inverse relationship exists between price and demand so when price increases demand decreases but quantity demand is another factor due to other factors like taste fashion incme expectations related goods etc

   a. Law of demand
   b. Microeconomics
   c. Market structure
   d. Macroeconomics

18. _____ is defined as the measure of responsiveness in the quantity demanded for a commodity as a result of change in price of the same commodity. It is a measure of how consumers react to a change in price. In other words, it is percentage change in quantity demanded as per the percentage change in price of the same commodity.
   a. Power III
   b. 180SearchAssistant
   c. Price elasticity of demand
   d. 6-3-5 Brainwriting

Chapter 20. Considerations in Price Planning

19. _____ is a broad label that refers to any individuals or households that use goods and services generated within the economy. The concept of a _____ is used in different contexts, so that the usage and significance of the term may vary.

A _____ is a person who uses any product or service.

a. Consumer
b. Power III
c. 6-3-5 Brainwriting
d. 180SearchAssistant

20. In economics, _____ is the ratio of the percent change in one variable to the percent change in another variable. It is a tool for measuring the responsiveness of a function to changes in parameters in a relative way. Commonly analyzed are _____ of substitution, price and wealth.

a. ACNielsen
b. Intellectual property
c. Elasticity
d. Opinion leadership

21. Price _____ is defined as the measure of responsiveness in the quantity demanded for a commodity as a result of change in price of the same commodity. It is a measure of how consumers react to a change in price. In other words, it is percentage change in quantity demanded as per the percentage change in price of the same commodity.

a. Elasticity of Demand
b. AMAX
c. ADTECH
d. ACNielsen

22. _____ is anything that is intended to save time, energy or frustration. A _____ store at a petrol station, for example, sells items that have nothing to do with gasoline/petrol, but it saves the consumer from having to go to a grocery store. '_____' is a very relative term and its meaning tends to change over time.

a. Convenience
b. MaxDiff
c. Demographic profile
d. Marketing buzz

23. _____ of consumer products (often supermarket goods) are distinguished by the absence of a brand name. They are identifed more by product characterstics.

They may be manufactured by less [prominent companies], or manufactured on the same production line as a 'named' brand. _____ are usually priced below those products sold by supermarkets under their own brand (frequently referred to as 'store brands' or 'own brands'.)

a. Generic brands
b. Micro ads
c. Gross Margin Return on Inventory Investment
d. M80

24. A _____ is a collection of symbols, experiences and associations connected with a product, a service, a person or any other artifact or entity.

_____s have become increasingly important components of culture and the economy, now being described as 'cultural accessories and personal philosophies'.

Some people distinguish the psychological aspect of a _____ from the experiential aspect.

a. Brandable software
b. Store brand
c. Brand equity
d. Brand

25. _____, in marketing, consists of a consumer's commitment to repurchase the brand and can be demonstrated by repeated buying of a product or service or other positive behaviors such as word of mouth advocacy. True _____ implies that the consumer is willing, at least on occasion, to put aside their own desires in the interest of the brand. _____ has been proclaimed by some to be the ultimate goal of marketing.
   a. Brand loyalty
   b. Trade Symbols
   c. Brand implementation
   d. Brand awareness

26. In economics, business, retail, and accounting, a _____ is the value of money that has been used up to produce something, and hence is not available for use anymore. In economics, a _____ is an alternative that is given up as a result of a decision. In business, the _____ may be one of acquisition, in which case the amount of money expended to acquire it is counted as _____.
   a. Variable cost
   b. Fixed costs
   c. Transaction cost
   d. Cost

27. _____ is a form of government regulation which protects the interests of consumers. For example, a government may require businesses to disclose detailed information about products--particularly in areas where safety or public health is an issue, such as food. _____ is linked to the idea of consumer rights (that consumers have various rights as consumers), and to the formation of consumer organizations which help consumers make better choices in the marketplace.
   a. Federal Bureau of Investigation
   b. Consumer Protection
   c. Trademark dilution
   d. Sound trademark

28. The _____ is an independent agency of the United States government, established in 1914 by the _____ Act. Its principal mission is the promotion of 'consumer protection' and the elimination and prevention of what regulators perceive to be harmfully 'anti-competitive' business practices, such as coercive monopoly.

The _____ Act was one of President Wilson's major acts against trusts.

   a. 6-3-5 Brainwriting
   b. Power III
   c. Federal Trade Commission
   d. 180SearchAssistant

29. The _____ of 1914 (15 U.S.C §§ 41-58, as amended) established the Federal Trade Commission (FTC), a bipartisan body of five members appointed by the President of the United States for seven year terms. This Commission was authorized to issue Cease and Desist orders to large corporations to curb unfair trade practices. This Act also gave more flexibility to the US congress for judicial matters.
   a. Product liability
   b. Gripe site
   c. Comparative negligence
   d. Federal Trade Commission Act

30. _____ exists when sales of identical goods or services are transacted at different prices from the same provider. In a theoretical market with perfect information, no transaction costs or prohibition on secondary exchange (or re-selling) to prevent arbitrage, _____ can only be a feature of monopoly and oligopoly markets, where market power can be exercised. Otherwise, the moment the seller tries to sell the same good at different prices, the buyer at the lower price can arbitrage by selling to the consumer buying at the higher price but with a tiny discount.

Chapter 20. Considerations in Price Planning

a. Resale price maintenance
b. Price
c. Penetration pricing
d. Price discrimination

31. _____ is an agreement between business competitors to sell the same product or service at the same price. In general, it is an agreement intended to ultimately push the price of a product as high as possible, leading to profits for all the sellers. _____ can also involve any agreement to fix, peg, discount or stabilize prices.
   a. Price competition
   b. Non-price competition
   c. Price fixing
   d. Direct competition

32. The _____ requires the Federal government to investigate and pursue trusts, companies and organizations suspected of violating the Act. It was the first United States Federal statute to limit cartels and monopolies, and today still forms the basis for most antitrust litigation by the federal government.
   a. 180SearchAssistant
   b. Power III
   c. Sherman Antitrust Act
   d. 6-3-5 Brainwriting

33. _____ is the act of consigning, which is placing a person or thing in the hand of another, but retaining ownership until the goods are sold or person is transferred. This may be done for shipping, transfer of prisoners, or for sale in a store (i.e. a _____ shop.)

Features of _____ are as follows: 1)The Relation between the two parties is that of consignor and consignee and not that of buyer and seller 2)The consignor is entitled to receive all the expenses in connection with _____ 3)The consignee is not responsible for damage of goods during transport or any other procedure.

   a. Consignment
   b. Self service
   c. History of pawnbroking
   d. Garage sale

34. _____ are final goods specifically intended for the mass market. For instance, _____ do not include investment assets, like precious antiques, even though these antiques are final goods.

Manufactured goods are goods that have been processed by way of machinery.

   a. Free good
   b. Durable good
   c. Power III
   d. Consumer Goods

35. The (manufacturer's) suggested retail price (MSRP or SRP), _____ or recommended retail price (RRP) of a product is the price the manufacturer recommends that the retailer sell it for. The intention was to help to standardize prices among locations. While some stores always sell at, or below, the suggested retail price, others do so only when items are on sale or closeout.
   a. Power III
   b. Predatory pricing
   c. 180SearchAssistant
   d. List price

36. A _____ is a type of wholesale merchant business that buys goods and bulk products from importers, other wholesalers and then sells to retailers. _____s can deal in any commodity destined for the retail market. Typical categories are food, lumber, hardware, fuel, and textiles.

a. Chief privacy officer
b. Tacit collusion
c. Refusal to deal
d. Jobbing house

37. The _____ of 1936 (or Anti-Price Discrimination Act, 15 U.S.C. Â§ 13) is a United States federal law that prohibits what were considered, at the time of passage, to be anticompetitive practices by producers, specifically price discrimination. It grew out of practices in which chain stores were allowed to purchase goods at lower prices than other retailers.
a. Fair Debt Collection Practices Act
b. Registered trademark symbol
c. Trademark infringement
d. Robinson-Patman Act

38. A _____ is a type of department store, which sell products at prices lower than those asked by traditional retail outlets. Most discount department stores offer wide assortments of goods; others specialize in such merchandise as jewelry, electronic equipment, or electrical appliances. _____s are not dollar stores, which sell goods at a dollar or less.
a. Discount store
b. Strip mall
c. Gruen transfer
d. Sales per unit area

39. A _____ or leader is a product sold at a low price (at cost or below cost) to stimulate other, profitable sales. It is a kind of sales promotion, in other words marketing concentrating on a pricing strategy. The price can even be so low that the product is sold at a loss.
a. Loss leader
b. Penetration pricing
c. Price shading
d. Resale price maintenance

40. _____ is the practice of selling a product or service at a very low price, intending to drive competitors out of the market, or create barriers to entry for potential new competitors. If competitors or potential competitors cannot sustain equal or lower prices without losing money, they go out of business or choose not to enter the business. The predatory merchant then has fewer competitors or is even a de facto monopoly, and can then raise prices above what the market would otherwise bear.
a. List price
b. Power III
c. 180SearchAssistant
d. Predatory pricing

41. False advertising or _____ is the use of false or misleading statements in advertising. As advertising has the potential to persuade people into commercial transactions that they might otherwise avoid, many governments around the world use regulations to control false, deceptive or misleading advertising. Truth in labeling refers to essentially the same concept, that customers have the right to know what they are buying, and that all necessary information should be on the label.
a. Misleading advertising
b. Fine print
c. Power III
d. Deceptive advertising

42. _____ is a branch of philosophy which seeks to address questions about morality, such as how a moral outcome can be achieved in a specific situation (applied _____), how moral values should be determined (normative _____), what moral values people actually abide by (descriptive _____), what the fundamental semantic, ontological, and epistemic nature of _____ or morality is (meta-_____), and how moral capacity or moral agency develops and what its nature is (moral psychology.)

Chapter 20. Considerations in Price Planning

Socrates was one of the first Greek philosophers to encourage both scholars and the common citizen to turn their attention from the outside world to the condition of man. In this view, Knowledge having a bearing on human life was placed highest, all other knowledge being secondary.

a. AMAX	b. Ethics
c. ACNielsen	d. ADTECH

43. The _____ is an economic and political union of 27 member states, located primarily in Europe. It was established by the Treaty of Maastricht on 1 November 1993 upon the foundations of the pre-existing European Economic Community. With almost 500 million citizens, the _____ combined generates an estimated 30% share (US$16.8 trillion in 2007) of the nominal gross world product.

a. ACNielsen	b. ADTECH
c. Eurozone	d. European Union

44. A grey market or _____ is the trade of a commodity through distribution channels which, while legal, are unofficial, unauthorized, or unintended by the original manufacturer. In contrast, a black market is the trade of goods and services that are illegal in themselves and/or distributed through illegal channels, such as the selling of stolen goods or illegal items such as heroin or unregistered handguns.

The two main types of grey market are imported manufactured goods that would be normally unavailable or more expensive in a certain country and unissued securities that are not yet traded in official markets.

a. Zone pricing	b. Customs union
c. Green market	d. Gray market

45. _____ is when a large distribution channel member (usually a retailer), buys from a manufacturer in bulk and puts its own name on the product. This strategy is only practical when the retailer does very high levels of volume. The advantages to the retailer are:

- more freedom and flexibility in pricing
- more control over product attributes and quality
- higher margins (or lower selling price)
- eliminates much of the manufacturer's promotional costs

The advantages to the manufacturer are:

- reduced promotional costs
- stability of sales volume (at least while the contract is operative)

- Kumar, Nirmalya; Steenkamp, Jan-Benedict E.M., Private Label Strategy - How to Meet the Store Brand Challenge. Harvard Business Press 2007

- private label
- brand management
- brand
- product management
- marketing

a. Customization
c. Promotion
b. Private branding
d. Rural market

46. _____ Management is the succession of strategies used by management as a product goes through its _____. The conditions in which a product is sold changes over time and must be managed as it moves through its succession of stages.

The _____ goes through many phases, involves many professional disciplines, and requires many skills, tools and processes.

a. Chain stores
c. Customer satisfaction
b. Product life cycle
d. Supplier diversity

47. A supply chain is the system of organizations, people, technology, activities, information and resources involved in moving a product or service from _____ to customer. Supply chain activities transform natural resources, raw materials and components into a finished product that is delivered to the end customer. In sophisticated supply chain systems, used products may re-enter the supply chain at any point where residual value is recyclable.

a. Product line extension
c. Rebate
b. Bringin' Home the Oil
d. Supplier

48. _____ is a term used in business to indicate a state of intense competitive rivalry accompanied by a multi-lateral series of price reduction. One competitor will lower its price, then others will lower their prices to match. If one of them reduces their price again, a new round of reductions starts.

a. Pricing objectives
c. Competitor indexing
b. Resale price maintenance
d. Price war

Chapter 21. Developing and Applying a Pricing Strategy

1. The phrase _____ refers to the aspect of corporate strategy, corporate finance and management dealing with the buying, selling and combining of different companies that can aid, finance, or help a growing company in a given industry grow rapidly without having to create another business entity.

An acquisition, also known as a takeover or a buyout, is the buying of one company (the 'target') by another. An acquisition may be friendly or hostile.

a. 180SearchAssistant
b. Power III
c. 6-3-5 Brainwriting
d. Mergers and acquisitions

2. _____ is one of the four Ps of the marketing mix. The other three aspects are product, promotion, and place. It is also a key variable in microeconomic price allocation theory.

a. Pricing
b. Competitor indexing
c. Price
d. Relationship based pricing

3. A _____ is a plan of action designed to achieve a particular goal.

_____ is different from tactics. In military terms, tactics is concerned with the conduct of an engagement while _____ is concerned with how different engagements are linked.

a. 180SearchAssistant
b. Power III
c. 6-3-5 Brainwriting
d. Strategy

4. _____ or goals give direction to the whole pricing process. Determining what your objectives are is the first step in pricing. When deciding on _____ you must consider: 1) the overall financial, marketing, and strategic objectives of the company; 2) the objectives of your product or brand; 3) consumer price elasticity and price points; and 4) the resources you have available.

a. Transfer pricing
b. Competitor indexing
c. Discounts and allowances
d. Pricing objectives

5. In economics, _____ is the desire to own something and the ability to pay for it. The term _____ signifies the ability or the willingness to buy a particular commodity at a given point of time.

a. Market dominance
b. Market system
c. Discretionary spending
d. Demand

6. _____ is the pricing technique of setting a relatively low initial entry price, often lower than the eventual market price, to attract new customers. The strategy works on the expectation that customers will switch to the new brand because of the lower price. _____ is most commonly associated with a marketing objective of increasing market share or sales volume, rather than to make profit in the short term.

a. Penetration pricing
b. Competitor indexing
c. Price war
d. Fee

7. The _____ of 1936 (or Anti-Price Discrimination Act, 15 U.S.C. § 13) is a United States federal law that prohibits what were considered, at the time of passage, to be anticompetitive practices by producers, specifically price discrimination. It grew out of practices in which chain stores were allowed to purchase goods at lower prices than other retailers.

a. Trademark infringement
b. Robinson-Patman Act
c. Registered trademark symbol
d. Fair Debt Collection Practices Act

8. _____ in economics and business is the result of an exchange and from that trade we assign a numerical monetary value to a good, service or asset. If I trade 4 apples for an orange, the _____ of an orange is 4 - apples. Inversely, the _____ of an apple is 1/4 oranges.
   a. Pricing
   b. Contribution margin-based pricing
   c. Discounts and allowances
   d. Price

9. In economics, business, retail, and accounting, a _____ is the value of money that has been used up to produce something, and hence is not available for use anymore. In economics, a _____ is an alternative that is given up as a result of a decision. In business, the _____ may be one of acquisition, in which case the amount of money expended to acquire it is counted as _____.
   a. Cost
   b. Variable cost
   c. Transaction cost
   d. Fixed costs

10. The break-even point for a product is the point where total revenue received equals the total costs associated with the sale of the product (TR=TC.) A break-even point is typically calculated in order for businesses to determine if it would be profitable to sell a proposed product, as opposed to attempting to modify an existing product instead so it can be made lucrative. _____ can also be used to analyse the potential profitability of an expenditure in a sales-based business.

In _____, margin of safety is how much output or sales level can fall before a business reaches its break-even point (BEP).

   a. Pay Per Sale
   b. Price skimming
   c. Contribution margin-based pricing
   d. Break even analysis

11. _____ is a pricing method used by companies. It is used primarily because it is easy to calculate and requires little information. There are several varieties, but the common thread in all of them is that one first calculates the cost of the product, then includes an additional amount to represent profit.
   a. Break even analysis
   b. Loss leader
   c. Relationship based pricing
   d. Cost-plus pricing

12. In economics, _____ are business expenses that are not dependent on the activities of the business They tend to be time-related, such as salaries or rents being paid per month. This is in contrast to variable costs, which are volume-related (and are paid per quantity.)

In management accounting, _____ are defined as expenses that do not change in proportion to the activity of a business, within the relevant period or scale of production.

   a. Marginal cost
   b. Variable cost
   c. Transaction cost
   d. Fixed costs

13. In economics and finance, _____ is the change in total cost that arises when the quantity produced changes by one unit. It is the cost of producing one more unit of a good. Mathematically, the _____ function is expressed as the first derivative of the total cost (TC) function with respect to quantity (Q.)

Chapter 21. Developing and Applying a Pricing Strategy

a. Transaction cost
c. Variable cost
b. Fixed costs
d. Marginal cost

14. _____s are used in open sentences. For instance, in the formula x + 1 = 5, x is a _____ which represents an 'unknown' number. _____s are often represented by letters of the Roman alphabet, or those of other alphabets, such as Greek, and use other special symbols.
a. Personalization
c. Variable
b. Book of business
d. Quantitative

15. _____s are expenses that change in proportion to the activity of a business. In other words, _____ is the sum of marginal costs. It can also be considered normal costs.
a. Marginal cost
c. Fixed costs
b. Transaction cost
d. Variable cost

16. In mathematics, an _____, or central tendency of a data set refers to a measure of the 'middle' or 'expected' value of the data set. There are many different descriptive statistics that can be chosen as a measurement of the central tendency of the data items.

An _____ is a single value that is meant to typify a list of values.

a. ADTECH
c. AMAX
b. ACNielsen
d. Average

17. _____ is an economics term used to describe the total fixed costs (TFC) divided by the quantity (Q) of units produced.

_____ is a per-unit measure of fixed costs. As the total number of goods produced increases, the _____ decreases because the same amount of fixed costs are being spread over a larger number of units.

a. ADTECH
c. ACNielsen
b. Average variable cost
d. Average fixed cost

18. In economics, _____ is equal to total cost divided by the number of goods produced (the output quantity, Q.) It is also equal to the sum of average variable costs (total variable costs divided by Q) plus average fixed costs (total fixed costs divided by Q.) _____s may be dependent on the time period considered (increasing production may be expensive or impossible in the short term, for example.)
a. ADTECH
c. ACNielsen
b. Average variable cost
d. Average cost

19. _____ is an economics term to describe a firms variable costs (labor, electricity, etc.) divided by the quantity (Q) of total units of output.

Where:

- TVC = Total Variable Cost
- _____ = Average variable cost
- Q = Quantity of Units Produced

_____ plus average fixed cost equals average total cost:

_____ + AFC = ATC.

a. ACNielsen
c. Average variable cost
b. Average fixed cost
d. ADTECH

20. _____ involves disseminating information about a product, product line, brand, or company. It is one of the four key aspects of the marketing mix. (The other three elements are product marketing, pricing, and distribution). P>_____ is generally sub-divided into two parts:

- Above the line _____: Promotion in the media (e.g. TV, radio, newspapers, Internet and Mobile Phones) in which the advertiser pays an advertising agency to place the ad
- Below the line _____: All other _____. Much of this is intended to be subtle enough for the consumer to be unaware that _____ is taking place. E.g. sponsorship, product placement, endorsements, sales _____, merchandising, direct mail, personal selling, public relations, trade shows

a. Cashmere Agency
c. Promotion
b. Davie Brown Index
d. Bottling lines

21. In economics, and cost accounting, _____ describes the total economic cost of production and is made up of variable costs, which vary according to the quantity of a good produced and include inputs such as labor and raw materials, plus fixed costs, which are independent of the quantity of a good produced and include inputs (capital) that cannot be varied in the short term, such as buildings and machinery. _____ in economics includes the total opportunity cost of each factor of production in addition to fixed and variable costs.

The rate at which _____ changes as the amount produced changes is called marginal cost.

a. Hoarding
c. Product proliferation
b. Household production function
d. Total cost

22. _____ is the process of estimation in unknown situations. Prediction is a similar, but more general term. Both can refer to estimation of time series, cross-sectional or longitudinal data.

Chapter 21. Developing and Applying a Pricing Strategy

a. 6-3-5 Brainwriting
b. Power III
c. 180SearchAssistant
d. Forecasting

23. _____ exists when sales of identical goods or services are transacted at different prices from the same provider. In a theoretical market with perfect information, no transaction costs or prohibition on secondary exchange (or re-selling) to prevent arbitrage, _____ can only be a feature of monopoly and oligopoly markets, where market power can be exercised. Otherwise, the moment the seller tries to sell the same good at different prices, the buyer at the lower price can arbitrage by selling to the consumer buying at the higher price but with a tiny discount.

a. Resale price maintenance
b. Price discrimination
c. Penetration pricing
d. Price

24. _____ Management is the succession of strategies used by management as a product goes through its _____. The conditions in which a product is sold changes over time and must be managed as it moves through its succession of stages.

The _____ goes through many phases, involves many professional disciplines, and requires many skills, tools and processes.

a. Supplier diversity
b. Chain stores
c. Product life cycle
d. Customer satisfaction

25. _____ is systematic determination of merit, worth, and significance of something or someone using criteria against a set of standards. _____ often is used to characterize and appraise subjects of interest in a wide range of human enterprises, including the arts, criminal justice, foundations and non-profit organizations, government, health care, and other human services.

Depending on the topic of interest, there are professional groups which look to the quality and rigor of the _____ process.

a. ACNielsen
b. AMAX
c. ADTECH
d. Evaluation

26. _____ is the process of understanding, anticipating and influencing consumer behavior in order to maximize revenue or profits from a fixed, perishable resource This process was first discovered by Dr. Matt H. Keller. The challenge is to sell the right resources to the right customer at the right time for the right price. This process can result in price discrimination, where a firm charges customers consuming otherwise identical goods or services a different price for doing so.

a. Yield management
b. Multi-level marketing
c. Cross-selling
d. Service provider

27. _____ is defined by the American _____ Association as the activity, set of institutions, and processes for creating, communicating, delivering, and exchanging offerings that have value for customers, clients, partners, and society at large. The term developed from the original meaning which referred literally to going to market, as in shopping, or going to a market to sell goods or services.

_____ practice tends to be seen as a creative industry, which includes advertising, distribution and selling.

Chapter 21. Developing and Applying a Pricing Strategy

a. Marketing myopia
b. Product naming
c. Customer acquisition management
d. Marketing

28. Competitiveness is a comparative concept of the ability and performance of a firm, sub-sector or country to sell and supply goods and/or services in a given market. Although widely used in economics and business management, the usefulness of the concept, particularly in the context of national competitiveness, is vigorously disputed by economists, such as Paul Krugman .

The term may also be applied to markets, where it is used to refer to the extent to which the market structure may be regarded as perfectly _____.

a. Free trade zone
b. Geographical pricing
c. Customs union
d. Competitive

29. _____ is a broad label that refers to any individuals or households that use goods and services generated within the economy. The concept of a _____ is used in different contexts, so that the usage and significance of the term may vary.

A _____ is a person who uses any product or service.

a. 180SearchAssistant
b. Consumer
c. Power III
d. 6-3-5 Brainwriting

30. _____ is the study of when, why, how, where and what people do or do not buy products. It blends elements from psychology, sociology,social psychology, anthropology and economics. It attempts to understand the buyer decision making process, both individually and in groups. It studies characteristics of individual consumers such as demographics and behavioural variables in an attempt to understand people's wants. It also tries to assess influences on the consumer from groups such as family, friends, reference groups, and society in general.

a. Communal marketing
b. Multidimensional scaling
c. Consumer confidence
d. Consumer behavior

31. _____ or price ending is a marketing practice based on the theory that certain prices have a psychological impact. The retail prices are often expressed as 'odd prices': a little less than a round number, e.g. $19.99 or Â£6.95 (but not necessarily mathematically odd, it could also be 2.98.) The theory is this drives demand greater than would be expected if consumers were perfectly rational.

a. First-mover advantage
b. Psychological pricing
c. Supplier diversity
d. Chain stores

32. A _____ or leader is a product sold at a low price (at cost or below cost) to stimulate other, profitable sales. It is a kind of sales promotion, in other words marketing concentrating on a pricing strategy. The price can even be so low that the product is sold at a loss.

a. Price shading
b. Loss leader
c. Resale price maintenance
d. Penetration pricing

Chapter 21. Developing and Applying a Pricing Strategy

33. _____ is an agreement between business competitors to sell the same product or service at the same price. In general, it is an agreement intended to ultimately push the price of a product as high as possible, leading to profits for all the sellers. _____ can also involve any agreement to fix, peg, discount or stabilize prices.
   a. Non-price competition
   b. Price competition
   c. Direct competition
   d. Price fixing

34. _____ is an economics term used to describe the system of firms setting prices of their goods the same to all buyers regardless of the sellers location, even if their transportation costs to the locations are different.

This means that if the destinations are far apart and have considerably different costs of transportation, each will still be charged the same price.

Although some consider this a form of collusion between the selling firms (it lowers the ability of buying firms to gain a competitive advantage by location or private transportation), it is common practice in the steel and automotive industries.

   a. Price war
   b. Base point pricing
   c. Price markdown
   d. Price shading

35. _____ is a marketing strategy that involves offering several products for sale as one combined product. This strategy is very common in the software business (for example: bundle a word processor, a spreadsheet, and a database into a single office suite), in the cable television industry (for example, basic cable in the United States generally offers many channels at one price), and in the fast food industry in which multiple items are combined into a complete meal. A bundle of products is sometimes referred to as a package deal or a compilation or an anthology.
   a. Product bundling
   b. Technology acceptance model
   c. Primary research
   d. Psychographic

36. _____ is the study of the Earth and its lands, features, inhabitants, and phenomena. A literal translation would be 'to describe or write about the Earth'. The first person to use the word '_____' was Eratosthenes .
   a. 6-3-5 Brainwriting
   b. 180SearchAssistant
   c. Power III
   d. Geography

37. _____s is the social science that studies the production, distribution, and consumption of goods and services. The term _____s comes from the Ancient Greek oá¼°κονομῖα from oá¼¶κος (oikos, 'house') + vĺŒμος (nomos, 'custom' or 'law'), hence 'rules of the house(hold)'. Current _____ models developed out of the broader field of political economy in the late 19th century, owing to a desire to use an empirical approach more akin to the physical sciences.
   a. ADTECH
   b. Economic
   c. ACNielsen
   d. Industrial organization

38. _____ is the level of inventory that minimizes the total inventory holding costs and ordering costs. The framework used to determine this order quantity is also known as Wilson _____ Model. The model was developed by F. W. Harris in 1913.
   a. ADTECH
   b. ACNielsen
   c. AMAX
   d. Economic order quantity

Chapter 21. Developing and Applying a Pricing Strategy

39. An overprint is the addition of text (and sometimes graphics) to the face of a postage stamp (or banknote) after it has been printed (although some overprints are solely in the selvedge area of souvenir sheets.) Overprints have been used for many purposes over the years. They have been used as _____s, commemorations, and control marks.
   a. Moratorium
   b. Comparison-Shopping agent
   c. Surcharge
   d. Consumption Map

40. _____ is a lightweight markup language, originally created by John Gruber and Aaron Swartz to help maximum readability and 'publishability' of both its input and output forms. The language takes many cues from existing conventions for marking up plain text in email. _____ converts its marked-up text input to valid, well-formed XHTML and replaces left-pointing angle brackets ('<') and ampersands with their corresponding character entity references.
   a. Power III
   b. 180SearchAssistant
   c. 6-3-5 Brainwriting
   d. Markdown

41. _____ is a form of communication that typically attempts to persuade potential customers to purchase or to consume more of a particular brand of product or service. 'While now central to the contemporary global economy and the reproduction of global production networks, it is only quite recently that _____ has been more than a marginal influence on patterns of sales and production. The formation of modern _____ was intimately bound up with the emergence of new forms of monopoly capitalism around the end of the 19th and beginning of the 20th century as one element in corporate strategies to create, organize and where possible control markets, especially for mass produced consumer goods.
   a. Advertising
   b. ACNielsen
   c. AMAX
   d. ADTECH

Chapter 22. Pulling It All Together: Integrating and Analyzing the Marketing Plan

1. _____ is an advertisement in which a particular product specifically mentions a competitor by name for the express purpose of showing why the competitor is inferior to the product naming it.

This should not be confused with parody advertisements, where a fictional product is being advertised for the purpose of poking fun at the particular advertisement, nor should it be confused with the use of a coined brand name for the purpose of comparing the product without actually naming an actual competitor. ('Wikipedia tastes better and is less filling than the Encyclopedia Galactica.')

In the 1980s, during what has been referred to as the cola wars, soft-drink manufacturer Pepsi ran a series of advertisements where people, caught on hidden camera, in a blind taste test, chose Pepsi over rival Coca-Cola.

a. Heavy-up
b. GL-70
c. Cost per conversion
d. Comparative advertising

2. _____ is a form of communication that typically attempts to persuade potential customers to purchase or to consume more of a particular brand of product or service. 'While now central to the contemporary global economy and the reproduction of global production networks, it is only quite recently that _____ has been more than a marginal influence on patterns of sales and production. The formation of modern _____ was intimately bound up with the emergence of new forms of monopoly capitalism around the end of the 19th and beginning of the 20th century as one element in corporate strategies to create, organize and where possible control markets, especially for mass produced consumer goods.

a. ADTECH
b. ACNielsen
c. Advertising
d. AMAX

3. A _____ is a written document that details the necessary actions to achieve one or more marketing objectives. It can be for a product or service, a brand, or a product line. _____s cover between one and five years.

a. Disruptive technology
b. Prosumer
c. Marketing plan
d. Marketing strategy

4. _____ is a marketing term, and involves evaluating the situation and trends in a particular company's market. _____ is often called the 'three c's', which refers to the three major elements that must be studied:

- Customers
- Costs
- Competition

The number of 'c's' is sometimes extended to four, five, or even six, with 'Collaboration', 'Company', and 'Competitive advantage'.

- Marketing mix
- SWOT analysis

a. Power III
b. 180SearchAssistant
c. 6-3-5 Brainwriting
d. Situation analysis

5. _____ is a broad label that refers to any individuals or households that use goods and services generated within the economy. The concept of a _____ is used in different contexts, so that the usage and significance of the term may vary.

A _____ is a person who uses any product or service.

- a. Consumer
- b. Power III
- c. 6-3-5 Brainwriting
- d. 180SearchAssistant

6. _____ is the study of when, why, how, where and what people do or do not buy products. It blends elements from psychology, sociology, social psychology, anthropology and economics. It attempts to understand the buyer decision making process, both individually and in groups. It studies characteristics of individual consumers such as demographics and behavioural variables in an attempt to understand people's wants. It also tries to assess influences on the consumer from groups such as family, friends, reference groups, and society in general.

- a. Communal marketing
- b. Multidimensional scaling
- c. Consumer confidence
- d. Consumer behavior

7. _____ is a measure of the strength of a brand, product, service relative to competitive offerings. There is often a geographic element to the competitive landscape. In defining _____, you must see to what extent a product, brand, or firm controls a product category in a given geographic area.

- a. Discretionary spending
- b. Productivity
- c. Market system
- d. Market dominance

8. _____ is a list for goods and materials held available in stock by a business. It is also used for a list of the contents of a household and for a list for testamentary purposes of the possessions of someone who has died. In accounting _____ is considered an asset.

- a. ADTECH
- b. Ending Inventory
- c. Inventory
- d. ACNielsen

9. _____ is defined by the American _____ Association as the activity, set of institutions, and processes for creating, communicating, delivering, and exchanging offerings that have value for customers, clients, partners, and society at large. The term developed from the original meaning which referred literally to going to market, as in shopping, or going to a market to sell goods or services.

_____ practice tends to be seen as a creative industry, which includes advertising, distribution and selling.

- a. Marketing
- b. Product naming
- c. Customer acquisition management
- d. Marketing myopia

10. _____, also referred to as i-marketing, web marketing, online marketing is the marketing of products or services over the Internet.

The Internet has brought many unique benefits to marketing, one of which being lower costs for the distribution of information and media to a global audience. The interactive nature of _____, both in terms of providing instant response and eliciting responses, is a unique quality of the medium.

Chapter 22. Pulling It All Together: Integrating and Analyzing the Marketing Plan

a. ACNielsen
b. ADTECH
c. AMAX
d. Internet marketing

11. _____ is understood as a business unit within the overall corporate identity which is distinguishable from other business because it serves a defined external market where management can conduct strategic planning in relation to products and markets. When companies become really large, they are best thought of as being composed of a number of businesses (or _____s.)

In the broader domain of strategic management, the phrase '_____' came into use in the 1960s, largely as a result of General Electric's many units.

a. Corporate strategy
b. Business strategy
c. Cost leadership
d. Strategic business unit

12. _____ is an organization's process of defining its strategy and making decisions on allocating its resources to pursue this strategy, including its capital and people. Various business analysis techniques can be used in _____, including SWOT analysis (Strengths, Weaknesses, Opportunities, and Threats) and PEST analysis (Political, Economic, Social, and Technological analysis) or STEER analysis involving Socio-cultural, Technological, Economic, Ecological, and Regulatory factors and EPISTEL (Environment, Political, Informatic, Social, Technological, Economic and Legal)

_____ is the formal consideration of an organization's future course. All _____ deals with at least one of three key questions:

1. 'What do we do?'
2. 'For whom do we do it?'
3. 'How do we excel?'

In business _____, the third question is better phrased 'How can we beat or avoid competition?'. (Bradford and Duncan, page 1.)

a. Power III
b. 6-3-5 Brainwriting
c. 180SearchAssistant
d. Strategic planning

13. In economic models, the _____ time frame assumes no fixed factors of production. Firms can enter or leave the marketplace, and the cost (and availability) of land, labor, raw materials, and capital goods can be assumed to vary. In contrast, in the short-run time frame, certain factors are assumed to be fixed, because there is not sufficient time for them to change.

a. 180SearchAssistant
b. 6-3-5 Brainwriting
c. Power III
d. Long-run

14. A _____ is a process that can allow an organization to concentrate its limited resources on the greatest opportunities to increase sales and achieve a sustainable competitive advantage. A _____ should be centered around the key concept that customer satisfaction is the main goal.

A _____ is most effective when it is an integral component of corporate strategy, defining how the organization will successfully engage customers, prospects, and competitors in the market arena.

a. Marketing strategy
c. Psychographic
b. Societal marketing
d. Cyberdoc

15. _____ in organizations and public policy is both the organizational process of creating and maintaining a plan; and the psychological process of thinking about the activities required to create a desired goal on some scale. As such, it is a fundamental property of intelligent behavior. This thought process is essential to the creation and refinement of a plan, or integration of it with other plans, that is, it combines forecasting of developments with the preparation of scenarios of how to react to them.

a. 6-3-5 Brainwriting
c. Power III
b. 180SearchAssistant
d. Planning

16. A _____ is a plan of action designed to achieve a particular goal.

_____ is different from tactics. In military terms, tactics is concerned with the conduct of an engagement while _____ is concerned with how different engagements are linked.

a. 180SearchAssistant
c. Power III
b. Strategy
d. 6-3-5 Brainwriting

17. The U.S. _____ is an independent agency of the United States government which holds primary responsibility for enforcing the federal securities laws and regulating the securities industry, the nation's stock and options exchanges, and other electronic securities markets. The SEC was created by section 4 of the Securities Exchange Act of 1934 (now codified as 15 U.S.C. § 78d and commonly referred to as the 1934 Act.)

a. Power III
c. 6-3-5 Brainwriting
b. 180SearchAssistant
d. Securities and Exchange Commission

18. _____ is a branch of philosophy which seeks to address questions about morality, such as how a moral outcome can be achieved in a specific situation (applied _____), how moral values should be determined (normative _____), what moral values people actually abide by (descriptive _____), what the fundamental semantic, ontological, and epistemic nature of _____ or morality is (meta-_____), and how moral capacity or moral agency develops and what its nature is (moral psychology.)

Socrates was one of the first Greek philosophers to encourage both scholars and the common citizen to turn their attention from the outside world to the condition of man. In this view, Knowledge having a bearing on human life was placed highest, all other knowledge being secondary.

a. Ethics
c. AMAX
b. ACNielsen
d. ADTECH

19. The _____ is generally accepted as the use and specification of the four p's describing the strategic position of a product in the marketplace. One version of the origins of the _____ starts in 1948 when James Culliton said that a marketing decision should be a result of something similar to a recipe. This version continued in 1953 when Neil Borden, in his American Marketing Association presidential address, took the recipe idea one step further and coined the term 'Marketing-Mix'.

Chapter 22. Pulling It All Together: Integrating and Analyzing the Marketing Plan

a. Power III
b. 180SearchAssistant
c. 6-3-5 Brainwriting
d. Marketing mix

20. Competitiveness is a comparative concept of the ability and performance of a firm, sub-sector or country to sell and supply goods and/or services in a given market. Although widely used in economics and business management, the usefulness of the concept, particularly in the context of national competitiveness, is vigorously disputed by economists, such as Paul Krugman .

The term may also be applied to markets, where it is used to refer to the extent to which the market structure may be regarded as perfectly _____.

a. Customs union
b. Geographical pricing
c. Free trade zone
d. Competitive

21. _____ is, in very basic words, a position a firm occupies against its competitors.

According to Michael Porter, the three methods for creating a sustainable _____ are through:

1. Cost leadership - Cost advantage occurs when a firm delivers the same services as its competitors but at a lower cost;

2.

a. Competitive advantage
b. Power III
c. 6-3-5 Brainwriting
d. 180SearchAssistant

22. _____ is one of the four Ps of the marketing mix. The other three aspects are product, promotion, and place. It is also a key variable in microeconomic price allocation theory.

a. Price
b. Relationship based pricing
c. Competitor indexing
d. Pricing

23. A _____ is a business that is independently owned and operated, with a small number of employees and relatively low volume of sales. The legal definition of 'small' often varies by country and industry, but is generally under 100 employees in the United States and under 50 employees in the European Union. In comparison, the definition of mid-sized business by the number of employees is generally under 500 in the U.S. and 250 for the European Union.

a. Time to market
b. Product support
c. Small Business
d. Customer centricity

24. The _____ is a United States government agency that provides support to small businesses.

The mission of the _____ is 'to maintain and strengthen the nation's economy by enabling the establishment and viability of small businesses and by assisting in the economic recovery of communities after disasters.'

Chapter 22. Pulling It All Together: Integrating and Analyzing the Marketing Plan

The _____ makes loans directly to businesses and acts as a guarantor on bank loans. In some circumstances it also makes loans to victims of natural disasters, works to get government procurement contracts for small businesses, and assists businesses with management, technical and training issues.

a. Power III
b. 180SearchAssistant
c. 6-3-5 Brainwriting
d. Small Business Administration

25. _____ is a business term meaning the market segment to which a particular good or service is marketed. It is mainly defined by age, gender, geography, socio-economic grouping, technographic, or any other combination of demographics. It is generally studied and mapped by an organization through lists and reports containing demographic information that may have an effect on the marketing of key products or services.

a. Category Development Index
b. Brando
c. Market specialization
d. Distribution

26. _____ is the process of comparing the cost, cycle time, productivity, or quality of a specific process or method to another that is widely considered to be an industry standard or best practice. The result is often a business case for making changes in order to make improvements. The term _____ was first used by cobblers to measure ones feet for shoes.

a. Strategic group
b. Benchmarking
c. Switching cost
d. Business strategy

27. _____ is the management of the flow of goods, information and other resources, including energy and people, between the point of origin and the point of consumption in order to meet the requirements of consumers (frequently, and originally, military organizations.) _____ involves the integration of information, transportation, inventory, warehousing, material-handling, and packaging. _____ is a channel of the supply chain which adds the value of time and place utility.

a. Logistics
b. Power III
c. 6-3-5 Brainwriting
d. 180SearchAssistant

28. _____ consists of the sale of goods or merchandise from a fixed location, such as a department store or kiosk in small or individual lots for direct consumption by the purchaser. _____ may include subordinated services, such as delivery. Purchasers may be individuals or businesses.

a. Warehouse store
b. Retailing
c. Thrifting
d. Charity shop

29. The _____ is an English-language international daily newspaper published by Dow Jones ' Company in New York City with Asian and European editions. As of 2007, It has a worldwide daily circulation of more than 2 million, with approximately 931,000 paying online subscribers. It was the largest-circulation newspaper in the United States until November 2003, when it was surpassed by USA Today.

a. Wall Street Journal
b. 6-3-5 Brainwriting
c. 180SearchAssistant
d. Power III

30. _____ is one of the four elements of marketing mix. An organization or set of organizations (go-betweens) involved in the process of making a product or service available for use or consumption by a consumer or business user.

The other three parts of the marketing mix are product, pricing, and promotion.

Chapter 22. Pulling It All Together: Integrating and Analyzing the Marketing Plan

a. Japan Advertising Photographers' Association
b. Comparison-Shopping agent
c. Better Living Through Chemistry
d. Distribution

31. _____ is a market coverage strategy in which a firm decides to ignore market segment differences and go after the whole market with one offer.it is type of marketing (or attempting to sell through persuasion) of a product to a wide audience. The idea is to broadcast a message that will reach the largest number of people possible. Traditionally _____ has focused on radio, television and newspapers as the medium used to reach this broad audience.
   a. Cyberdoc
   b. Marketspace
   c. Business-to-consumer
   d. Mass marketing

32. _____ is a term used to denote a section of the media specifically designed to reach a very large audience such as the population of a nation state. It was coined in the 1920s with the advent of nationwide radio networks, mass-circulation newspapers and magazines, although _____ were present centuries before the term became common. The term public media has a similar meaning: it is the sum of the public mass distributors of news and entertainment across media such as newspapers, television, radio, broadcasting, which may require union membership in some large markets such as Newspaper Guild, AFTRA, ' text publishers.
   a. Power III
   b. 180SearchAssistant
   c. 6-3-5 Brainwriting
   d. Mass media

33. The _____ is an economic indicator that measures the satisfaction of consumers across the U.S. economy. It is produced by the National Quality Research Center (NQRC) at the University of Michigan in Ann Arbor, Michigan.

The _____ interviews about 80,000 Americans annually and asks about their satisfaction with the goods and services they have consumed.

   a. ADTECH
   b. ACNielsen
   c. American Customer Satisfaction Index
   d. AMAX

34. _____, a business term, is a measure of how products and services supplied by a company meet or surpass customer expectation. It is seen as a key performance indicator within business and is part of the four perspectives of a Balanced Scorecard.

In a competitive marketplace where businesses compete for customers, _____ is seen as a key differentiator and increasingly has become a key element of business strategy.

   a. Supplier diversity
   b. Customer base
   c. Psychological pricing
   d. Customer Satisfaction

35. In economics, business, retail, and accounting, a _____ is the value of money that has been used up to produce something, and hence is not available for use anymore. In economics, a _____ is an alternative that is given up as a result of a decision. In business, the _____ may be one of acquisition, in which case the amount of money expended to acquire it is counted as _____.
   a. Cost
   b. Variable cost
   c. Transaction cost
   d. Fixed costs

Chapter 22. Pulling It All Together: Integrating and Analyzing the Marketing Plan

36. The _____ of 1936 (or Anti-Price Discrimination Act, 15 U.S.C. § 13) is a United States federal law that prohibits what were considered, at the time of passage, to be anticompetitive practices by producers, specifically price discrimination. It grew out of practices in which chain stores were allowed to purchase goods at lower prices than other retailers.
   a. Registered trademark symbol
   b. Trademark infringement
   c. Fair Debt Collection Practices Act
   d. Robinson-Patman Act

37. In accounting, _____ has a very specific meaning. It is an outflow of cash or other valuable assets from a person or company to another person or company. This outflow of cash is generally one side of a trade for products or services that have equal or better current or future value to the buyer than to the seller.
   a. ACNielsen
   b. AMAX
   c. Expense
   d. ADTECH

38. The _____ is a marketing term and refers to all of the forces outside of marketing that affect marketing management's ability to build and maintain successful relationships with target customers. The _____ consists of both the macroenvironment and the microenvironment.

The microenvironment refers to the forces that are close to the company and affect its ability to serve its customers.

   a. Psychographic
   b. Customer franchise
   c. Business-to-consumer
   d. Market environment

39. _____ refer to a collection of facts usually collected as the result of experience, observation or experiment or a set of premises. This may consist of numbers, words particularly as measurements or observations of a set of variables. _____ are often viewed as a lowest level of abstraction from which information and knowledge are derived.
   a. Pearson product-moment correlation coefficient
   b. Data
   c. Sample size
   d. Mean

40. The general definition of an _____ is an evaluation of a person, organization, system, process, project or product. _____ s are performed to ascertain the validity and reliability of information; also to provide an assessment of a system's internal control. The goal of an _____ is to express an opinion on the person/organization/system (etc) in question, under evaluation based on work done on a test basis.
   a. ACNielsen
   b. ADTECH
   c. Audit
   d. AMAX

41. _____ is a term used in marketing as well as the title of an important marketing paper written by Theodore Levitt. This paper was first published in 1960 in the Harvard Business Review; a journal of which he was an editor.

Some commentators have suggested that its publication marked the beginning of the modern marketing movement.

   a. Business marketing
   b. Marketing performance measurement and management
   c. Corporate image
   d. Marketing myopia

Chapter 22. Pulling It All Together: Integrating and Analyzing the Marketing Plan

42. _____ is the ongoing process of identifying and articulating market requirements that define a product's feature set.
   a. Market intelligence
   b. Brand parity
   c. Targeted advertising
   d. Product planning

43. _____ involves disseminating information about a product, product line, brand, or company. It is one of the four key aspects of the marketing mix. (The other three elements are product marketing, pricing, and distribution). P>_____ is generally sub-divided into two parts:

   - Above the line _____: Promotion in the media (e.g. TV, radio, newspapers, Internet and Mobile Phones) in which the advertiser pays an advertising agency to place the ad
   - Below the line _____: All other _____. Much of this is intended to be subtle enough for the consumer to be unaware that _____ is taking place. E.g. sponsorship, product placement, endorsements, sales _____, merchandising, direct mail, personal selling, public relations, trade shows

   a. Promotion
   b. Davie Brown Index
   c. Bottling lines
   d. Cashmere Agency

44. A _____ is a subgroup of people or organizations sharing one or more characteristics that cause them to have similar product and/or service needs. A true _____ meets all of the following criteria: it is distinct from other segments (different segments have different needs), it is homogeneous within the segment (exhibits common needs); it responds similarly to a market stimulus, and it can be reached by a market intervention. The term is also used when consumers with identical product and/or service needs are divided up into groups so they can be charged different amounts.
   a. Production orientation
   b. Customer insight
   c. Commercial planning
   d. Market segment

45. A _____ is an entity formed between two or more parties to undertake economic activity together. The parties agree to create a new entity by both contributing equity, and they then share in the revenues, expenses, and control of the enterprise. The venture can be for one specific project only, or a continuing business relationship such as the Fuji Xerox _____.
   a. Joint venture
   b. Trademark attorney
   c. Consumer protection
   d. Gripe site

46. _____ is that area of marketing research which focuses on customers' perceptions with their shopping or purchase experience.

Many firms are interested in understanding what their customers thought about their shopping or purchase experience, because finding new customers is generally more costly and difficult that servicing existing or repeat customers.

Many people are familiar with 'business to customer' (B2C) or retail-level research, but there are also many 'business to business' (B2B) or wholesale-level projects commissioned as well.

   a. Power III
   b. 6-3-5 Brainwriting
   c. 180SearchAssistant
   d. Customer satisfaction research

Chapter 22. Pulling It All Together: Integrating and Analyzing the Marketing Plan

47. A personal and cultural _____ is a relative ethic _____, an assumption upon which implementation can be extrapolated. A _____ system is a set of consistent _____s and measures that is soo not true. A principle _____ is a foundation upon which other _____s and measures of integrity are based.
   a. Package-on-Package
   b. Perceptual maps
   c. Value
   d. Supreme Court of the United States

48. In economics, _____ is the desire to own something and the ability to pay for it. The term _____ signifies the ability or the willingness to buy a particular commodity at a given point of time .

   a. Demand
   b. Discretionary spending
   c. Market dominance
   d. Market system

ANSWER KEY

Chapter 1
1. d	2. a	3. d	4. a	5. c	6. d	7. d	8. b	9. d	10. b
11. a	12. c	13. b	14. a	15. b	16. d	17. b	18. d	19. d	20. d
21. a	22. c	23. a	24. d	25. a	26. b	27. d	28. d	29. d	30. d
31. d	32. c	33. d	34. c						

Chapter 2
1. a	2. c	3. b	4. b	5. b	6. d	7. b	8. d	9. d	10. d
11. a	12. d	13. c	14. b	15. b	16. c	17. b	18. d	19. b	20. a
21. c	22. d	23. b	24. c	25. d	26. d	27. d	28. d	29. d	30. b
31. d	32. c	33. b	34. c	35. a	36. d	37. b	38. c	39. a	40. d
41. a	42. d	43. d	44. b	45. d	46. c	47. d	48. d	49. d	50. a
51. d	52. b	53. c	54. d	55. d	56. d	57. d	58. d	59. d	

Chapter 3
1. b	2. d	3. b	4. b	5. c	6. a	7. d	8. d	9. d	10. d
11. d	12. d	13. d	14. d	15. b	16. a	17. d	18. d	19. d	20. a
21. b	22. b	23. c	24. d	25. c	26. c	27. c	28. d	29. d	30. d
31. c	32. c	33. d	34. b	35. d					

Chapter 4
1. d	2. b	3. d	4. a	5. d	6. b	7. d	8. d	9. b	10. d
11. d	12. d	13. a	14. d	15. d	16. a	17. b	18. b	19. d	20. d
21. d	22. a	23. d	24. b	25. d	26. c	27. c	28. b	29. d	30. a
31. d	32. c	33. b	34. a	35. b	36. a	37. d	38. b		

Chapter 5
1. d	2. b	3. d	4. d	5. d	6. d	7. d	8. d	9. d	10. c
11. a	12. d	13. c	14. d	15. a	16. d	17. d	18. b	19. d	20. d
21. d	22. d	23. d	24. c	25. d	26. d	27. c	28. d	29. b	30. b
31. a	32. a	33. d	34. d	35. b	36. d	37. d	38. d	39. b	40. d
41. d	42. d	43. d	44. d	45. d					

Chapter 6
1. d	2. d	3. d	4. d	5. c	6. b	7. d	8. d	9. b	10. d
11. a	12. d	13. d	14. d	15. c	16. c	17. d	18. d	19. d	20. b
21. d	22. d	23. c	24. a	25. b	26. d	27. d	28. b	29. a	30. b
31. d	32. d	33. d	34. a	35. a	36. b	37. d	38. d	39. d	40. d
41. d	42. d	43. b							

Chapter 7
1. d	2. d	3. c	4. d	5. a	6. b	7. d	8. c	9. d	10. d
11. d	12. d	13. c	14. d	15. d	16. a	17. b	18. b	19. c	20. d
21. d	22. a	23. d	24. d	25. a	26. d	27. c	28. a	29. b	30. d
31. d	32. c	33. b	34. c	35. d	36. d	37. a	38. b	39. d	40. b
41. b	42. d								

Chapter 8

1. b	2. c	3. a	4. d	5. a	6. b	7. c	8. c	9. b	10. a
11. d	12. c	13. d	14. a	15. c	16. c	17. b	18. c	19. b	20. a
21. b	22. c	23. d	24. d	25. d	26. b	27. d	28. d	29. b	30. a
31. b	32. a	33. b	34. d	35. b	36. a	37. d	38. d	39. c	40. d
41. d	42. d	43. d	44. d	45. d	46. d	47. d	48. b	49. d	50. d
51. c	52. d	53. c	54. c	55. a					

Chapter 9

1. a	2. d	3. d	4. d	5. c	6. d	7. d	8. d	9. d	10. d
11. b	12. c	13. b	14. b	15. d	16. c	17. d	18. b	19. a	20. d
21. b	22. d	23. b	24. d	25. c	26. d	27. d	28. c	29. a	30. d
31. d	32. c	33. c	34. a	35. b	36. c	37. d	38. a	39. d	40. a
41. c									

Chapter 10

1. b	2. d	3. d	4. d	5. d	6. b	7. d	8. a	9. c	10. d
11. d	12. d	13. a	14. d	15. d	16. a	17. d	18. d	19. c	20. b
21. d	22. c	23. d	24. d	25. d	26. d	27. a	28. d	29. d	30. d
31. b	32. d	33. a	34. b	35. d	36. c	37. d	38. a	39. a	

Chapter 11

1. d	2. b	3. d	4. d	5. d	6. d	7. a	8. a	9. a	10. d
11. b	12. c	13. d	14. d	15. d	16. d	17. a	18. d	19. b	20. c
21. d	22. d	23. d	24. d	25. a	26. d	27. d	28. d	29. d	30. c
31. d	32. d	33. d	34. a	35. d	36. d	37. b	38. d	39. b	40. b
41. b	42. d	43. d	44. a	45. b	46. b	47. d	48. b	49. d	50. b
51. a	52. d	53. a	54. d	55. d	56. d	57. c	58. d	59. d	

Chapter 12

1. d	2. c	3. d	4. d	5. d	6. d	7. b	8. d	9. d	10. a
11. b	12. d	13. d	14. c	15. d	16. d	17. b	18. d	19. d	20. b
21. a	22. a	23. d	24. c	25. d	26. d	27. a	28. d		

Chapter 13

1. c	2. c	3. d	4. b	5. b	6. d	7. d	8. b	9. d	10. d
11. d	12. d	13. b	14. d	15. d	16. d	17. d	18. d	19. d	20. a
21. a	22. d	23. d	24. d	25. c	26. d	27. c	28. d	29. d	30. d
31. a	32. b	33. d	34. a	35. b	36. d	37. d	38. d	39. b	40. d
41. d	42. d	43. d	44. d	45. c	46. c	47. d			

ANSWER KEY

Chapter 14

1. d	2. d	3. d	4. c	5. d	6. b	7. d	8. d	9. a	10. d
11. d	12. c	13. b	14. a	15. c	16. d	17. b	18. d	19. c	20. d
21. a	22. a	23. d	24. d	25. b	26. d	27. d	28. c	29. a	30. d
31. b	32. d	33. c	34. d	35. c	36. a	37. b	38. b	39. c	40. d
41. a	42. b	43. d	44. d	45. d	46. c	47. b	48. b	49. d	50. d
51. c	52. d	53. b	54. d	55. d					

Chapter 15

1. a	2. d	3. d	4. c	5. b	6. a	7. d	8. d	9. a	10. b
11. d	12. b	13. c	14. b	15. d	16. d	17. c	18. d	19. a	20. d
21. d	22. d	23. b	24. d						

Chapter 16

1. b	2. d	3. c	4. d	5. d	6. c	7. d	8. d	9. b	10. d
11. b	12. c	13. d	14. d	15. b	16. c	17. c	18. d	19. d	20. d
21. d	22. a	23. d	24. d	25. d	26. b	27. c	28. c	29. d	30. b
31. a	32. d	33. d	34. c	35. b	36. d	37. a	38. d	39. a	40. d
41. c	42. d	43. c	44. d	45. d	46. b				

Chapter 17

1. c	2. d	3. a	4. d	5. d	6. d	7. d	8. a	9. d	10. d
11. c	12. a	13. c	14. d	15. b	16. d	17. c	18. d	19. b	20. c
21. d	22. d	23. d	24. a	25. b	26. a	27. d	28. c	29. c	30. a
31. c	32. d	33. d	34. d	35. a	36. d	37. d	38. d	39. c	40. d
41. d	42. d								

Chapter 18

1. b	2. c	3. b	4. d	5. b	6. d	7. c	8. b	9. c	10. d
11. b	12. a	13. b	14. d	15. d	16. b	17. d	18. a	19. d	20. a
21. a	22. c	23. d	24. d	25. b	26. c	27. b	28. d	29. d	30. d
31. d	32. a	33. b	34. d	35. b	36. d	37. a	38. a	39. c	40. d
41. b	42. b	43. d							

Chapter 19

1. c	2. d	3. d	4. a	5. a	6. d	7. d	8. d	9. b	10. a
11. d	12. b	13. d	14. c	15. c	16. d	17. c	18. d	19. d	20. d
21. d	22. b	23. b	24. a	25. d	26. a	27. c	28. b	29. b	30. b
31. d	32. d	33. a	34. d	35. c	36. d	37. b	38. a	39. c	40. a
41. d	42. d	43. c							

Chapter 20

1. a	2. b	3. b	4. a	5. d	6. d	7. a	8. c	9. a	10. d
11. c	12. b	13. a	14. a	15. d	16. d	17. a	18. c	19. a	20. c
21. a	22. a	23. a	24. d	25. a	26. d	27. b	28. c	29. d	30. d
31. c	32. c	33. a	34. d	35. d	36. d	37. d	38. a	39. a	40. d
41. d	42. b	43. d	44. d	45. b	46. b	47. d	48. d		

Chapter 21

1. d	2. a	3. d	4. d	5. d	6. a	7. b	8. d	9. a	10. d
11. d	12. d	13. d	14. c	15. d	16. d	17. d	18. d	19. c	20. c
21. d	22. d	23. b	24. c	25. d	26. a	27. d	28. d	29. b	30. d
31. b	32. b	33. d	34. b	35. a	36. d	37. b	38. d	39. c	40. d
41. a									

Chapter 22

1. d	2. c	3. c	4. d	5. a	6. d	7. d	8. c	9. a	10. d
11. d	12. d	13. d	14. a	15. d	16. b	17. d	18. a	19. d	20. d
21. a	22. d	23. c	24. d	25. c	26. b	27. a	28. b	29. a	30. d
31. d	32. d	33. c	34. d	35. a	36. d	37. c	38. d	39. b	40. c
41. d	42. d	43. a	44. d	45. a	46. d	47. c	48. a		

www.ingramcontent.com/pod-product-compliance
Lightning Source LLC
Chambersburg PA
CBHW081351230426

43667CB00017B/2801